TURKEY, ISLAMISTS AND DEMOCRACY

TURKEY, ISLAMISTS AND DEMOCRACY

Transition and Globalization in a Muslim State

YILDIZ ATASOY

I.B. TAURIS

LONDON · NEW YORK

Published in 2005 by I.B. Tauris & Co Ltd
6 Salem Road, London W2 4BU
175 Fifth Avenue, New York NY 10010
www.ibtauris.com

In the United States of America and Canada distributed by
Palgrave Macmillan a division of St. Martin's Press
175 Fifth Avenue, New York NY 10010

ISBN 1 85043 758 0
EAN 978 1 85043 758 1

Library of Modern Middle East Studies 48

A full CIP record for this book is available from the British Library
A full CIP record for this book is available from the Library of Congress

Library of Congress catalog card: available

Printed and bound in Great Britain by MPG Books Ltd, Bodmin, Cornwall.
Camera-ready copy edited and supplied by the author

For my parents,
Fatma and Mehmet Nedim Atasoy,
And for my husband,
Ken Jalowica,
With love and gratitude

Contents

List of Tables

Acknowledgements

During my graduate education and subsequent research it became increasingly clear how important it is to understand world historical context and to overcome the limitations of conventional ways of thinking about social life. It was while writing my dissertation at the University of Toronto that I first had an opportunity to integrate these insights into my work. At that time, I became deeply engaged in examining transnationally linked, yet locally distinct, Islamist practices. As I developed my thoughts on the subject, my work came to reflect a particular theory of Islamic politics with a historical, comparative, and global perspective. My contention is that Islamic politics embodies historically situated social relations that express the material and discursive conditions associated with both domestic and international power dynamics.

Many people have contributed to my intellectual growth. The writings of Giovanni Arrighi, Fred Block, Harriet Friedmann, Philip McMichael, Kees van der Pijl, and Charles Tilly were particularly important to the development of my ideas. I am greatly indebted to Harriet Friedmann, my thesis supervisor at the University of Toronto, who helped me with the preliminary research and directed me to many previous works of political economy and historical comparative analysis. Specifically, Karl Polanyi's *The Great Transformation* and Fred Block's *The Origins of International Economic Disorder* were central to the overall project. These texts enabled me to fashion a research strategy that incorporates the seemingly disparate dynamics of political Islam into a larger structural framework for understanding the underlying process of global transformations. I am also indebted to Philip McMichael of Cornell University, who has provided me with insightful commentary on my work.

This book was written while I was teaching, advising graduate students, and completing another project on Muslim women's veiling in Canada and Turkey. The support of my colleagues at Simon Fraser University made it possible for me to push ahead with the book despite the demands of teaching. In the planning stages of the book I benefited from the suggestions of Robert Brym of the University of Toronto, William K. Carroll of the University of Victoria, and Gerardo Otero of Simon Fraser University. I also owe many thanks to the Muslim intellectuals and students whom I met during my research in Turkey. They kindly shared their views on Islamist politics in the many fascinating conversations I had with them.

I would like to thank Jane Springer for her helpful comments on the initial organization of the text. I am also grateful to Lesley Cameron for copy editing the manuscript and to Wilson Nam for his technical assistance in typesetting. In addition, I have benefited from the comments of several anonymous reviewers. Portions of Chapter 6 were first published in *Studies in Political Economy* (Volume 71/72 Autumn 2003/Winter 2004). Parts of Chapter 7 have been previously published in *Global Shaping and Its Alternatives*, edited by Yildiz Atasoy and William K. Carroll (Aurora and Bloomfield: Garamond Press and Kumarian Press, 2003).

Without Ken Jalowica, my husband, I can only wonder when this book would have been completed. I am very grateful for his willingness to spend countless hours reading and editing multiple drafts of this work, while he himself was very busy teaching at Kwantlen University College. Ken gave freely of his time to discuss many highly challenging issues and helped me to express my ideas more clearly. His patience, enthusiasm, and faith in this project were remarkable.

My greatest debt is to my wonderful parents, Fatma and Mehmet Nedim Atasoy. They sent me out into the world to experience it for myself and have always given me their unconditional support. The Ata *gecekondu* district in Dikmen, Ankara where I was raised deserves special mention. From my childhood, the inhabitants of this shantytown neighbourhood have inspired me with their work ethic and enduring spirit. Their unwavering determination to achieve the best for themselves and their children, despite being marginalized and impoverished, motivates me to this day.

1

Islam in Global Politics: Theoretical Perspectives

The 11 September 2001 attacks on the World Trade Center and Pentagon unleashed a global furor over the 'terrorist' activities of the al-Qaeda network and the Taliban. President Bush immediately identified members of these groups as 'wicked evildoers' who represent a grave threat to the United States. A worldwide campaign was launched against terrorism and all those who are, as Bush put it, 'against us'. Journalists, politicians, policy-makers, scholars, and the general public became engaged in a fierce debate over Islamists and their ideologies. It has become commonplace for commentators to portray Islamists as violent fundamentalists committed to eliminating liberal democratic institutions and individual freedoms in favour of anti-Western theocracies. The ongoing debate is intense and emotionally charged. 'Militant Islam', 'Islamic terrorism', and 'Islamic fundamentalism' are among the terms now frequently used to describe Islam as one of the world's most dangerous political movements.

Scholars who study Islamic politics can be roughly divided into two groups. One group is highly pessimistic about the role of Islam in Muslim societies (Afshar 1998; Moghadom 1991). Influenced by the miserable record of Islamic regimes in Iran and Afghanistan, this group argues that Islam has instigated an anti-modern desire to return to the past. In order to contain this movement, they believe, Muslim societies must pursue programmes directed towards Western conceptions of political liberalism, citizenship, and secularism. The other group is more sceptical of the uniform application of Western modernity to non-Western societies, arguing that Islam is an expression of local indigenous cultures (Ahmed 1992; Hoodfar 1997; Mernissi 1991). For these scholars, Islam represents a distinct culture that underpins morality, lifestyle choices, and, ultimately, resistance to Western domination. Although the two groups display divergent reactions to Islamic politics, both analyse Islam in terms of the dilemmas characteristic of non-Western post-colonial societies. They point to the power struggles and conflicts over modernization, its relation to westernization, and Islam's relevance to local cultures (Bozdogan and Kasaba 1997; Chatterjee 1993; Prakash 1995).

Islam in non-Western societies appears to be caught in an ideological struggle between the pursuit of the global project of modernity and the local project of 'authenticity'. This recalls the dichotomous view of culture between global and local posited in social theory. For example, Barber (1995) expects local cultures to form a reactionary counter-movement against Western modernity. For Ritzer (2000), these cultures will disappear under the conditions of greater global integration. Alternatively, for Escobar (1995), local cultures will provide the basis for an emancipatory politics against globalization. For Gulalp (1997) and Majid (2000), the mobilization of local cultures is a form of identity politics. For Ahmed (1992) and Mernissi (1991), these cultures are sources of alternative modernities.

It is undeniable that Islamic political movements now challenge the ideas, practices, and political dominance of westernizing political elites. Some Islamist groups claim to locate their activities within the realm of 'authentically' Muslim cultural traditions. Does this mean that Islamic politics represent a counter-cultural assertion of Islamic principles and identities against the Western idea of modernization? Are we experiencing a clash of world-views?

Many commentators view the Islam of today as a political movement that aspires to replace Enlightenment principles. Even though 'capitalism' and 'socialism' were antagonistic modernization projects during the Cold War, both adhered to the universal conception of modernity and progress that emerged from the Enlightenment. Hobsbawm (1994) argues that Cold War modernization projects contained 'indigenous' cultures within the concept of a 'universal modernity'. However, the end of the Cold War in 1991 exposed the internal tensions within nation-states between traditional local and modern universal cultural values. Various culturally framed infranational movements emerged. Nation-states now find themselves pulled in opposite directions by the universalizing forces of the global economy and localizing infranational movements (Gill 1992). This points to the disintegration of a political programme of modernity based on the liberal ideology of progress (Wallerstein 2000). At a time when we are witnessing the disintegration of a universal modernity, religious fundamentalism constructs an ideology with a claim to the 'authentic' local culture of the past.

We live in an era of great uncertainty. At present there are no effective international mechanisms to contain anti-modern political movements and rival fundamentalist strategies. We do little more than label these newly emerging politics as dangerous, anti-modern forms of religious fundamentalism. Islam is undoubtedly a new factor in global politics. But how exactly is an Islamic political movement constituted? Does Islam formulate a clear political strategy? Is it an aggressive, anti-Western, and xenophobic religion? Is its goal to eventually replace a universal conception of modernity? These are among the questions that surround a meaningful analysis of the political significance of Islam.

There are different Islamic movements, and radical Islamist groups make up only one variety. These groups frame the rise of infranational movements in terms of an intense cultural encounter between Islamic and Western relations (Tibi 1998). They insist that there is only one true Islam, that it is applicable to all times and places, and that it is one of the pillars of an emerging global system with its own conception of universalism. Huntington (1996) goes so far as to suggest that Islam epitomizes those particularistic ideologies that are undermining the liberal democratic aspirations of Western civilization around the globe. From this perspective, Islam is an example of an Eastern civilization that seriously threatens Western cultural dominance and the culturally homogenizing tendencies of globalization.

In contrast, Halliday (1994) dismisses as nonsense any claim that Islam constitutes a challenge to the West. Islamic politics is 'not about inter-state relations at all, but about how these Islamic societies and states will organize themselves and what the implications of such organization for relations with the outside world will be' (Halliday 1994: 92).

Recent post-colonial theory has elaborated on the importance of local cultural specificities in the quest for an alternative non-Western modernity. Proponents of this position question the Eurocentric bias in notions of modernization (Rist 1997) and highlight the possibility of combining local cultures with Western culture in instituting another concept of modernization (Escobar 1995; Pigg 1992). They regard Islam as diverting modernity away from its association with Western cultures (Ahmed 1992; Narayan 1997). This emphasis on local/national differences in politico-cultural experience decentres our understanding of modernization from its European origins. Escobar (1995) argues that the dominant project of modernity is nothing short of the globalization of Western ways. He sees the mobilization of 'indigenous' local cultures and experiences as essential to developing alternative conceptions. In directing our attention to Islamic movements in the more 'modernized' Muslim countries of Iran, Egypt, and Tunisia, Esposito (1992) argues that Islam projects an alternative vision for moulding society and the state, although the question of what constitutes that vision may be disputed.

How do Islamists actually situate themselves between the universality of Western modernity and the locality of cultural authenticity? I respond to this question by examining Islamic politics in Turkey. My hope is to unravel the tensions and conflicts that mark the interplay between local cultures and global projects of modernization. My argument is that Islamic movements cannot be analyzed without historically contextualizing them in the wider relations of global politics. Political Islam is very much embedded in the processes of active incorporation of Western modernity into local cultural practices. This assumes 'hybrid' patterns of social change that reposition cultures within interactive processes that can no longer be defined as exclusively authentic or inauthentic. The present work breaks down the rigid categorizations of 'Western' versus 'local' and considers the implications of this for situating Islam in the global political economy.

There is no doubt that Islam plays an important role in the local cultures and lifestyles of Muslims. It is also mobilized as an anti-Western political ideology that challenges the cultural foundations of a Western-dominated global system. However, radical Islamists and Western commentators on the 'Islamic threat' have both got it wrong. There is no unchanging 'Islam' that exists as a single entity outside of history. There are broad ideological differences among various Islamist groups. Members of these groups include highly educated professionals, teachers, engineers, lawyers, bureaucrats, and scientists. They are immersed in the world of modern science and technology and want to formulate a competitive strategy for achieving social transformation through the acquisition of state power. This power is necessary for Islamists to become politically engaged in the global economy, such that the West represents a competitive partner rather than a cultural model for emulation (Atasoy 2003a).

I take issue with the long tradition in Western thought of distinguishing between the global or modern and the local or traditional. In the context of scholarship dealing with Islamic movements this division between the local-global and traditional-modern has come under increasing scrutiny (Abu-Lughod 1997; Al-Azmeh 1993). Nonetheless, current social theory still feeds on this dichotomous conception. Ritzer (2000), for example, expects an increasingly homogenized world and the disappearance of the local under the influence of a consumer culture emerging around globally produced and consumed commodities. Both Barber (1995) and Huntington (1996), on the other hand, expect a cultural contestation pitting local against global. They see Islam as an aspect of local Muslim cultures that counteracts global homogenization. Ahmed (1992) also sees Islam as a source of authentic local culture and alternative practices to Western ways. Such conceptualizations of culture would have us believe that there is a growing cultural clash between Islam and Western ways.

I argue that it is untenable to conceptualize Islam as representing traditional local values, and globalization as having a modernizing impact on 'traditional' societies. Many social scientists argue that 'all cultures are more fragmented than coherent, and that the Weberian image of culture providing a systematic set of ideas and values by which people orient their behaviour is fundamentally misleading' (Griswold 2004: 44). According to Abu-Lughod (1997) and Kandiyoti and Saktanber (2002), Western culture figures in Islamist thinking in more complex ways than a reference to global and local differences enables us to comprehend. Islamists are quite capable of participating in the competitive relations of the global economy.

I study Islamic politics in broader terms, as an element of globalization wherein global and local dynamics interact and interconnect (Atasoy 2003a). Islamists think of themselves as belonging to a global system within which they share modern values and lifestyles. Their participation in the global economy is part of the cultural complexity that is constitutive of globalization. The Islamic political movement in Turkey has attracted a growing number of engineers, business people, industrialists, teachers, bureaucrats, and lawyers, many of whom are not only graduates of reputable universities in Turkey but also hold postgraduate degrees from universities in western Europe and the United States. Their central goal is to reposition themselves in the highly competitive relations of the national and global economy, working alongside, and sometimes in coalition with, secular political elites. This locates Islamist groups as participants in a culturally polycentric world.

Such an interpretation of Islamic politics is, of course, controversial. It breaks the long-standing ideological connection between Western cultural patterns and the capitalist economy established by Max Weber in his explanation of the origins of capitalism in western Europe. Rather than assuming that cultures are dominant sites of conflict that produce a 'clash of civilizations', I argue that we should grasp the contingency, variety, and indeed the 'modernity' of Islamic politics in the reorganization of the global economy. It seems to me that the key question is *how* Islamic politics enters into the process.

As for the question of who participates in an Islamic movement, my starting point would be to revisit theories of modernization that elaborate the question of agency in terms of a context-bound interpretation of modernity and the self. For the moment, let us consider the view of the modern and the Islamic as cultural opposites. Such a view seeks to explain Islamic politics in terms of a traditional opposition of lower classes against the modernizing influences of a capitalist market economy. Here Islam becomes the repository of local traditions experienced by rural and urban lower classes and other marginal segments in society. These classes and marginal groups understand their disadvantaged position in life as resulting from the reorganization of traditional society around the principle of market competition. They feel a loss of community and culture, and harbour a sense of anxiety and insecurity. Politically, these sentiments are expressed in the form of opposition based on local cultural values. This is the essence of the modernization theory that became the dominant paradigm of post-war scholarship.

Modernization theory tries to relate Islam to the cultural anxieties of the lower classes but Islam is not restricted to the politics of the marginalized and economically weak. Increasing numbers of well-educated professionals are now part of the pro-Islamic political movement in Turkey, using Islam as a strategic resource for building frames of reference and cross-class alliances. It therefore makes no sense to even try to describe their politics as a resistance movement based on cultural traditions that oppose the global capitalist economy. Max Weber has shown in his study of the relationship between Protestant beliefs and the advent of capitalism in western Europe that culture as a systematic set of ideas and values mediates economic activity. I would depart from this interpretation and suggest that studying Islamic politics in functional terms does not provide evidence of a significant link between changes in state power, class politics, and religion in regenerating meanings for action within the global political economy.

The electoral success story of the pro-Islamic party compels us to study the ways in which Islamists interact with the deployment of state power to affect the shape of that power and to influence economic strategy. In the national elections of November 2002 the pro-Islamic AKP (the Justice and Development Party founded in 2001 and the sixth pro-Islamic party to be established in Turkey since the late 1960s) won a majority government by obtaining close to 35 per cent of the popular vote. The Constitutional Courts have closed down four pro-Islamic parties, in 1971, 1980, 1998, and 2001. There is currently one other pro-Islamic party actively competing with the AKP, the Prosperity Party (*Saadet Partisi*). In total, 20 parties entered the 2002 elections but only the intensely secular Republican People's Party has been able to obtain parliamentary representation. The AKP succeeded in forming a majority government for the first time in Turkey after eleven long years of highly fragile coalitions. It is a party of young Islamists who define themselves as modern and pro-Western. Their leader prefers the AKP to be known as a 'democratic conservative' party on the centre-right of the political spectrum.

The emergence of this new party presents us with a different picture of Islamic politics. The AKP supports Turkey's military alliance with the United States, promises to advance Turkey's claim to European Union membership, and pledges to build a rapprochement with Greece. Yet it is at odds with Turkey's powerful military bureaucracy and the official state ideology of secularism.

Islamists are actively reconfiguring their position in the economy and state structure. The very name of the AKP, Justice and Development, invokes principles of social justice and connotes a response to economic inequality and state oppression. Islam is in part a political protest movement expressing the grievances of the poorest and most marginal segments of the population as well as a newly emerging fraction of the middle classes. These groups believe they are excluded from the benefits of economic development and power positions in society (Onis 1997). Why is it then that Islam in particular, rather than other forms of protest such as leftist movements or popular nationalism, would appeal to these groups?

To answer this question, I begin by referring to Serif Mardin's (1997) assertion of a connection between political protest and religious beliefs. Mardin argues that Islam is a social bond and a strategic resource for a variety of groups that, despite having different goals, are all seeking some form of social justice. This multifaceted role, however, is not inscribed within the ahistorical conception of Islam held by commentators who speak of an authentic culture from an earlier golden age. The positioning of cultures on opposite poles of a continuum between authentic-traditional and global-modern tells us remarkably little about the actual content of their ideas, their construction, and their political direction. There are many different Islamist groups throughout the Muslim world with diverse interests and goals. They act in different, changing contexts, and face new challenges and choices. This range of expression compels us to rethink Islam and its existing economic and political relations.

Social theory often tends to reduce a complex social reality to a single essence. By grossly distorting the complexities of Islamic politics, this tendency can negatively influence our perception and undermine our understanding of other people's struggles for a better life. There is nothing natural or inevitable in the association between Islamic beliefs and protest movements. I am convinced that political parties and the political elite, including civil and military bureaucrats, actively forge these connections. Sufi religious orders, such as the Naqshbandi, and religious communities, such as the *Nurcu cemaati* and *Fethullahcilar*, are also actively involved in creating cultural repertoires for steering political action. Choices that are made by state managers, political parties, Sufi orders, and other religious communities shape the main features of an Islamic culture that binds various groups to the political project of social justice.

I argue for the development of new conceptual models to help us understand Islam and the complex relations of contemporary globalization. Global political and economic conditions are transforming human experience throughout the world and influencing the local conditions of life. At the same time, global relations are being transformed by the penetration of local influences. Islam is constitutive of a global politics wherein global and local dynamics interact and interconnect.

It may be easy for some to describe Islamists as fundamentalist 'evildoers'. But Muslims, like everyone else in the world, have aspirations, fears, and disappointments. Only a handful of scholars, including Mardin (1997), Saktanber (2002), and White (2002), have examined Islamic politics from the point of view of those who embrace it. C. Wright Mills (1959) alerted us many years ago to the importance of analysing a social phenomenon in relation to both global conditions of material existence and individuals' own personal histories. One can only assume that Islamists, like other social groups, go through a process of deliberation and self-reflection before they develop a political project. An inquiry into Islamic politics, therefore, should include an investigation of the interplay between societal and personal histories. I do not dwell primarily on the personal narratives and practices of Islamist individuals, but I do refer to their life stories from time to time in order to gain an understanding of how Islamic ideological orientations are configured.

This book aims to answer the following question: How do Islamists situate themselves and their politics within the political context of Turkey and the general conditions of global transformation?

Islam and Turkish politics

Much current social theory seeks to answer the above question by examining the discordance between Islam and Western ways. However, this leaves serious students of Islamic politics dissatisfied. On the world stage Turkey occupies a strategic location, situated between the West and the Islamic world. An important player in the North Atlantic Treaty Organization (NATO) and in the regional alliances of the Middle East, it has also formally applied to join the European Union (EU), and stands at the crossroads of almost every issue of importance to the United States and the EU on the Eurasian continent. An interesting consequence of these political and military relations is that Turkey is the only Muslim country that has been integrated into Western political, economic, and cultural structures. On the other hand, Turkey differs from other Muslim countries in its domestic politics. Unlike Iran, Algeria, and Egypt, Turkey has achieved a political compromise between secular and Islamic political elites by incorporating Islam into the secular state structure (Atasoy 2003a: 134). In short, Turkey is both a Muslim and a Western country. Because of its unique position in global affairs, Turkey offers us an opportunity to move beyond a simplistic view of Islam as possessing distinct cultural characteristics that stand in opposition to global modernity.

Three major theoretical perspectives explain the rise of Islamic politics in Turkey: modernization, centre-periphery, and world systems. Despite the differences, there is an impressive similarity in these approaches. For modernization theorists, modern and traditional characteristics are deeply embedded in cultural traits, and the modern/traditional dichotomy is synchronistic with an urban/rural antagonism. Rural populations are seen to be religious and resistant to cultural patterns that occur in Western societies. Urbanites, in contrast, are cosmopolitan, literate, and open to cultural transformations originating in the West.

Modernization theory treats wealth creation and accumulation as a uniquely Western process, presumably rooted in the technologically and culturally superior values of market competition. Non-Western societies must therefore adopt Western values and institutions in order to shake off their cultural backwardness. Daniel Lerner (1958), for example, believes that the adoption of Enlightenment ideals is necessary to create a modern psyche. These ideals include efficiency, instrumental rationality, preparedness for change, physical and social mobility, energetic enterprise, alertness to opportunities, individualism, and self-reliance. According to modernization theory, Muslims appear to be 'sleeping beauties', waiting for Western cultural values to awaken them to the process of modernization. They must choose between modernity and Islam, between the emulation of technologically superior Western ways and the idealization of a traditional culture.

Why should Islam even be a choice? For centre-periphery theorists, the Turkish attempt to bring about modernization by imposing a westernization project did not carry the masses along with it. Serif Mardin (1973), the main proponent of this perspective, argues that westernizing modernity failed to win the hearts of Muslims because of state repression and the abuse of power by westernizing bureaucrats. In the absence of politically dominant landed and commercial classes, civil and military bureaucratic cadres constitute the centre in Turkey, wielding state power over a weak 'periphery'. This political structure was inherited from the Ottoman Empire, a legacy that perpetuates intense cultural encounters between bureaucrats and peripheral groups in society. Islam thus becomes a strategic tool for peripheral forces in the development of a critical view of the state as a source of repression.

This approach is useful in directing attention to the cultural-ideological forms of state domination that generate feelings of resentment, estrangement, and hostility in the 'periphery'. Mardin (1986) explains Islamic politics as having emerged from a particular path of modernization followed in Turkey since the founding of the Turkish Republic in 1923. Kemalism, named after the founder of the republic, Mustafa Kemal, is the official ideology of the Turkish state and central to Turkish modernization projects. Kemalism encourages a westernizing populism to replace traditional social arrangements, often through abusive bureaucratic power. However, this undermines community and culture, resulting in acute feelings of insecurity among the masses. Mardin argues that Kemalism has provided no viable means to make life meaningful for the majority of the population. It has failed to create a social ethos that appeals to the heart as well as to the mind.

Nonetheless, for Mardin (1991), Islam does not represent an anti-modern reactionary movement for the insecure and disoriented masses. Rather, it provides a 'world-view'. Religious groups take the task of formulating a world-view seriously and make Islamic teachings accessible to the masses without emptying them of their enchanting, mystic qualities. This may be a very eloquent interpretation, but it does not tell us how and why these disillusioned individuals rally around religion as a response to their cultural impoverishment. The centre-periphery approach also fails to appreciate the fact that Islamic politics is not restricted to a small religious group on the periphery of society. Islam has instead become integral to the production of a new sector of highly educated and Islamically-oriented political and economic elites striving to obtain state control.

Although superior to the modernization approach, which essentially views religiously oriented people and rural populations as backward and ignorant, the centre-periphery perspective still leaves important questions unresolved. It assumes a homogeneity within the bureaucratic cadres and peripheral forces, which in turn suggests a necessarily conflictual relationship between the state and the periphery. This makes it very difficult to recognize the reality of diverse interests and demands arising from within both the periphery and the centre. This approach falls short of explaining the political construction of peripheral 'marginality' and the entrance of these marginals into the political process. The strength of Islam lies not merely in its ability to provide a sense of social justice for the culturally impoverished masses, but also in its ability to facilitate a negotiated consensus among various segments of the periphery and bureaucratic cadres. I believe the politics surrounding the formation of a political category of marginality is a central issue in the study of contemporary Islam.

World systems theory focuses on the peripheral position of Turkey in the world capitalist system, and the economic and political conditions that produce unemployment, poverty, constant economic crises, high-level rural migration, and political authoritarianism. Building on these negative consequences of capitalist development, Islamists advance a critique of modernity and the Enlightenment ideals of progress. Keyder (1997) argues that the Islamist strategy in Turkey grows out of the failures of the state in implementing the liberal principles of the Enlightenment. From its beginning in the 1920s, the state has delimited the scope of modernization among the masses and, therefore, failed to achieve the goal of emancipating its citizenry from the inertia of traditional religious culture. The result is a political void readily filled by Islam.

World systems theory suggests that Islamists appeal to the urban poor by emphasizing the principles of equality, justice, and freedom. Islamists have successfully organized a coherent ideology of opposition to explain the causes of poverty. They point to the dependent position of Turkey in the world economy, the lack of national independence, and the influence of Western imperialism. But there is nothing uniquely Islamic about these issues. The Left also invokes them. According to Keyder, though, Islamists appear to be more successful than the Left in using 'anti-imperialist' rhetoric because the state systematically represses the Left. Islamists are thus able to take on the role of bearers of a nationalist critique of Western imperialism and capitalism. The Islamist formulation of a culture of opposition against the westernizing mission of Kemalism displaces the secular and modernizing ideologies of the Left. However, one obvious question remains: How do Islamists translate these issues of social justice, equality, and national independence into specifically Islamic political projects?

Most discussion around this question is speculative, revealing a strong fear that Islam threatens the very survival of the secular nation-state. This fear results from the supposed link between Islamic ideas and the ignorance of rural populations and the urban poor. These masses are subject to exploitation by their patron landlords, the bourgeoisie, right-wing political parties, and conservative religious leaders, to the extent that they develop a false consciousness around an Islamist 'fabrication' of cultural empowerment. To prevent the spread of Islam among these populations, Keyder proposes further westernization and modernization. Implicit in this suggestion is the view that state managers are independent of societal influences and unified around progressive aspirations. Unfortunately, this state-centred view assigns the secular segments of state bureaucracy the role of political tutelage over society; but the centre-periphery approach has already shown that this has historically led Kemalist bureaucrats to abuse state power and repress segments of largely rural populations.

The cultural transformation brought about by the modernizing mission of Kemalism has profound implications for the reconfiguring of Islam. Islamists do not represent a group of uneducated, 'backward' elements in society. There are many Muslim capitalists, business people, and educated professionals who are perfectly in tune with and adept at participating in the global economy. Their behaviour is completely consistent with Western notions of instrumental rationality and efficiency directed towards the goal of capital accumulation (Atasoy 2003a). What does further westernization and modernization mean then in political terms? Who benefits and who loses? Do different categories of people benefit from these projects in the same way? The world systems perspective of Turkey seems to remain silent on the Islamist creation of cross-class alliances and the populist political programme of economic and social justice.

None of the three theories has produced a satisfactory answer to our question on the role of Islamic politics in global affairs. They all fail, in my view, because they regard a certain pattern of development taken by European states as a universal model to be emulated by Turkey. These theories identify the distinctive features in the European pattern and then proceed to explain the causes of variation within the Turkish experience. Even though the centre-periphery approach acknowledges the historical and cultural specificity of Turkey, a comparison between Turkish and western European experience is the dominant feature of the analysis.

In all three theories the rise of Islamic politics results from a departure in the Turkish experience from a Western trajectory of change. In concrete terms this means that when these theories analyse Islamic politics they refer to it as a deviation from an ideal model of modernization. Yet this elevates a historically specific European pattern of change to the level of a general explanation. A historical process experienced in western Europe becomes a totalizing explanation of global affairs. If social theory is to contribute to an understanding of Islamic politics, it must chart a range of cultural possibilities for reconstituting society.

There is now a sizeable body of literature devoted to formulating an approach to political struggles about cultural 'identity' (Gole 1996; Gulalp 1997; Navaro-Yashin 2002; White 2002). It responds to the inadequacies of the three theories and examines the resurgence of Islam in the 1980s and 1990s. While scholars delineate particular domestic political, economic, and cultural circumstances, as well as international events, these factors most commonly appear as background forces that, individually or in combination, contribute to the rise of Islamic identity politics. Gole (1996) explains Islamic identity politics in terms of opposition to a politically imposed Western modernity. She differentiates between political and cultural orientations towards an Islamic lifestyle. Political Islam advocates a complete transformation of society and the seizure of political power. Cultural Islam formulates an Islamic identity by asserting the meanings and world-views of society and its individuals. The Islamists in Gole's study are veiled women engaged in cultural Islam. They are highly educated, young, urban, upwardly mobile, and activist. Their veiling activity helps them to distance themselves from traditionalism and customary Islam while at the same time challenging Western modernity and the power domain of Kemalist elites. The Golden Age of Islam, which existed during the reign of the first four caliphs, provides the reference point for these women in their adoption of a uniquely Islamic way of living. The veil integrates their quest for a distinct self with an Islamic lifestyle.

Gulalp (1997) situates Islamic identity formation and the transformation of dominant normative standards within the Islamist critique of modernization. He argues that the failure of modernity to realize the promises of the Enlightenment prompted a 'post-modern' search for alternatives to the homogenizing tendencies of global capitalism. Islamic identity politics is a post-modern cultural reaction to modernity, rooted in the failure of the state to deliver economic prosperity and equality. The result is resentment and disappointment on the part of the lower classes over the modernization project. Islamists transform popular resentment of the poor and marginalized segments of society into a counter-hegemonic critique of the destructive effects of Western capitalism on the human soul and the natural environment. Gulalp's study of the writings of a small group of Islamist intellectuals reveals that disenchanted groups often generate meanings, and make sense of their existence, by reference to the Golden Age of Islam. This, according to Gulalp, parallels the 'post-modern' recognition of local cultural diversity and the right to multiple paths of modernity. Islamists challenge the centrality of Western modernity as a model to be replicated elsewhere and reassert the specificity and distinctiveness of Islam.

White (2002) argues that an Islamist attempt to distance a specifically Islamic modernity from Western modernity and customary Muslim practices opens the way for an alternate path. But Islamists are not a homogeneous group; they hold different views on what is uniquely Islamic. Social class differences, cultural practices, and cleavages in rural and urban lifestyles, as well as gender issues, affect their understanding of Islamic identity. Nevertheless, there does seem to be a broad consensus on what constitutes an Islamic lifestyle. For White, the Islamist elite plays a dominant role in formulating a consensus politics. Highly educated, urban, upwardly mobile, young activists facilitate the process—and are supported by the newly emerging Islamist capitalist classes.

According to Navaro-Yashin (2002), a consensual Islamic politics of identity is built into the process of consumerism. Islamists are reshaping their cultural being through the medium of the market by consuming products distinct from those used by secularists. For Navaro-Yashin, the emergence of an Islamic cultural context of consumerism contributes to the construction of a counter-hegemonic image of Islamic community. This process expands Islamist middle-class lifestyles and tastes into the normative domain of the devout popular classes disenfranchised by neoliberal globalization. Navaro-Yashin argues that this does not produce an alternative image of society, but highlights commonalities between the seemingly diverse elite projects of Islamic and secular cultural identity around the creation of a market for consumption.

For me, social theory must provide more than the claim that Islamists take part in the formation and expansion of a market economy. Islamic politics did not suddenly emerge during the 1980s and 1990s under the conditions of neoliberal globalization. It has roots in the Ottoman Empire and has been incorporated into the secular structure of the Turkish state in ways far more complex than is often assumed. If social theory is to contribute to an understanding of historical possibilities of change, it must give us a systematic account of how an Islamist connection between culture and the social world is formed by the relations between the market economy and the state.

World systems theory makes a useful contribution to our understanding of Turkey's experience on the margins of the capitalist world economy and the impact of global systemic pressures on Turkey's class structure and political regimes. However, this explanation still does not provide the analytical tools necessary for combining the unique realities of Turkey with the general regularities of its world context. World systems theory expects a unity of experience in Third World societies given their dependent position in a capitalist world economy. But the domestic context of each state is unique and each state is uniquely situated within the state system. Turkey occupies a primary position in terms of military and political-strategic relations in the state system, although it is marginal in its economic significance. Its strategic importance in the Middle East and NATO produces results for Turkey's domestic politics, including Islam, while at the same time its distinct national dynamics are of crucial significance for the emergent patterns of global power.

The interplay between domestic and international politics creates both opportunities and constraints for various political projects. Governments are involved in negotiating consensus, while shaping the demands and desires of various social groups along the way. This possibility presupposes active political engagement on the part of state managers, social classes, and political factions involved in the remaking of a political culture. Such a possibility is not fixed within a universal account of a Western pattern or a Third World experience, but is constantly negotiated within a specific conjuncture of geopolitical events in the world economy. The present work explains how Islamic projects are conceived in the links between participation in global structures of power and the moral claims of different groups in society. Indeed, it argues that behind Islamic ideas are political strategies for mediating domestic and international politics.

I believe it is important to reveal historical specificity rather than assuming a theoretical divide between a universal modernity and Islam. My work recounts the existing relations of power that have played a major role in the emergence of Islamist groups. As world systems theory has shown, the position of the state in the international division of labour is critical, but only in so far as it creates the necessary opportunities for, and constraints against, the articulation of distinct politico-cultural projects. The centre-periphery perspective's conceptualization of the state as a source of coercive power is also useful in understanding the power of Islam as a day-to-day discourse of the powerless. My own position is not a synthesis of the existing literature.

Current scholarship rarely reveals the discontinuities, recurrences, and resolutions in capital accumulation arrangements, the organization of states and political alliances, and the cultural dynamics that help us understand the patterns and outcomes of Islamic movements. Clearly, Islamic politics is part of exceptionally complex, multifaceted historical events. A closer examination of these events reveals different aspects of global processes that have resulted in the disintegration of empires, opened the way for the emergence and consolidation of national states, and produced further critical changes in the state system. What cannot be emphasized enough is that these changes do not present a 'fixed' political role for Islam that repeats itself from one historical period to the next. What is more, there are no sharply defined categories of 'Islamic' and 'secular', nor are there wild swings between secular and Islamic periods in Turkish history. Rather, there is a complex reworking and blurring of both Western and Islamic ways that makes such rigid categorizations impossible.

I consider the following range of questions in developing an alternative explanation of Islamic politics within the global system:

1) How do various domestic motives, historical legacies, and international processes enter into the fashioning of Islamic projects and how do they change over time?

2) What are the chief forms of domination (economic and non-economic) taken by the state as credible ideological devices for the common people? Why and how do these forms change?

3) What determines the responsiveness of the state to the needs, demands, and desires of its citizens? How does this responsiveness interact with competing claims and conceptions of citizenship as political projects contend for power?

4) How does the heightened fear of 'Islamic fundamentalism', especially since 11 September 2001, influence this process?

5) What non-national or non-state forms of power are contesting the rule of the state in general and the Islamic world in particular?

6) If these forms of power succeed, what institutional shapes could they take? What forms of rule are prefigured by present Islamic politics? Would the idea of a nation-state system still apply in revised form to a world governed by transnational Islamist parties and, presumably, other transnational forces?

I argue that Islamic politics must be understood in terms of the material relations of global capitalism, the reorganization of states, political alliances, and cultures. These factors are crucial to understanding the historically specific reinterpretation of Islam and the reconfiguration of Islamic politics. There are many complicated cultural effects that result from integrating a uniquely Western pattern of social change with the specific local arrangements of Turkey. Local and global relations are mutually constitutive. Therefore, rather than giving support to arguments that bear on global cultural homogenization, or, alternatively, theories that view the local and the global as cultural opposites, we should examine the complexity that emerges from the dynamics of Islamist incorporation of Western ways into specific political projects. If we wish to understand the position of Islamists in relation to global political economy, we must look at history from a different perspective and question the relevance of the distinction between West and non-West.

The present work is an account of the local and global dynamics of power. It examines their points of intersection through an analysis of economic, cultural, political, and military factors. This process shapes the reorganization of major social classes and their relations to the state. It also significantly affects strategies employed by the wielders of state power, the opposition they face, and the political struggles that result. Various ideas about what makes sense in society influence the balance of power among competing groups. In addition, people's understanding of their social position in society influences the way they mobilize themselves to realize certain goals. It is not enough, therefore, to speculatively construct universal cultural categories of modernity against which we can measure Islamic politics.

Situating Islam: the relevance of the West

In the *Great Transformation*, Karl Polanyi (1944) develops a historical critique of the 'universal modernity' thesis. The concept of 'universal modernity' suggests that the self-regulating market economy is inevitable and natural. However, Polanyi insists that human economic activity is always embedded in the social and cultural arrangements of society (Block 1990). This is significant because it helps to redirect our understanding of Islamic politics beyond a dichotomous conception of local-traditional and universal-modern.

Polanyi explains the rise of fascism in Europe as a protective counter-movement against the market principle. The nineteenth-century conditions of political interaction between a naturalized view of the market economy and the alternative view of the economy's cultural embedment produced two opposing movements. The first was laissez-faire, which sought to free economic activity from political regulation. This caused widespread insecurity and social anxiety. The second was the spontaneous counter-movement of social forces demanding protection from the market. Diverse social groups fearful of a destructive market will invariably resist the unrestricted penetration of capital relations and press the state for protection. This helps explain the social bases of fascism in Europe. Following a similar line of reasoning, some may also interpret Islamic politics as representing Muslim claims for protection against the homogenizing influence of the global market economy. The suggestion is that Islam is a repository of local traditions that spontaneously fashions a protective response to global market forces. Such an argument once again posits an unchanging Islam that exists outside of politics and history, a view that essentially conflates ideology and history.

What is important for our purposes is Polanyi's insistence that cultural politics must be situated in the nexus between national political strategies and shifting patterns in the global economy of capitalism. Cultural movements, Islamist or otherwise, are not 'autonomous' agents of social change operating in a vacuum. They are embedded in the dynamic interplay between domestic political strategies and global relations of power. Domestic strategies are part and parcel of the state-to-state relations involved in defining and managing a time-specific international order (Block 1977; van der Pijl 1984). The organization of an international order is always partial and unstable because of the ongoing political struggles within the boundaries of each state. On the other hand, shifting patterns in the state system with regard to production, trade, and military relations present opportunities and constraints for domestic political struggles and cultural movements. These struggles take place within the historically specific conjuncture of the political and geo-military events that govern the capitalist world economy (McMichael 2000).

The state is an important element in these interactions. States are the institutional manifestations of the link between global relations of power and the domestic political and cultural responses to it. Domestic political compromises, achieved within the state structure through various forms of multi-class populist alliances, mediate the link. This active political process involves constant negotiation, bargaining, and compromise within the specific conjuncture of world historical events. State policy must balance domestic political compromises with those formed in the international order (Block 1986). This balancing act structures many of the opportunities for and constraints against cultural movements. In a Muslim context, a political imagining of the links between participation in the global structures of power and cultural claims hinges on a particular perception of the West. In the process of such an imagining, Islamic ways become either comparable or opposed to those experienced in the West.

There is another approach to situating Islam in global politics, an alternative to the construction of a theoretical divide between 'universal modernity' and Islam. The very articulation of culture in a Polanyian sense is constitutive of the economy. The economy as an instituted process is organized within the larger relations of political, military, and ideological processes. Implicit here is the idea that the state distils the tension between international and domestic relations of power. This reflects evolving domestic political compromises in the state structure. The state modifies the impact of global economic, political, and geo-military forces on domestic politics by responding to the needs and demands of various social groups. This view of the state allows us to conceptualize Islamic politics as a relational phenomenon.

This belies any suggestion that the global market economy is homogenizing the world through the spread of a universal conception of Western modernity. More specifically, it refutes the notion that local religious traditions spontaneously consolidate into protective movements mobilized against the process of homogenization. Instead, this approach sees Islamic politics as entering into the domestic political compromises achieved within the state, becoming a player in the rethinking of links between national space and the outside world.

Polanyi formulated his ideas on the rise of a spontaneous protective response in the nineteenth century to the conditions of an emergent market economy in western Europe. In a non-Western context, the issue is that of a peripheral state embracing Western military and economic power in instituting a world capitalist market economy. We know from Polanyi that state policies must balance domestic political concerns with those in the international order. For Turkey, a country strategically located on the margins of western Europe and the Muslim world, the economic, political, and military-strategic encounters between the West and non-West are key to understanding Islamic politics.

We cannot, however, distinguish between the West and Islam in terms of a civilizational divide, traceable to unchanging cultural essences. Gellner (1983) has pointed out that cultural production involves arbitrarily chosen, even fabricated, cultural premises. Anderson (1991), on the other hand, argues that cultures cannot be distinguished by their falsity or genuineness, but only by the style in which they are imagined. He has shown that they are actually constituted through capitalism's historical trajectory of geographical expansion. What matters is the social construction of cultural traits that are real and powerful enough to create a strong sense of belonging in a community. This solidarity is also an ideological device that creates apprehensiveness towards others who happen to be outside of this particular 'imagined community'. The concern here is with figuring out how 'the West and non-West' operates in an Islamist imagining of domestic and global politics.

The Islamist encounter with Western dominance

Islam does not possess a cultural essence outside history. It is a category for understanding politics, society, and history, drawing on themes commonly encountered in populist and nationalist ideologies. According to Edward Said (1995), the idea of 'Islam and the West' corresponds to powerful ways of each knowing the other, which European colonial powers historically structured not only through political and economic domination but also through the production of knowledge in philosophy, literature, art, and colonial administration. The West, in large measure, implies a detached superiority for a handful of values and ideas, none of which has much meaning outside the history of conquest (Said 1993). Both the West and Islam know themselves as essentially different from each other, but in ways that assume the superiority of the West.

The issue for Islamists, therefore, concerns the ways in which Western economic and political-military dominance was established over Muslim societies and how they can respond to these claims of Western superiority. Islamists have developed two alternatives to Western domination—Islamic modernism and Islamic radicalism—whose roots lie in the colonial history of the Arab world and the Indian subcontinent of the late nineteenth and early twentieth centuries. Jamal al-Din al Afghani (1839–97), born in Iran and educated in Iran and British India, was a pioneer of Islamic modernism and radicalism. He was a modernist in that he believed in the necessity of reforming Islam so that Muslim societies could resist the West and restore their independence (Keddie 1994). He was also a radical anti-imperialist activist who wanted to organize a transnational Islamist liberation movement against Western encroachment.

According to Afghani, the reassertion of Islamic identity and solidarity was essential for the survival of Muslims. Afghani believed that Muslim solidarity was essential at both the national and international levels for the restoration of Muslim independence and self-sufficiency. His ideas contributed to the pan-Islamic programme of Ottoman Sultan Abdulhamit II (1878–1908), although it was Namik Kemal, an Ottoman Muslim intellectual, who first wrote on the importance of Islamic unity against Western imperialism. Abdulhamit prefigured a transnational political Islam under the political leadership of the Ottoman Empire. The Islamists of today continue to find appeal in Afghani's ideas on Muslim self-sufficiency and unity against Western domination.

Egyptian-born Sheikh Muhammed Abduh (1849–1905) was a follower of Afghani but departed from transnationalist pan-Islamism. Abduh gave priority to the promotion of national interests through reform measures. He believed this was essential for enhancing the position of a Muslim state within the international system. His ideas form the basis of Islamic modernism. Despite differences in strategy, modernist and radical strands of the Islamic movement agreed on the dominant motif of European colonial control of Muslim societies. Both had an imperialist image of the West, attaching great importance to the international system in determining Muslim subordination within it.

Islamic modernism responds to the challenge of Western imperialism by reforming Muslim societies. According to Abduh, reform has to come from within Islam, not from emulating Western ways (Haddad 1994). Moreover, Islam, correctly understood and interpreted, is perfectly compatible with the instrumental reason of modern science and technology. In order to strengthen Muslim societies, Muslims must first recognize the scientific and economic dynamism of Western societies, and then use this power themselves to reformulate Islam in such a way that they can counter Western dominance. This means making Islam relevant to modern ideas and institutions. For Abduh, Islam is a religion with strong rational elements that can serve as the basis for life in the modern world. A reinterpretation of the Koran's meaning would make Islam the champion of progress and development. Abduh argues that Muslims should not simply follow tradition blindly but should use their reason in interpreting Islam. They should think creatively about the revelation and become knowledgeable about the laws and principles that govern the universe. This would provide a foundation for the empowerment and revival of Muslim societies. Islamic modernism, then, must lead the way in playing 'catch-up' with European powers through a 'modernizing' reform programme. Abduh was greatly impressed with European progress ideology and the application of instrumental reason (Brown 2000), but his primary goal was to redefine Islam for the twentieth century rather than blindly emulate Western ways.

Neither Islamic modernism nor the radicalism of the nineteenth century advocated a return to a golden age of the past. Both, however, acknowledged the need for change on the basis of the cultural legacy of Islam. In challenging Western dominance, they denied that Islam implies a fixed cultural essence that is incompatible with changing social conditions. These ideas, which came about in the nineteenth century during the expansion of a capitalist market economy into the non-Western world, produced a long-lasting legacy for Islamic politics. The compatibility of Islam and modernity is not an issue here. Most Islamists would acknowledge the acceptability of Islamic reform (Cooper et al 2000; Hassan 2002). Islamists would disagree, however, over the meaning of Western influence for a Muslim society. They have very different views regarding the direction, method, and degree of change necessary for reorganizing society. This difference of opinion makes sense in the ideological context of a political movement which has some members who advocate accommodation with the West and others who push for self-sufficiency and independence.

During the height of the Cold War some Islamist thinkers came to question a universal conception of Islamic politics. Although they developed a critique of Western imperialism, capitalism, and materialism in relation to Islamic values, their critique reflects the possibility of choice on how to use existing forms of state power. For example, the radical Islamism of Mawlana Mawdudi (1903–79), founder of the Jamaat-I Islami movement on the Indian subcontinent, and Sayyid Qutb (1906–66), a major figure of the Muslim Brotherhood of Egypt, regards Islam as a unique world-view that must be distinguished from other belief systems. This includes a rejection of nationalism and the nation-state, which Mawdudi believed misled Muslims and undermined Muslim unity. Consequently, the writings of these radical Islamists took on a more communitarian tone. Their vision was one of total self-sufficiency guided by political organizations such as the Muslim Brotherhood and the Jamaat-I Islami.

The Islamic modernism of Ali Shariati (1933–77) of Iran, on the other hand, accepted much from the West, including the Enlightenment principles of freedom, equality, justice, and progress. For Shariati, the national space of the state was the arena of a historical struggle between justice and injustice. In the quest to free society from repressive political regimes and the injustices of a capitalist economy, Shariati expected Islamic intellectuals to spearhead revolutionary national liberation movements (Rahnema 1994; Shepard 1987). His writings were an attempt to formulate an Islamic ideology of freedom, equality, and justice by articulating Islam's compatibility with other revolutionary ideologies, including socialism.

The radical Islamism of Mawdudi and Qutb involves a complete rebuilding and reorientation of Muslim society. Mawdudi's writings reflect a strong preference for a transnational Muslim community and a dislike of nationalism. His work emphasizes the universalism of Islam and the comprehensiveness of Islamic life. Mawdudi envisions a form of globalization in which Islamic unity is severed from all local cultural and political ties with national states. For him, the conflict is between Islam and the non-Islamic, which consists of the West and the local cultural traditions practised in Muslim societies. This struggle between Islam and the non-Islamic would eventually culminate in an Islamic revolution and the creation of an Islamic state. A gradual Islamization of society through Islamic education would facilitate such a revolution, eliminating the need for a violent political uprising. An Islamic modernist like Shariati, on the other hand, would only refashion Muslim society and the nation-state. The Islamic modernist stand in relation to westernization is nationalist, with independence and economic development as its ideological foundation (Piscatori 1986).

Both radical and modernist Islamic ideologies were put forward more forcefully in the Cold War era, when other Third Word independence movements also mobilized against Western imperialism and domination. What appears to be a current 'resurgence of Islam' is actually a political struggle over the future direction and social meaning of Islamic culture in reorganizing Muslim societies. This is a struggle that brings the relevance of Islam to the current processes of globalization. It incorporates the urban poor, rural masses, and other marginalized segments of society into the rewriting of a new history of Muslim culture in the post–Cold War international system.

Competing conceptions of society and related power struggles enter into the articulation of an Islamic ideology that imagines society either as parallel to or distant from Western ways. That Islamic politics takes a particular form at a particular time reflects a process of mediation and shifting domestic political alliances responding to the pressure of global relations of power within the conjuncture of geopolitical events. It is never an outcome predetermined by the ideological content of Islam or the West. As I have demonstrated, Islam takes a variety of ideological forms in its dealings with modernity and the West.

The well-educated Islamist engineers, industrialists, and business groups who emerged as a new fraction of capitalists in the political context of the 1980s and 1990s are struggling to reposition themselves in the highly competitive relations of the global economy. Their ideas and aspirations can hardly be grouped within a 'Third Worldist' perspective that, during the Cold war, popularized notions of national self-sufficiency and decoupling from the capitalist world economy. This new group of Islamists possesses a cultural disposition of openness to the world based on an Islamic morality that facilitates their participation in the global economy.

Organization of the book

This book views Islam as a multidimensional construct in which politics, ideology, and the economy form an interrelated whole. A broad historical model is used to articulate these dimensions at the global, regional, and local levels, thereby allowing us to interpret the national dynamics of the political economy and culture of the Turkish state and Islam. The analysis is organized around three themes: 1) global relations of power including development strategies and political and military relations that govern the organization of the global economy; 2) domestic political-cultural responses to these relations; and 3) opportunities and constraints presented to citizens within these larger mechanisms of change. The book draws these themes from the double movement argument of Karl Polanyi (1944). It suggests that various forms of multi-class populist alliances in the state structure mediate the link between global power relations and domestic responses to them. This dynamic political process incorporates daily life experience into the negotiations and compromises that take place within a specific conjuncture of global events.

The book provides an overview of the political economy of a declining Ottoman Empire in the nineteenth century and the subsequent political and economic changes of the Turkish state, from its founding around the Kemalist principles of secularism in the 1920s to the current era. All of this is examined in the context of a changing global system.

The ordering of the seven chapters enables us to explore the historically variable articulation of Islam in Turkey in relation to the exercise of state power. By exposing the powerful forces confronting the state, a framework is developed for interpreting the dynamics of Islam within contemporary Turkey. Also illuminated are the historical forms of capital fractions and political interests, including patterns of elite formation, and their incorporation into the state. Finally, each chapter provides empirical evidence for the articulation of Islam not only by the political elite, including the military, but also by Muslims confronting changes in their day-to-day activities. We see how Islam becomes a critical resource for the state and for Muslims themselves in reconfiguring specific social relations and frames of reference, rather than merely a moral force for prescribing social behaviour.

One thing is certain: The most appropriate question to ask in relation to research on Islamic politics is not whether Islam constitutes a fundamentalist rejection of the West and modern ways of living. Rather, we should ask: What lies behind the dynamics of Islamic ideology construction, who constructs it, how is it shaped over time, and how does it enter into the organization of the global economy? This book describes a pattern of recurrence in the shaping of Islamic politics in Turkey. The central link is straight-forward: Islamic politics is a product of interactions between domestic and global political economy. This interaction depends on the domestic political alliances formed within the state. But how do changes in state strategies and the wider military and economic relations of power relate to each other? What are the outcomes? The rise of political Islam is one possibility, but Islamists figure in Turkish politics in complicated ways and are undoubtedly making a long-term difference to the history of the Turkish state. Clearly, the links between the power configurations of the state, political regimes, and Islam vary significantly from one period to the next. Exactly how and why Islam appears to be a credible ideology over such a long period of time is discussed in later chapters.

2

A Secular Vision of Modernity

My review of the long history of Islamic politics in Turkey traces the debate on the role of Islam back to the second half of the nineteenth century. During the Tanzimat period (1839–76) Ottoman reformers undertook a series of policies to restructure the Ottoman state along secular principles. In their minds, the term 'secular' did not constitute something wholly independent from Islamic referents. Islamists opposed the 'secularization' project of the Tanzimat. They advocated the adoption of Western technology, but not its culture. Islamists argued that a nation that turned its back on its own culture could only produce a rootless imitation. For them, this was a call for disaster. Nevertheless, Islamists were not wholly against the adoption of Western ways. They reworked the relationship between Western and Islamic culture so that the Ottoman Empire could regain its competitive power. The controversy was settled temporarily during the formative years of the Turkish nation-state in the 1930s, when the founding leaders of the Turkish Republic eliminated any possibility of opposition. For them, development required the wholesale adoption of Western cultural values.

The 'secularism' project of the early republican period reflects a synthetic approach to Western modernity as a model for emulation, but a comprehensive analysis of Ottoman history reveals an attempt to elevate a specific western European experience to a level of universally replicable 'modernity'. The long-standing debate over the meaning of modernity informs the dynamic interplay between Islamic and secular politics in a way that translates into the rhythms of class formation, new configurations of power, and interstate rivalries. Via political and cultural struggles, Esteva and Prakash (1998) write, modernity is defined by a capacity to apply the Western culture of progress, science, and technology to the market-economic credo. A uniquely western European experience thus becomes transformed into a universal belief in modernity.

Ottoman reformers had considerable experience in combining Islamic and Western ways, and any representation of their efforts as a matter of merely choosing between two competing sets of practices misses the point. These reformers were responding to the institution of a global market economy, and their response was tied to a specific image of the West.

What exactly are 'the West' and the 'Western model'? Perhaps if we acknowledge the challenge of other states contending for dominance in Europe in the late nineteenth century, as we grant Britain the status of dominant world power in the eighteenth century, we might see that the West cannot be characterized as an unproblematic entity. Fierce historical struggles in each state culminated in the emergence of various trajectories of state formation in Europe (Tilly 1990). Their outcomes in producing the Western model were far from obvious (Zubaida 1994). Still, the Ottoman elite viewed the West as a largely unchallenged homogeneous notion that impinged on a project of 'modernity' idealizing Enlightenment principles. Tanzimat imagery contrasted the Ottoman-Islamic legacy with a newly constructed knowledge of the West. In the minds of the reformers, the West was a source of inspiration, while the Ottoman Empire was a bureaucratically oppressive and economically and militarily weak.

This understanding of the West is accurate in so far as it points to the discursive primacy of the West in the fields of science and technology (Kandiyoti 1996). Nevertheless, the characterization overlooks complex, multifaceted encounters involving trade, diplomacy, and war (Arrighi and Silver 1999). These encounters were entangled with the search for a model that would strengthen the Ottoman state. A deeper understanding of the military-diplomatic engagements and political struggles of the late nineteenth and early twentieth centuries might enable us to conclude, then, that we have good reason to subvert the binary view of the West and Islam.

The Ottoman merging of Islam and Western modernity

Although 'pan-Islamism' is an old concept referring to the union of all Muslims, it only emerged as a political ideology in the second half of the nineteenth century. The Young Ottomans, the earliest advocates of pan-Islamism, were part of a new urban class of literati from Istanbul, including Sinasi (1826–71), Ali Suavi (1839–78), and Namik Kemal (1840–88). In addition to receiving an Islamic education, many of them attended European-style schools, established during the Tanzimat era, where they learned foreign languages and came under the influence of European liberal principles. Most Young Ottomans had family backgrounds in the Ottoman bureaucracy and worked for the government in the Translation Office of the Sublime Porte. The Translation Office, founded in 1821, was the first educational body in the Ottoman Empire in which government officials received a Western-style education (Somel 2001: 21). Working in the Translation Office, the Young Ottomans were well acquainted with European thought and European political and administrative systems. Sinasi, for example, studied public finance and literature in Europe.

All Young Ottomans were concerned about the disintegration of the Ottoman Empire and believed that European liberal ideas needed to be incorporated into an Islamic theory of the state (Mardin 1962). They saw this integration as necessary to strengthen the Ottoman state in the face of Western encroachment onto Muslim lands. The unifying theme among Young Ottoman intellectuals was reform for Ottomans, by Ottomans, and along Islamic lines, even though they were inspired by Western liberal ideals (Tunaya 1952: 94). They hoped to institute constitutional rule and to create an ideology of Ottoman unity under Islam. What they envisaged was a consultative and responsible government that derives its power from God, turned into a Western theory of government that emphasizes popular representation and sovereignty. However, this was a difficult task given that the Young Ottomans lacked a workable theory of political opposition and a clear distinction between state, individual, and community. Although they praised the Enlightenment idea of progress for contributing to material advances in Europe, they still believed that the Koran was a fundamental source of social cohesion and that it offered the greatest guaranty of individual freedom. For the Young Ottomans, there was 'no discrepancy between the theory that the King's power comes from God and the theory that it arose by a contract with the people' (Mardin 1962: 401).

The Young Ottomans were forerunners of those who hold the idea that Islamic culture is compatible with Western liberal principles. Their emphasis on the compatibility of Islam with European modernity reappears in the writings of Islamic modernists such as Afghani and Abduh. As patriots, the Young Ottomans defended Muslim lands from the West. They protested the abusive power of ruling bureaucratic cadres but were not against the sultanate. Their concern was that 'the people' be protected from bureaucratic abuses. 'The people', for the Young Ottomans, were the lower and lower-middle classes who received few if any of the material benefits promised by the secularizing reforms of the Tanzimat.

The print media became the means by which Young Ottomans disseminated their critical ideas. While in exile in Paris and London, they started newspapers such as the *Muhbir* and the *Hurriyet*. Because they sought to communicate with the general population in the Ottoman Empire, they wrote in spoken Turkish, a clear departure from the writing style of the Ottoman era—a mixture of Arabic, Persian, and Turkish. When they returned from exile in 1871 they continued their criticism in Istanbul newspapers such as the *Ibret* and the *Basiret,* contributing greatly to political debate in the empire (Turkone 1991).

Intellectuals from other Muslim lands also became familiar with Young Ottoman writings, including Muslim refugees who came to Istanbul as a result of the European colonization of India (Ozcan 1997). Afghani was among the intellectuals most influenced by the Young Ottoman idea of combining Islam with Western ways. He stayed in Istanbul during 1870 and 1871 (Turkone 1991: 35–6).

It is noteworthy that an article published in *Basiret* on 12 April 1872 opened a discussion for the first time on the policy of pan-Islamism in the Ottoman Empire (Ozcan 1997: 35–8). The article was followed by a general upsurge of Islamist activity. This included the writing and distribution of pamphlets, letters, and articles, the publication of a book in 1899 by Esat Efendi entitled *Ittihad-I Islam* (Unity of Islam), and the founding of the Society for the Geography of Muslim Lands (Memalik-Islamiye Cografya Cemiyeti) by Hoca Tahsin Efendi. All emphasized the need for Muslim unity around the Ottoman sultan-caliph in confronting European colonialism. While these activities cannot all be attributed to the Young Ottomans, their writings certainly encouraged the general population to become more enthusiastic about Muslim unity.

The Young Ottomans generally, and Namik Kemal in particular, were ardent critics of Tanzimat period reforms. They were not against the constitution of a rational bureaucratic state (Findley 1980), but they vehemently opposed the transformation of the central state into a monolithic and authoritarian apparatus controlled by secular bureaucrats. Much of their criticism was levelled against the granting of equal status and rights to non-Muslims. The goal of Tanzimat bureaucrats was to achieve a unified Ottoman nation through the concept of mass citizenship, unbroken by creed, religious affiliation, or nationality. As Gocek (1996: 85) demonstrates, this unity was only realized to a limited extent. Nevertheless, Tanzimat reforms, at least in theory, extended the principle of equality before the law to cover areas of educational opportunity, government appointments, and the administration of justice, as well as matters concerning taxation and the military (Davison 1993: 64). This is exactly what the Young Ottomans opposed.

The Young Ottomans protested against an Ottoman autocracy that they perceived to be a tool of Western imperial domination in the design and enforcement of reforms. They believed the government was catering to the expectations of Western powers in a manner that would define the rights of its Christian subjects as distinct from those of Muslims. The 1839 reform programme (Hatti-Sheriff of Gulhane), dictated by the British, and the Hatti Humayun of 1856, imposed by the Treaty of Paris, required the Ottoman government to accept the religious privileges of its Christian subjects and undertake a number of reforms to guarantee their security. The 1861 treaty extended foreign involvement in Ottoman reforms and forced the government to recognize France, for example, as the protector of Ottoman Catholic subjects. Similarly, Russia claimed to be a protector of the rights of Greek and Russian Orthodox faiths and Slavic speakers in the Ottoman Empire.

According to the Young Ottomans, *sharia* law assured Muslim dominance in the state (Turkone 1991). There were two main *millets*, consisting of Muslims and non-Muslims. Regardless of language differences, Muslims were the dominant *millet*. Non-Muslims were the ruled *millet*, divided into separate religious communities. They lived in separate quarters of the city under the headship of their own religious leaders who represented their community before the government (Inalcik 1994: 150–1). Non-Muslim *millets* had no right to access ruling positions in the central bureaucracy unless they converted to Islam. They were also prohibited from serving in the military, although they had to pay an exemption tax. The Young Ottomans believed that Tanzimat reforms granted equal citizenship rights to all, while maintaining special religious community privileges for non-Muslims at the same time (Mardin 1962: 14–5). This contradiction, Young Ottomans argued, resulted from the fact that foreign states imposed reforms on the government, yet extended legal assurances to non-Muslim *millets* and non-Muslim mercantile groups affiliated with European commercial interests. Namik Kemal was thus moved to call the reforms 'charters of concessions' to non-Muslims (Turkone 1991: 68).

The Young Ottoman opposition to Tanzimat reforms underscores the dominant role of foreign powers in designing these reforms. For example, diplomatic pressure imposed by the British ambassador, Lord Stratford de Redcliffe, was instrumental in this regard (Palmer 1992). Britain favoured a strong, centralized Ottoman state to curb the unpredictability of future Great Power politics in redrawing the map of Europe. Britain hoped that the reforms would strengthen the central authority of the government and undercut Russian influence in the Balkans over Slavic-speaking members of the Orthodox faith (Marriot 1924). It was also believed that the reforms would help contain the expansionist ambitions of France (Kasaba 1993).

It is not fair, however, to claim that the reformers were passive recipients of Western-imposed prescriptions. Tanzimat bureaucrats were determined to revivify the empire and fend off growing foreign influence. Ottoman military power had been weakened by Balkan insurrections and the Ottoman–Russian wars of 1768–74, 1787–92, 1806, 1809–12, 1828–29, and 1854–56. Particularly after the defeat of the Ottoman army by Russia in the Crimean war of 1854–56, it became necessary to 'modernize' the army and navy. This, in turn, required that Ottomans accept the military superiority of guns, heavy artillery, and armoured warships produced through the application of techniques developed during the Industrial Revolution. Convinced of the need to acquire Western scientific thinking and catch up with Western technological advances, Tanzimat bureaucrats gave priority to Western-style education.

Western-style education in the Ottoman Empire

The government opened the first Western-style educational institutions in 1773, during the military emergency created by the Ottoman-Russian war of 1768–74 (Somel 2001: 21–2). These were military schools designed to train officers, where students learned mathematics, geometry, and the natural sciences. In the 1830s the government began to open schools for civil servants in order to train a professional class of civil bureaucrats. The new educational policies resulted in a significant increase in the number of military and civil bureaucrats graduating from Western-style, government-built schools. Many of these officers and civil servants, whom Gocek (1996: 44–86) refers to as the Ottoman bureaucratic bourgeoisie, were Ottoman Muslims.

Prior to the 1830s, Ottoman education consisted mainly of religious training, with Koran schools at the elementary level and *medreses* at the higher level. These were civil educational institutions established for Ottoman Muslims. They were financed by *vakifs* (charitable endowments) and directed by members of the lower *ulema* (Singer 2002). The *rusdiyye* public schools, founded in 1839, were the first schools to provide a mixed religious and practical curriculum. These were advanced primary level schools attended mainly by Muslims. Their graduates were seen as potential civil servants. The Young Ottoman intellectuals and many founding members of the Turkish Republic, including Mustafa Kemal, received their education at the *rusdiyye* schools.

Non-Muslims attended Western-style schools, founded by their own religious communities, European states, and missionaries, where they received a mixed education in the modern sciences and the religious culture of their particular denomination. Ineligible for the bureaucratic posts traditionally allocated to Muslims, non-Muslims developed into a new social group, the Ottoman commercial bourgeoisie (Gocek 1996: 86–116).

The 1856 reform package brought about a major shift in educational policy. Equal opportunity for all subjects was mandated, thereby allowing admittance of non-Muslims to Ottoman civil and military schools. Although the educational system was being secularized in order to increase non-Muslim presence in the Ottoman bureaucracy, the reformers did not rid education of its Islamic religious content. Rather, they began to institute a mixed curriculum of Islamic studies and modern sciences for Muslim students, while acknowledging the right of every religious community to establish its own schools (Somel 2001: 49). This marks the emergence of an Ottoman brand of education based on the perceived need for both scientific-technical knowledge and religious moral values. Reformers saw such an educational programme as essential for the growth of a competitive Ottoman power-base with the capacity to fend off foreign political and cultural interference (Fortna 2002). This emphasis on increasing Ottoman competitiveness through education became more explicit during the Abdulhamit era of pan-Islamism.

As reforms unfolded after 1839, the curriculum of the sultan's schools changed to accommodate courses on commerce and the sciences as well as Islamic studies. Nevertheless, Islam and moral education continued to be an important pillar of Tanzimat educational ideology. The earliest government-backed textbook *Ahlak Risalesi* (Treaties of Morality) was used between 1847 and 1876. Written by Sadik Rifat Pasha, it sought to inculcate the core values deemed necessary for a pupil's moral education. These included: religiosity, obedience, respect, cleanliness, discipline, preservation of health, generosity, self-control, patience, good manners, benevolence, and duty. The *Ahlak Risalesi* was designed to ensure that students maintained their religious devotion and patriotic fervour.

It is not an exaggeration to say that Ottomans welcomed Western liberal principles in the hope of strengthening state power. But they were also suspicious of the wholesale adoption of Western cultural values. In fact, they attributed the growth of secessionist movements among non-Muslims to those values.

Non-Muslims were not interested in remaining in the empire as equal citizens of the state, nor were they interested in being trained for the civil service in sultan schools. They objected strenuously to the principle of equal taxation and the abolition of all community privileges and exemptions (such as serving in the military). For the first time, non-Muslims would have to pay considerably higher taxes (Inalcik 1994). After the Ottoman-Russian war of 1877 and the Berlin Treaty of 1878, it was clear that the Christian communities of Greek and Slavic-speakers were not even interested in a kind of federal equality with the empire.

Intellectuals and ruling bureaucratic cadres concluded that the Tanzimat project of achieving Ottoman unity around secular principles of citizenship was dead. Given the increase in the Muslim population of the empire, the sultan began to promote the idea of Muslim unity. The empire lost most of its Balkan lands and the Christian population but there was a massive influx of Muslim refugees from territories that had fallen under British, Russian, and French rule in India, Central Asia, and North Africa. As a result, by the end of the 1870s more than 70 per cent of the population in the Ottoman Empire was Muslim (Ozcan 1997: 44). The sultan's pan-Islamic appeal was also popular among the Muslims of Central Asia and India living in communities under colonial attack by Russia and Britain.

The Russian war and the Berlin Treaty had reinforced the idea that Ottomans had to rely on their own resources and co-author their own trajectory of social change. Sultan Abdulhamit undertook a programme to expand the education of Muslims by merging Islamic religion with modern science and technology. In addition to the traditional Koran schools, new Western-style elementary level *ibtidai* schools were built, as well as advanced primary level *rusdiyye* and secondary level *idadi* schools. The number of new-style schools constructed during the Abdulhamit reign approached 10,000 (Fortna 2002: 99). The secondary level *idadi* schools, designed in the tradition of French lycées, exposed imperial bureaucratic cadres to western European culture and rational scientific thinking, but without neglecting the role of Islamic culture and moral principles. In 1868, the Galatasaray Lycée (Mekteb-I Sultani) was established in Istanbul by the French for the education of the bureaucratic elite. It set the example for Abdulhamit's *idadi* schools. Under the directorship of Ali Suavi, the Galatasaray Lycée shifted its curriculum to prevent students from becoming preoccupied with Western ideas and philosophy at the expense of Islamic teachings.

A Western-style education combining knowledge of science and technology with the precepts of Islam was also advocated for the general population. The press, especially the *Basiret*, the *Sabah*, and the *Vakit*, were all mobilized to promote the idea of Muslim unity through education and moral guidance. Education for the general public, however, actually meant education for Muslim men. The students being trained in these schools for positions in state management were all male. Girls began to receive education in state schools as early as the 1840s, but their education remained at the primary level; very few women entered state employment, and those who did worked as teachers (Quataert 2000: 66).

Under Sultan Abdulhamit, education was given the highest priority in order to develop skills in practical, religious, and moral matters. The educational system was central to the production of civil servants as well as Muslim commercial classes. Reformers redesigned the educational system so that Muslims could become competitive with the non-Muslim commercial classes who were already receiving a mixed education abroad or in the community schools opened by their religious leaders (Fortna 2002).

Sultan Abdulhamit also mobilized Sufi orders and sent Muslim clerics into the countryside to rally Muslim support for religious and practical education. With the spread of railways from about 1870 onwards, there was a sharp increase in the number of Sufi dervishes and other Muslim clerics travelling back and forth between Ottoman and other Muslim lands. The Naqshbandi order, in particular, was mobilized to organize popular support for Muslim unity (Gunduz 1983).

The Naqshbandi order had a strong organizational structure. It formed small community-based networks based on personal relations and linked them to a strong, centrally organized structure. This strategy also defined the way in which knowledge applied to the task of Muslim mobilization was to be acquired (Algar 1983). Such knowledge—defined as the pursuit of self-purification— was to be gained through absolute conformity to the teachings of the sheikh residing in one's community. In Naqshbandi thought there are three sources of knowledge: the book, the memory, and the practice of *rabita*. Acquiring knowledge is not seen as a solitary practice involving only the study of religious texts. The spiritual leader or master plays a crucial role in the learning process. Schimmel (1975: 366) writes that the centre of Naqshbandi education is the silent *dhikr* (recollection of God in the heart) inspired by the spiritual leader. The second characteristic is *sohbet,* an intimate spiritual conversation between master and disciple. The close relation between master and disciple reveals itself in *rabita* (linking the heart of the follower to the heart of the leader) and results in the experience of spiritual unity and purification. It is this system of interpersonal linkages established for the exercise of *sohbets* and *dhikrs* that distinguishes the organizational strategy of the Naqshbandi and underpins its political success (Mardin 1991). Recognizing the tremendous potential in the Naqshbandi organizational strategy, Sultan Abdulhamit encouraged Naqshbandi disciples to appeal to the hearts and minds of Muslims throughout the empire and mobilize them against Western encroachment.

The Naqshbandi order also successfully used the print media that had been introduced into the intellectual life of Ottoman Muslims during the early eighteenth century. The wide circulation of letters and books has always been a very important component of Naqshbandi political activism (Schimmel 1975: 367). Ottoman Naqshbandi Sheikh Gumushanevi published his own book, *Cami'ul-Usul,* and many journals were printed and circulated, including *Ceride-I Sufiyye, Tasavvuf, Muhibban, Hikmet, Mirsad,* and *Mihrab.* An association known as Cem'iyet-I Sufiyye was founded for the purpose of publishing books, building a library, and organizing conferences (Kara 1979: 17–20). Similarly, the Gumushanevi convent built four libraries, purchased a printing machine, and distributed books to Muslims free of charge (Gunduz 1983: 184–90).

The Naqshbandi emphasis on Islamic education was complementary to Abdulhamit's educational programme. The sultan, along with leading figures of the period, saw the roots of European economic and military power in the rational sciences, which they believed were inextricably tied to technological achievement (Fortna 2002: 87–130). The substance of, and continuities between, the sultan's and the Tanzimat's goals of education are clear: to create and maintain a Muslim bourgeoisie equipped with the culture of modern science and technology and capable of facing a competitive market economy, all within the regulatory function of government schools.

Despite the continuities, there was also discontinuity with the Tanzimat project. The sultan's intense devotion to Muslim unity was part of the self-fashioning of the Ottoman Empire. The Ottoman nation-building that began with the Tanzimat's secular citizenship concept was transformed under Abdulhamit, placing Ottomans under Islamic moral regulation. Still, both converge in their ambivalent response to Western modernity: Ottomans rejected Western imperial domination but drew from Western liberal principles and cultural values. As Coronil (1997) has observed in relation to Venezuela, the nineteenth-century Ottoman project of co-authoring its own path decentres the European model of social change.

To understand how this preoccupation with self-fashioning shaped the path of Ottoman reforms, we must go beyond simplistic conceptions of

Western imitation or rejection. Going beyond such dichotomous views is key to understanding the emergence of historical differences as products of interrelated histories. More precisely, it is the history of free trade imperialism that put Europe and the Ottoman Empire on separate trajectories of social change.

Peripheralization of the state: free trade

To the extent that states regularly interact with each other and to the degree that their interaction affects the behaviour of each state is what makes state relations a system (Tilly 1990: 162). In Polanyi's (1944) view, from the 1815 Peace of Vienna until 1914, Britain fashioned a distinctive system of states based on a balance of power policy. The balance of power system, established by the Peace of Westphalia in 1648, became an instrument of British dominance in the nineteenth century via the Concert of Europe. It guaranteed consultation, co-operation, and thus the interdependence of nations (Arrighi and Silver 1999: 58–9). The balance of power policy was integral to the British reorganization of the world economy. The essential component of this reorganization was overseas colonial expansion, creating what McMichael (2000: 18–23) has called a division of labour between raw material and food production in the colonies and industrial production in Europe. By combining colonial expansion overseas with industrialization at home, Britain emerged as the dominant world power.

The adoption of the gold standard in 1870 set the monetary framework for the institution of a global free-trade regime (Eichengreen 1996: 7–44). The gold standard also fostered collaboration between central banks—usually privately owned institutions—and governments. It created a balance in great power politics, or in Polanyi's words, a hundred years' peace in Europe that secured open markets. The openness of markets and the operation of the colonial division of labour allowed Britain to recycle wealth from the colonies into capital investment all over the world. While the recycling of wealth enhanced London's central position in the global circulation of finance capital, it also supported the gold standard as an adjustment mechanism in world trade.

The importance of achieving a balance in power politics for the institution of a global market economy was most evident in the Western imposition of reforms on the Ottoman Empire. The Tanzimat project of secularism was premised on the formation of a powerful central state. Its most novel aspect was the granting of equal status and rights to non-Muslim subjects in order to prevent their separation from the empire. The territorial unity of the empire was considered essential for the maintenance of a power balance between European states.

However, a careful 'unpacking' of Tanzimat and subsequent Ottoman reforms erases any notion that the empire was a passive recipient of a Western-led reform programme. In actual fact, the Ottomans were engaged in refashioning their own historical trajectory. Ottoman reformers found the state to be entangled in a global process that demarcated Western from non-Western in a hierarchical manner, with Europeans dominating non-Europeans. Reformers discovered that the global process was unitary and entailed the constitution of a market economy. Rather than coming into conflict with Western progress ideology and the culture of science and technology—perceived to be keys to advancement—Ottomans decided to focus on Islamic morality in their adaptation to the market economy. To better understand the politics of Ottoman reforms, we must closely examine the Ottoman reworking of Western ways, from the Tanzimat period onwards.

Starting with the Anglo-Ottoman Commercial Convention of 1838, the Ottoman Empire adopted an economic model based on free trade. The convention sought to reduce the authority of the Ottoman government in imposing import tariffs and controls that would inhibit the free circulation of goods in the empire (Kasaba 1993). It allowed British merchants to purchase goods anywhere in the empire without paying taxes or dues other than a very small sum for import/export duties (Issawi 1980: 74–5). Other European states also became part of the Convention, which led to the expansion of cash-crop production on plantation-like farms for export to the industrial centres of Europe (Inalcik 1969: 115).

In the name of trade liberalization and equality, most barriers to trade were removed, economic concessions were granted to Europeans, and other treaties were imposed on the Ottoman Empire. This deeply polarized the Ottoman populace. Tariff concessions exposed domestic handicraft production to the competition of industrially manufactured European goods. The inability of government to protect domestic manufacturing hastened its decline (Barkan 1975). At the same time, concessions encouraged the production of raw materials and foodstuffs for export to Europe. Ottoman Muslims in handicraft production were transformed into unskilled labour (Inalcik 1987), while non-Muslim Ottoman merchants and agricultural producers became dominant in cash-crop production and trade with European business (Gocek 1996: 96-7).

The beginning of private ownership of land for cash crop production and the expansion of plantation-like farms, following adoption of the Land Code of 1858, were crucial elements in this process. The Ottoman state lost its traditional control over land and its revenues. Under these circumstances, it was no longer possible for the Ottoman government to raise the funds required for its wars from internal sources.

The Ottoman Empire also experienced a significant balance of payments deficit with Britain and other European states. This resulted not only from it becoming an exporter of raw materials and foodstuffs and importer of manufactured goods (Keyder 1987: 37–48), but also from the army's growing need for cash to wage increasingly industrialized wars. The empire desperately needed to borrow money. But the possibility of Russian military advances into the Mediterranean and Central Asia affected British and French willingness to lend money to the empire (Marriot 1924). The Ottoman loss to Russia in the Crimean War (1854–56) was a turning point in the relationship between private money-lending networks in London and Paris and the Ottoman balance of payments deficit.

By connecting Ottoman territorial security concerns to loans from London and Paris-centred private capital groups, Britain governed the process of Ottoman incorporation into the world free-trading regime as a 'peripheral state'. The 'Report on the Financial Condition of Turkey', written in 1860 by Lord Hobart and Mr. Foster, and approved by the British Parliament, required that the Ottoman Empire withdraw its paper money from circulation and adjust its currency to the international gold standard (Kiray 1990: 255–6). The convertibility of currency was to rest on the further liberalization of the Ottoman economy. Liberalization was key to foreign investment and trade, and also provided stability for Ottoman balance of payments vis-à-vis European capital.

In 1856 the Ottoman Bank was established by a group of London bankers. In 1863 it was reorganized with the entry of French financiers as co-owners. The bank was a focal point for the harmonization of policies between the Ottoman Empire and its creditors. Acting as a private central bank, it channelled loans from London and Paris money markets to the empire and issued treasury bonds against gold reserves in exchange for loans.

Between 1854 and 1875, 15 loans totalling 220 million British pounds were issued. This resulted in a large Ottoman foreign debt with an average rate increase of 5 million pounds per year (Baxter 1871: 71). The burden of foreign debt grew heavier with annual service charge increases, from 10 per cent of total government revenues in the early 1860s to 67 per cent in 1874 (Kiray 1990: 255). Unable to pay off these loans, the Ottoman government defaulted on foreign debt charges in 1875.

Between 1875 and 1881 the Ottoman Empire became a peripheral debtor state. To administer the Ottoman foreign debt, the Decree of Mouharrem was negotiated in 1881. In 1882 the government of pan-Islamic Sultan Abdulhamit allowed the establishment of the Public Debt Administration (PDA). After negotiating a 56 per cent debt reduction, the Ottoman government ceded certain state revenues to the PDA and granted them the right to administer, collect, and hold in deposit these revenues for the servicing of the debt (Blaisdell 1929: 80–93). The PDA was a private transnational organization representing private capital interests, negotiated bilaterally between the Ottoman government and the non-official representatives of its creditors. It became a large independent bureaucracy run by creditors, employing some 5,000 officials until its demise in 1928 (Quataert 2000: 71).

The PDA marked a crucial turning point in Ottoman history, with the Ottoman state virtually relinquishing much of its economic sovereignty. The PDA was formed to provide greater security for European private investors holding Ottoman bonds than that provided by the government. Ottoman revenue from custom duties, taxes, and tobacco production was designated as collateral in loan negotiations, and foreign moneylenders were able to establish claims on the future revenues of the Ottoman government. This effectively eroded the sultan's ability to claim and protect these revenue sources.

Under the PDA, increased revenues generated through the market expansion of cash crop production were shifted to private European creditors and investors as Ottoman debt payments (Pamuk 1987). The PDA also acted as an intermediary in the reinvestment of capital by foreign railroad companies. It paid railroad companies with the income generated from its collection of tithes, which the Ottoman government had assigned as pledges for a kilometric guarantee. The Decree of Mouharrem and the capital from railroad construction enabled the PDA to control about one third of the total public revenue of the Ottoman state (Keyder 1987: 40). More significant than the percentage of revenues controlled by the PDA was the fact that the liquid resources of the Ottoman Empire were in its hands.

Amidst the complexities of nineteenth-century power politics, Ottoman reformers constantly struggled over the alignment of the state with the market economy. Although outcomes differed in the Tanzimat and Abdulhamit periods, reformers did not conceive of secular and Islamic approaches as oppositional forms of modernity. Rather, they believed it was possible to merge the two to formulate a distinctly Ottoman brand of market competitiveness. This was their strategy to protect the empire from disintegration. Reformers attempted to merge Western culture and Islamic referents under the conditions of the global market economy.

The Tanzimat's secularism and Abdulhamit's pan-Islamism were both examples of the Ottoman reworking of Western modernity so that the state could regain control over the economy and create a unified Ottoman bourgeoisie out of the highly polarized commercial classes. In their adaptation of Western modernity, reformers engaged in a refashioning of Islam and secularism in order to create a common vision of Ottoman society for different cultural and religious groups. Central to this theorizing, then, was a conception of culture that simultaneously reproduced both Western and Islamic elements in the formation of an Ottoman bourgeoisie.

The problem was that material conflicts of interest had already intensified among various religious communities. Not only Christians but also Muslim-Arabs in the empire pushed for separation, while Ottoman reformers sought nationhood. It was after recognizing the futility of Ottoman unity that a group of intellectuals known as the Young Turks developed what they believed to be a solution. Broadly speaking, some Young Turks supported the emulation of Western ways while others made reference to Islam in modeling the empire's future. Ahmet Riza was representative of the former group and Murat Mizanci the latter. Young Turks also promoted Turkish nationalism as a rival ideology. They linked the reproduction of Western modernity to the creation of a unified Turkish bourgeoisie and economy by curbing the economic power of non-Muslims. Ziya Gokalp occupies a pivotal role in this formulation. Although Gokalp never developed an ideology to completely eliminate Islamic or Ottoman referents, the future adaptation of his thought by the founders of the Turkish Republic represents a break from previous Ottomanist projects. Ottomans had either refused the writing of a 'national' history or never defined the national as Turkish history (Yinanc 1969).

The Young Turks devoted themselves to the construction of a mythology from which Turks would find their national history. Hungarian anthropologist Vambery and the Polish-born Mustafa Celaleddin Pasha based this history on the belief that the Turks belong to a larger race of people known as *Turan*, which also includes Finns, Hungarians, and the Turkic people of Central Asia and the Caucasus (Behar 1992: 64–5). Gokalp added a linguistic nationalism to *Turan* by synthesizing Western modernity, Islamic morality, and Turkish history (Berkes 1959: 72–4, 103, 284–5). This set the stage for the production and reproduction of a distinct political culture for the emergent 'Turkish' bourgeoisie and the economy. In the 1930s nationalism played an even greater role in providing a vision of unity for the newly emerging national bourgeoisie in Turkey.

The global free-trade regime relegated the Ottoman Empire to a peripheral position in the world economy and intensified the divisions among Ottoman commercial groups along cultural and religious lines. Kemalism, named after Mustafa Kemal, the founder of the Turkish Republic, put forward a unified conception of the Turkish state, national economy, and bourgeoisie. What we have here is the case of a peripheral state embracing the global free-trade regime at the very moment when the framework for that economy was collapsing in the 1920s and 1930s.

Kemalist secularization of the state

The Turkish nation-state was established after a near century-long journey of trial and error with Ottoman reforms. The journey ended on 29 October 1923 when the Grand National Assembly declared Turkey a republic and Mustafa Kemal was elected its first president. The declaration of the Turkish Republic sealed the end of the imperial government that had signed the Treaty of Sèvres in 1920. The treaty required the Ottoman state to surrender political sovereignty of its territories, renounce its rule of Cyprus and the Arab provinces in the

Middle East, and give up its administration of parts of western Anatolia. The War of Independence (1919–22), waged against the dismemberment of Anatolia by the Sèvres Treaty, and the military victory that resulted in the Lausanne Peace Treaty (1923), ended the First World War for Turkey. The Lausanne Treaty secured the territorial integrity of Anatolia and confirmed the abolition of capitulations that Ottoman governments had granted to foreign powers. In exchange for its sovereignty and the right to national self-determination, the government of the Turkish Republic renounced its rule over Arab provinces and accepted the British annexation of Cyprus. With two exceptions, the Lausanne Treaty finalized Turkey's present borders. In 1926 it was decided that Mosul would remain part of Iraq under British mandate. And in 1938 a dispute with France over Hatay-Alexandretta was resolved when it was decided that the region would remain in Turkey. The 15 years of Mustafa Kemal's republican presidency, from 1923 to his death in 1938, saw a series of political and cultural reforms, called Kemalism.

Kemalism endeavoured to end the dual character of Ottoman reforms that oscillated between Western modernity and Islamic culture. The abolition of the sultanate in 1922 was followed by the abolition of the caliphate in 1924. The *sharia* courts and office of the Seyh'ul-Islam (the highest religious official in the Ottoman Empire) were also closed. In 1928 the constitutional clause that proclaimed Islam the state religion was repealed. These reforms transformed the state structure, redirected social change onto a secular trajectory, and altered the symbolic framework of social and cultural life in Turkey (Bozdogan and Kasaba 1997).

Attempts were made to penetrate the lifestyle and customs of the population in the hope of eventually displacing Islam from the public sphere. Issues related to choice of clothing, where and how to live, what to eat, and what kind of music to listen to were all subject to Kemalist scrutiny. In 1925 the wearing of caps and fezzes by men was outlawed as these were considered symbols of religious obscurantism. In the same year, the religious brotherhoods were disbanded, convents and sacred tombs closed, and religious titles such as sheikh and dervish abolished. In 1926, the Muslim lunar calendar was replaced by the Gregorian solar calendar, and Islam's *sharia* law was replaced by the Swiss civil code and the Italian penal code. In 1928 the Latin alphabet was adopted and the script changed from Arabic to Latin. Attempts were also made to 'cleanse' the Turkish language of Arabic and Persian words. Co-education for girls and boys was introduced in 1924. Religious schools and institutes were closed, and the educational system was restructured along strictly secular lines. The Faculty of Theology, which had previously been responsible for higher education in religion, was abolished, and the Institute of Islamic Research was established within the body of the Faculty of Arts at Istanbul University. Higher religious education was thus replaced by scientific research on religion. In addition, the

Islamic call to prayer (*ezan*) and the Koran were changed from Arabic to Latin-scripted Turkish. The legal code was actually changed to permit three-month jail sentences for those caught reading the Koran in Arabic (Tarhanli 1993: 20). In 1935 the weekly holiday was shifted from Friday to Sunday, and in 1937 secularism became a constitutional requirement enforceable by law.

The effect of these reforms was far-reaching. In addition to the legal enforcement and repression carried out by public prosecutors and gendarmes, a series of propaganda campaigns was launched to disgrace local representatives of the Ottoman imperial system (Meeker 2002: 286). One particular letter campaign warned local *hocas* and *kadis* (Islamic *sharia* law judges) of the severe consequences for preaching against the republic. After receiving such a letter, one Islamic scholar and *kadi* of Ayas–a town in central Anatolia near Ankara–decided that it was time to retire from public service entirely. His grandson informed me in a personal interview that under the threat of persecution the *kadi* destroyed all remnants of his allegiance to the Ottoman system by burning the books he had written on *sharia* law. The goal of these intimidation campaigns was clearly to dislodge Muslim Ottomanists from all public activities.

In 1924 the Directorate of Religious Affairs was established within the office of the prime minister for the purpose of establishing greater state control over religion. It was to be a government-funded and regulated institution (Tarhanli 1993). All mosques were placed under its control, and all religious personnel, *imams* (prayer leaders) and *hatips* (preachers), became employees of the state—members of the secular bureaucracy. The Directorate of Religious Affairs illustrates that secularism was not an issue involving separation of state and religion. It was about the creation of an 'official' Islam as part of the secular state apparatus. The role of the Directorate of Religious Affairs was to encourage the development of civic responsibility and the loyalty of the general population to secular state principles.

During the late 1920s and 1930s state-employed Muslim clergy wrote completely new versions of religious textbooks. The directorate commissioned these books with the intention of promoting the idea that good citizenship was both a virtue and a religiously sanctioned moral duty. According to the new texts, a good Muslim

> must love his country, respect the laws of the republic, submit to the progressive guidance of state officials, do his utmost to learn modern techniques, apply scrupulously the principles of good hygiene, consult a doctor in case of illness to avoid being the cause of epidemics, and work energetically for the development of the country (Dumont 1987: 3).

By inserting personal ethics and moral duty into the notion of citizenship, Kemalism defined a good Muslim through the secular state.

It should be noted that secularizing reforms would not have been successful through repression and legal enforcement alone. Kemalists were not ignorant of the role of public celebration in ensuring people's loyalty to the new values and norms of the republic. For example, republican day festivities were, and remain, among the most celebrated in Turkey, observed every year on 29 October. The celebrations include folk songs, dances, and thanksgiving festivities, followed by speeches from local authorities and teachers on the role of Mustafa Kemal and his comrades in securing Turkey's independence. Schoolchildren also perform plays re-enacting the War of Independence. Festivities continue until well after nightfall with folk dances performed around a large fire by local residents. The republican day celebration is such an important event for the town of Gudul—a small town near Ankara—that even former inhabitants who have migrated to nearby cities travel back home to participate in the activities.

These public cultural celebrations demonstrate the similarity and kinship between the people of Turkey and the Western world. One such celebration, falling on 19 May, is dedicated to youth in high school. This was the date in 1919 when Mustafa Kemal arrived in the Black Sea port city of Samsun for the initial coordination of a national resistance to foreign occupation. Another celebration, for younger elementary schoolchildren, falls on 23 April. On this date in 1920 the Grand National Assembly was opened in Ankara. The 19 May and 23 April public performances emphasize national health and vitality expressed through sport and the athleticism of youth. The sporting events are accompanied by the playing of Western classical music. These festivities are designed to reveal the naturalness of an identification with secular culture expressed through sport. Irving Goffman's (1959) explanation of the construction of self through everyday performance is very applicable to Kemalist activities. Student performances demonstrate the embrace of Western cultural artefacts while disclosing the incongruity of Islamic elements in the public performance of everyday life.

Kemalists displaced Islam from the public realm with a pervasive secular life—one that would include everything from manners and clothing to household articles and furnishings. In a 1937 parliamentary speech, the Turkish Minister of Internal Affairs, Sukru Kaya, stated: 'Our aim is to make sure that religion will not be part of material life and worldly affairs' (Tarhanli 1993: 19). Although it cannot be argued that Islam framed all aspects of Ottoman daily life (Faroqhi 2000), the Kemalist obsession with its presumed religious content—especially in the case of clothing—focussed on eliminating all identification with the empire. Emptied of its religious and Ottoman referents, the 'nation' was now to be conceived in terms of a collection of individuals linked directly to the state through the concept of mass political citizenship. The Turkish Historical Society (1931) and the Turkish Linguistic Society (1932) were both established specifically to remove Ottoman-Muslim culture from the public space of the republic. They advocated the 'Turkish History Thesis' and the 'Sun-Language Theory' to provide the people of Turkey with an entirely new foundation for understanding their history (Gologlu 1974).

Similar to the idea of the *Turan* developed by the Young Turks, the Turkish History Thesis, presented at the First Turkish History Congress in 1932, claimed that the Turks belonged to a 'race' of people who first emerged in Central Asia and then established great civilizations in Anatolia, the Aegean, and Mesopotamia (Behar 1992). The Hittites and Sumerians were also seen as Turkish forebears (Seton-Watson 1977: 259). The Sun-Language Theory, presented at the Second Turkish History Congress in 1937, argued that in the old shamanistic religion of Turks before the acceptance of Islam, the sun symbolized the power of nature against that of God. The evolution of Turkish culture is thus seen as having followed a path based not on Islam, but on a secular interpretation of nature (Besikci 1991: 131–69; Gunaltay and Tankut 1938). These theories portrayed Islam as an ethnic religion of Arabs associated with the Arabic language and traditions (Lewis 1988). Both theories sought to show that ancient Turkish culture was congruent with Western modernity. The role of the state, then, was to eliminate the foreign traditions of Islam from a Turkish way of life, and place Turkish people back on their 'natural' trajectory. Reminiscent of a thesis advanced by Max Weber (1971), Kemalists believed that Islam was incongruent with modernity because of a cultural aversion to instrumental rationality and a capitalist economy.

The Kemalists' task was not easy, especially because of a significant increase in the number of Muslims living in Turkey during the 1920s. Many Muslims immigrated to Turkey from the Balkans during the Balkan wars and from Russia during the Bolshevik Revolution. Christian Armenians suffered from compulsory migration in 1915, resulting in a staggering loss of lives in 1914–15. In 1923 and 1930 population exchange agreements with Greece required the departure of Christian Greeks from Turkey and the immigration of Muslims from Greece to Turkey (Keyder 1987: 66–8). As a result, more than 90 per cent of the people living in Turkey during the 1920s were Muslims (Jaschke 1972: 20). They included Circassians, Lazes, Arabs, Kurds, Turks, Georgians, and all other Turkic and Muslim cultural categories (Kilic Ali 1955). For these people, local ties based on kinship, village, or religion were often more important than a general Turkish identification (Lewis 1968: Ch. 10). Although it was rather easy to identify non-Muslims as minority groups in relation to their religious affiliation, it was not easy to identify diverse Muslim cultural groups as Turks and direct them to a path completely detached from an earlier Ottoman and Muslim orientation. This detachment was the key foundational issue of the Turkish state and strictly enforced during the 1930s.

Eliminating the opposition

Behind the Kemalist reproduction of Western modernity was an almost century-long process of transformation during which the Ottoman Empire was absorbed into Europe's periphery. In the nineteenth century the world market economy was constituted as a free-trade regime, the stability of which was ensured by the international gold standard. With the intensification of Anglo-German and French rivalries, as evidenced by the First World War and subsequent conflicts within the inter-state system, the nineteenth-century market economy disintegrated into protected imperial zones (Arrighi et al 1999). If we examine this period of disintegration, we can reconceptualize Kemalism as a double-sided movement that both mitigated and obscured the centrality of Western identification in Turkish state formation.

Kemalists greatly admired Western modernity. They sought to ground their detachment from the Ottomans in a perception of the West as sole bearer of modernity. Yet Kemalists also feared Western domination of non-Western societies and rejected the West's 'imperialistic' claims. This ambivalence influenced the creation of a unitary Turkish nation-state in ways that implied a fundamental change in the relations between rulers and ruled, the techniques of political control, and economic strategies.

The post-war territorial configuration of imperial domains reframed the Kemalist imperialist image of the West. The end of the war brought Britain new opportunities to expand its overseas territorial empire. Together with its European rivals, the United States also became an important player in the inter-state system. Chief rivalries were focussed on control of trade routes around the Suez Canal to allow easy access to the Indian Ocean and oil resources in the Middle East (Venn 1986).

A number of oil concessions made by the Ottoman government between 1912 and 1922 granted monopoly rights to companies appointed by Britain (Zahlan 1989: Ch. 2). In 1912 the Turkish Petroleum Company (TPC) was established with a 50 per cent British share. It held a monopoly over the Mosul-Kerkuk oil fields. The French did not share an interest in the TPC, but the Sykes-Picot Agreement of 1916 allowed France to engage in exploration for Middle East oil. It did so by envisaging the creation of two Arab states, one under French protection around Damascus, from north of Beirut to south of Tyre, and the other under British protection, from Baghdad to Aqaba. Palestine would become the joint responsibility of France and Britain (Palmer 1992: 236). The agreement was finalized in 1920 at the San-Remo Conference, with a 25 per cent share of the TPC going to France. In return, Britain received French support for the establishment of a mandate regime in Iraq (Kent 1976: 137–57). However, since the San Remo Conference did not include the interests of US companies, the United States rejected the British mandate in Iraq. Moreover,

President Wilson delivered a proclamation on the right to self-determination (Mejcher 1976: 110–2). It was only after Standard Oil began to extract oil in Mosul and Kerkuk that the United States decided to back British colonial endeavours in the Middle East and abandon the 'right to self-determination'.

The US government was more concerned with securing a base for a US oil company in the region than rejecting British colonial control in the Middle East. As long as Britain followed a liberal open door policy for US companies, the United States did not reject British colonial domains. Britain therefore granted Standard Oil a 23.7 per cent share of the TPC in exchange for US support of its mandate in Iraq (Boratav 1982: 28). In a countermove, Turkey granted oil concessions to another US company, the Chester group. But, with Standard Oil's success in securing a share of Turkish Petroleum, the Chester group became obsolete. In the end, Turkey lost Mosul to Britain (Hershlag 1968: 25).

In securing its imperial domains, Britain also mobilized groups that were in fundamental conflict with the nationalizing reforms of Mustafa Kemal. The Kurdish tribes were among these groups (Yildiz 1991). But Britain was more successful in provoking Kurdish-speakers of Alavi and Christian faiths than it was in inciting the majority Sunni Muslim Kurds (Mumcu 1994a). The 1921 revolt by the Alavi-Kurdish Kockiri tribe and the 1924 Christian-Kurdish Nasturi revolt were carried out with British support (Duru 1978: 160–1). The revolts were sporadic and easily suppressed by the Turkish military but they nonetheless provided an opportunity for Kemalist bureaucrats to consolidate an image of the West as 'imperialistic' and to translate this image into the reorganization of relations between rulers and ruled. The government adopted blatantly oppressive techniques of political control and deployed coercive powers against those opposed to secularization. The Sheikh Said Revolt of 1925 in particular, led by a Kurdish-Naqshbandi sheikh, was used as justification for the deployment of the state's coercive power. The revolt also provided a rationale for imposing significant constraints on opposition in the Grand National Assembly and bringing it under the direct political control of Mustafa Kemal's party.

The majority of delegates in the Grand National Assembly were former top-ranking Ottoman military commanders and bureaucrats, professionals, ulema, and sheiks from various religious brotherhoods. In fact, Mustafa Kemal and his close associates were a minority in the Grand National Assembly. High-level bureaucrats included Fevzi Cakmak (Chief of the General Staff of the Ottoman Army, who also served as the Chief of Staff in the War of Liberation), Rauf Orbay, Ali Fuat Cebesoy, Kazim Karabekir, and Refet Bele. Neither Mustafa Kemal nor his close associate Inonu was in the upper ranks of the Ottoman army hierarchy. High-ranking army commanders were therefore resentful of the greater concentration of political power in the hands of Mustafa Kemal and Inonu (Kandemir 1955). As noted by Karabekir (1951), Army Commander of the Eastern Frontiers, the reason for founding the Grand National Assembly was not to detach Turkey from its Ottoman-Islamic heritage but to ensure the independence of Muslim-Turkish lands. Top military officials expected to carry on with their jobs in the upper ranks of the political hierarchy just as they did in the Ottoman Empire. They organized and formed the Progressive Republican Party.

The Progressive Republican Party (1924–25) was a liberal party that fought for the protection of individual rights and freedoms against abusive state power (Tunaya 1952: 585, 611–8). The party's support for freedom of expression included religious beliefs. This support, however, was interpreted as creating a basis for Islamic opposition against state reforms, thereby threatening the security of the state. In parliament, Mustafa Kemal was prompted to declare: 'What is the outcome of granting people various political liberties? People will start to make a fuss and noise on the streets. Is this a desirable aim? No! First, we should grant the nation protection and independence from enemies of the state before thinking about individual liberties, gentlemen' (Betin 1951: 81–2).

Enemies of the state included external and internal elements. The external enemy was Western states engaged in fierce rivalries over the territorial reconfiguration of oil fields in the Middle East. The internal enemy was Islamic groups. The War of Independence was successful in defeating the external threat; now was the time to suppress the internal threat. Political control came to be defined as the exclusion from the political process of any real, potential, or imagined rivals to the political power of Mustafa Kemal and his close associates. Potential internal threats included high-level bureaucratic cadres of the former Ottoman state and influential religious figures (Atasoy 1986: Ch. 3 and 4). They were perceived as dangerous because of their attempt to bring the Ottoman-Muslim ethos into the forefront of the founding of the Turkish state. However, one of these supposed threats, the Caliph Abdulmecit, was hardly a rival to the Kemalist state-making project. He was a quiet, artistic man, who spent most of his time painting. Abdulmecit never involved himself in Turkish politics, and the abolition of the caliphate in 1924 had nothing to do with his activities. Rather, it signalled to the opposition in parliament the beginning of oppressive modernization in Turkey.

Islamic groups were not initially identified as rivals to Mustafa Kemal. The leader had even developed ties with Naqshbandi sheikhs when organizing the War of Independence. Many of them supported the abolition of the sultanate in 1922 in favour of a constitutional regime, hoping that the caliph would be the 'natural' focus of power in liberated Muslim lands (Misiroglu 1992). Inonu went even further by making assurances that 'the caliph will live in Istanbul under the protection of free Turkey' (Jaschke 1972: 119). The Naqshbandi order's support for the War of Independence was rooted in their belief that the conflict was an Islamic *jihad* directed against Western encroachment. Mustafa Kemal had also organized the Grand National Assembly as a place where Muslims could gather to discuss strategies for the restoration of Islamic sovereignty. Ata Efendi, the Naqshbandi sheikh of the Uskudar Ozbekler convent in Istanbul, played a crucial role in the war. He supplied money, arms, and information to the nationalists and offered them refuge in his convent. Even Ismet Inonu found refuge in the Ozbekler convent and was assisted by Ata Efendi in his efforts to join the War of Independence (Misiroglu 1992: 209–65). Said Nursi (founder of the *Nurcu* religious community) and Abdulhakim Arvasi (the most influential Naqshbandi sheikh of the period) also supported the War of Independence. Mustafa Kemal himself invited Said Nursi to take up membership in the Grand National Assembly (Sahiner 1988: 236–49).

The outbreak of the Kurdish Sheikh Said Revolt in 1925 provided the final justification for crushing all opposition. Opposition members were accused of inciting the revolt, even though no evidence was found linking them to it. The Sheikh Said Revolt was a direct response to the abolition of the caliphate. Its significance was threefold. After it was suppressed, opposition within the Grand National Assembly was virtually eliminated and the single party regime was established. It signified the beginning of militant secularism in Turkey. And the Naqshbandi order, which had played an important political role since Sultan Abdulhamit's inception of pan-Islamism, was banned and forced underground. Naqshbandi sheikhs also began to lose their leadership role among the Kurds. According to van Bruinessen (1992a; 1992b), this created room for the emergence of ethnic Kurdish nationalism in the 1970s. This period also saw the rise of a popular form of Islam in south-eastern Anatolia, where most of the Kurds in Turkey live. This version of Islam had long been articulated with local cultural practices, constituting a binding element in the world-view of Kurds. Significantly, the south-eastern provinces are the poorest in Turkey. The cities of Mus and Agri, for example, have a per capita income of only US\$ 660, while the more affluent western provinces enjoy a per capita income of up to US\$ 7,000 (Kazgan 1999: 359–60). This regional poverty has contributed to the economic and cultural grievances of Kurds and has motivated Kurdish demands for greater equality and cultural autonomy, although other groups living in the eastern provinces face considerable economic hardship as well. Kurdish Islam and pro-Islamic political parties have drawn on popular sentiments in the region since the 1970s. However, we cannot easily conceptualize Kurdish Islam as the political representation of an association between Islam and economic deprivation; it has a much longer gestation and embodies historically situated social relations including geopolitical dynamics. My point here is that the political economies and associated power relations hastened the growth of Kurdish nationalism and popular Islam. However, this important development and its implications for Turkish politics are beyond the scope of this book.

Kurdish Naqshbandi leaders interpreted the abolition of the caliphate as an anti-religious act. They wanted to institute the *sharia* in the state structure, and if they failed to accomplish that, they would pursue the establishment of an independent Kurdish state under Islamic law. With Sheikh Said as their leader, the Kurdish Independence Organization hoped to provide the means for achieving this goal (Mumcu 1994a: 57-8, 123–40) but the revolt was limited in scope because not all Kurdish leaders participated (van Bruinessen 1992b). And even though Naqshbandi sheikhs played a crucial role in organizing the revolt, not all sheikhs supported it. Said Nursi did not support it, and there was very little Turkish participation. The revolt evolved as a Kurdish nationalist movement as much as an Islamic *jihad* against the abolition of the caliphate.

Mustafa Kemal acted decisively in putting down the Sheikh Said Revolt. The government quickly passed the Law for the Maintenance of Order, which remained in effect from 3 March 1925 to 4 March 1929. This law gave the government almost absolute power, exercised through special courts known as Independence Tribunals. Kemalists used the opportunity to enact radical reforms that would otherwise be resisted, not only by the opposition in parliament but also by the general public. During the first two years of the Law for the Maintenance of Order, the Independence Tribunals sentenced over 500 people to death. In June 1925, the Progressive Republican Party was dissolved. With the suppression of the revolt in 1925, Mustafa Kemal silenced all opponents of the regime and established a single party system in Turkey which was to last until the end of the Second World War.

The religious intellectuals and orders were seen to be in fundamental conflict with Kemalist efforts to reproduce the Western concept of modernity. The ideas of one of these religious intellectuals, the Kurdish Said Nursi, continue to influence various currents of Islamist thought throughout Turkey.

Said Nursi and Western modernity

Said Nursi was an Ottomanist who believed that the Ottoman Empire was the last powerful Islamic state capable of unifying all Muslims under one nation, regardless of linguistic differences (Said Nursi 1990a: 91–162; 1990b: 247). He was also strongly constitutionalist because he rejected the arbitrary personal governance of rulers, whether sultans or republican presidents (Algar 1979: 316–7). Said Nursi supported the republican form of the state as the best guarantee of Islamic law free from arbitrary personal rule.

For Said Nursi, the nation is a religious community: 'Our nationality is like a body in which the spirit is Islam and the intelligence is the faith and Koran' (Said Nursi n.d.). The Koranic concept of nation, he thought, would suit the modern concept of the territorially defined nation-state. The Koran states: 'We created you from a single male and female, and made you into nations, that you may know each other ... in order to help and not to hate and quarrel with each other' (The Koran 49: 13). According to Said Nursi, the nation refers to the religious unity of various Muslim communities within the territorial boundaries of the state. A common language, common religion, and loyalty to the state all play an important role in bringing about that union. According to Said Nursi (n.d: 20–1), 'If the above elements are unified, the nation is truly strong. If any one of these factors is missing, it will be at the expense of national unity'. For him, it was a mistake to focus on linguistic and territorial unity without including religion because it would promote racism. And he believed Kemalism was making just such a mistake.

Said Nursi opposed the abolition of the caliphate and conveyed this in a speech delivered to the Grand National Assembly in 1923. He argued that nation-building on the basis of racial or linguistic grounds would cause political divisiveness and internal conflict within the country, resulting in the eventual exploitation of Muslims by foreign powers. Only Islam could provide the necessary anti-imperialist sentiments to protect Turkey from future Western encroachment. He believed that Muslims from various linguistic communities were also very interested in having state rulers devoted to Islam (Said Nursi 1939). This was particularly true for the Kurds.

Mustafa Kemal was strongly opposed to Said Nursi's idea of Islamic solidarity, and Said Nursi realized that Mustafa Kemal was not to be persuaded. Consequently, he left the Grand National Assembly and returned to Van, his homeland in eastern Anatolia, where he devoted himself to the cultivation of an Islamic inner life. While Said Nursi was in eastern Turkey, the Kurdish-Naqshbandi revolt led by Sheikh Said broke out in 1925.

Said Nursi never endorsed separatist Kurdish nationalism. His political activities were largely confined to promoting the educational, economic, and cultural development of the Kurdish population (van Bruinessen 1992a: 141–3). He was opposed to the founding of a separate Kurdistan. According to Said Nursi, Kurdish nationalism was a British strategy to divide Muslim solidarity in Turkey rather than a movement that would benefit the development of the Kurds. He believed that nationalism based on racial or linguistic unity would break Islamic bonds and weaken Muslim resistance to imperialism (Said Nursi 1990c: 303–5). Said Nursi's response to Sayyid Abdulkadir (founding leader of the Kurdish Liberation Organization established in 1918) on Kurdish independence is revealing:

> Allah states in the Koran that He will create a nation which loves Allah, and which He, in return, will love. I thought about this and concluded that this nation is the Turkish nation which has defended the Islamic flag on behalf of the entire Muslim world for a thousand years. I don't support the separatism of a few tribal groups as opposed to serving this victorious nation (Sahiner 1988: 229).

Said Nursi's reference to the 'Turkish' nation is a semantic one. He had no problem defining nationhood in relation to language as long as it was not detached from Islamic cultural and moral values. Sheikh Said's revolt, then, was a tribalist act and not a *jihad*. For Said Nursi, '*jihad* is a battle by Muslims against the external enemies of Islam and against the egoistic desires of the self. It is not a *jihad* if the fight is directed against other Muslim groups within the boundaries of a Muslim state' (Cakir 1990: 80). Since he rejected any form of nationalism divorced from Islam, he sought to achieve a kind of constitutional federation in Turkey that would unify various linguistic groups under the umbrella of *sharia* law.

While in seclusion in eastern Anatolia, Said Nursi was accused of inciting rebellion among the Kurds. He was exiled to Burdur in western Anatolia, which gave him the opportunity to separate himself entirely from active politics. After this, an overtly Islamic political movement went underground.

Kisakurek (1990) divides Said Nursi's political life into an early period (1873–1925) and a later period (1926–60). Before 1925 he was actively involved in politics; afterwards he withdrew completely from political life and began to write his *risales* (short treaties), the collection of which is known in Turkey as the *Risale-I Nur*. He wrote in Turkish, but his Turkish was very much influenced by the Ottoman language—a mixture of Turkish, Arabic, and Persian, written in Arabic script. During his later period, Said Nursi devoted his time to the development of a new Islamic theology, and the establishment of a university for religious education. The institution he envisioned was to be called the Medreset uz-Zehra. Although he pursued this project until 1951, his dream was never realized (Algar 1979: 315).

During his years of exile in Burdur, Said Nursi began to expand his network of followers. It became known as the *Nurcu cemaati* (community), also referred to as the *Risale-I Nur cemaati*. The early followers were small-producing local industrialists, artisans, small commercial groups, and middle peasantry. Particularly after the 1950s, the *cemaat* began to attract all kinds of people and today constitutes an important political faction in Turkey. The Fethullah Gulen *cemaati* of the present era follows the *Risale-I Nur*. The *Nurcu cemaati* reads and interprets the *Risale-I Nur* under the leadership of a master, referred to as *Nur talebesi* (Student of Nur), who has understood its meaning through extensive study. Through his writings, Said Nursi wanted to demonstrate that the Koran contained knowledge generated by the natural sciences. He developed his arguments, albeit rather crudely, through an examination of the laws of order and harmony found in nature as illuminated through Koranic verse. In contrast to the Kemalist reproduction of Western modernity, and consistent with the Ottoman Islamic tradition, Said Nursi was trying to show the congruity of Islam with the idea of material development and progress. This aligns him with the modernist-Islamic thinking of Afghani and Abduh.

For Said Nursi, the Koran was the only guide required for the development of rational and scientific thinking. His ideas contrasted sharply with Mustafa

Kemal's view that modernity required the wholesale adoption of Western cultural values. Said Nursi believed that Islamic values and Western modernity needed to interact to constitute an Islamic brand of modernity.

Said Nursi identified himself as an *imam* involved in religious renewal. If Muslims were to become 'modern' there was no place for the personalism and flexible reinterpretation of a sheikh. He stated: 'I am not a sheikh, I am an *imam* like Imam-I Ghazzali and Imam-I Rabbani. The time of ours is not the time for *tariqa*, it is now the time to save the faith' (Cakir 1990: 82). Said Nursi saw himself as a reviver of the universal principles of Islamic knowledge. He was committed to a process of Muslim engagement with scientific thinking and material progress. In contrast to the Naqshbandi tradition which places primary importance on a personal connection between sheikh and follower, Said Nursi called upon Muslim men and women to liberate themselves from static customs and display a willingness to adopt the values of rationality, efficiency, and progress. In his proposal for the Medreset uz-Zehra, Said Nursi advocated attitudinal change and new educational policies that would use Koranic knowledge in the fashioning of a unique Islamic discourse on 'development'. It is therefore not inaccurate to suggest that the Ottoman-Tanzimat project of reproducing Western modernity also preoccupied Said Nursi.

State oppression

The Kemalist project of reproducing Western modernity adopted repressive methods. Despite its declared intent to replicate Western experience, the absence of political liberalism in Kemalism greatly strengthened the power of state-ruling bureaucrats. According to Keyder (1997), this undermined the goal of westernization and modernization, placing Kemalism on an authoritarian path.

Populist nationalism was the organizing ideological principle of Kemalism and underpinned the single-party regime. According to Recep Peker, Secretary General of Mustafa Kemal's Republican People's Party, 'populism implied equality before the law among all citizens of the state ... [It also meant] accepting the people as a unified whole within the boundaries of the state, with no cultural difference and conflicting status or class interests among them' (Peker 1984: 54–5). For Prime Minister Inonu, a strong and unified nation required that 'individual life be sacrificed for society' (Melzig 1944: 190). The only acceptable basis for differentiation within society was occupational.

Populist nationalism was the most important ideological point in distinguishing Turkish modernity from the political arrangements of the Ottoman Empire. Contrary to the political accommodation of different cultural categories within the empire, the Kemalist project asserted a unity of 'the people'. In 1923, Mustafa Kemal and his close associates established the People's

Party, renamed the Republican People's Party (RPP) in 1924. The RPP became the bureaucratic means of linking the people directly to the state. It aimed to create solidarity and guarantee the harmonious integration of the population without giving rise to conflicts of interest in society (Giritlioglu 1965: 96).

The state had absolute power in society and the RPP was its close subordinate. The Minister of Internal Affairs, for example, was also Secretary General of the party, and local governors acted as chairs of local party branches (Atasoy 1986: 59–62). Even the directors and members of occupational associations were required to receive party approval. In fact, all citizens of the country were required to become party members. Those who did not were classified as dissidents and accused of inciting opposition. As one of the motions of the Secretary General (N. 262, 22 April 1934, quoted in Atasoy 1986: 61) stated: 'It is necessary to be watchful against those who have not become party members. From now on, they must be seen as part of the opposition.'

In order to extend party control over rural areas and facilitate party propaganda, 'people's houses' (halk evleri) were established (Atasoy 1986: 61–6). Recep Peker insisted that party membership in the villages be increased and that organizations established outside the party be eliminated. According to Peker:

> We have become aware of some attempts to establish clubs called the union of youth. If those who want to organize a union of youth are not party members, it is necessary to insure that they establish membership in the party. If the purpose of such activities is to organize opposition, we should be informed about [it] and the youth unions should be eliminated. The people should be encouraged to work within the party (Secret Memo of the Secretary General N. 345, 16 August 1934, quoted in Atasoy 1986: 62).

According to Peker, the best way of realizing harmonious relations in society was to unite around the political leader. Peker believed that a society should 'conform to the rules of its national chiefs' (Yetkin 1983: 158). 'It is only under the leadership of a national chief that the masses of individuals can be unified around the state and become one in thinking and acting. Only this can lead to a great independent existence within the fatherland' (Peker 1984: 48, 63). For Peker, the national chief must rule the nation by demanding obedience and maintaining a strong militaristic command structure. And for Inonu, the leader's duty was to neutralize the various interests of different groups in order to keep state authority safe (Inonu's speech on 26 December 1938, quoted in Kop 1945: 20–1).

The RPP was equated with the state while the general population was synonymous with the nation. The security of the state came to mean the security of the party, which was equivalent to the security of the nation. The RPP played a strategic role in the maintenance of this equation between party-state and people-nation. The division between the ruling elite and the masses was justified as part of a responsible authority structure. At the same time, it excluded any opposition to the RPP and prevented the use of politics as an arena for power struggles. Exclusionary politics was justified by reference to the alleged inability of the nation to sustain a plurality of ideologies. Consequently, all opposition parties were eliminated and Islam lost its political importance. The government became the dominant force in defining national culture, and the concept of a 'national security state' became the organizing principle in Kemalist modernity. The historical emergence of a repressive Kemalist modernity clearly coincided with the Sheikh Said revolt, but was not caused by it.

The creation of a national economy

There were two aspects to the economic policy of Kemalist nationalists: to build a national economy, and to make Muslim-Turkish commercial and industrial classes dominant within it. Kemalists believed that the Ottoman free-trade model resulted in the transfer of agricultural economic surplus from the empire, through non-Muslim merchants, to Western 'imperialist' states. This position was forcefully made in 1923 at the Izmir Economic Congress (17 February–4 March 1923). Congress participants advocated national wealth creation through export-oriented agricultural production by Turkish farmers (Okcun 1968).

The congress saw the nationalization of commercial classes as an essential component of Turkish national economic independence. Even though national economic independence was poorly defined, congress participants presented an argument similar to that of Samir Amin (1976: 72–8). His definition of a 'national economy' was the articulation between the capacity to produce and the capacity to consume in the national space. In the highly polarized social class structure of the Ottoman Empire, non-Muslims dominated manufacturing. As shown in Table 1 below, Muslims held only 15 per cent of capital invested in manufacturing and had only a 15 per cent participation rate in the labour force. Christian Greeks held 50 per cent of the capital and made up 60 per cent of the labour force. For congress participants, nationalization of the manufacturing industry was crucial for national economic independence.

Table 1: The Ethnic Distribution of Capital and Labour in Large Ottoman Manufacturing Industries, 1915

Ethnicity	Share in Capital (%)	Labour Force (%)
Muslim-Turkish	15	15
Greek	50	60
Armenian	20	15
Jewish	5	10
Foreign	10	-
Total	100	100

Kazgan (1999: 66).

By the mid 1920s the non-Muslim population had declined drastically and Turkey had lost most members of its commercial classes. This turned military-civil bureaucratic cadres into a major political power. Following the Kurdish-Islamic Sheikh Said Revolt of 1925, the bureaucratic class excluded those who were identified with Islam from the creation of a new commercial bourgeoisie, as well as those who belonged to other cultural-ethnic communities such as Kurds. The absence of commercial groups reinforced the view that political power belonged to state-ruling bureaucrats whose goal was to reproduce Western-style modernity in Turkey.

The official discourse of the national economy was still liberal, however. From the outset, the concept of Turkey as a nation was grounded in the creation of a social class base believed necessary to catch up with Western modernity. As a first step in that direction, the government appropriated property left by Greek and Armenian Christians and sold it to native-born and immigrant Muslims (Keyder 1981: 23). Other policies included government support for tractor purchases, the supply of fertilizers, and other agricultural inputs. In 1922, there were only three Fordson tractors in the cotton-producing region of Adana. By the beginning of the 1930s there were 2,000 (Tezel 1982: 374).

Railway construction was also an important element in the economic policy of Kemalist nationalists wanting to organize an internal market. The largest part of the existing railway network was concentrated in western Anatolia. Constructed from concessions given by the Ottoman state, the network was designed to link western Anatolian raw materials with western European industry, and to provide European manufactured goods to wealthy Anatolians. However, the transportation network between grain-producing regions of Anatolia and consuming cities was so poorly developed that imported grain was cheaper than grain produced in Anatolia. The cost of transporting one tonne of wheat from central Anatolia to Istanbul in 1924 was US$ 8.8, whereas it cost only US$ 5 to transport it from New York to Istanbul. Hence it seemed more rational to feed the population of Istanbul from Iowa rather than Ankara and Konya (Boratav 1981: 165). The government railroad construction policy aimed to reduce wheat imports, which accounted for about 20 per cent of total imported goods in 1925 (Mackie 1939: 445–6).

The abolition of the tithe tax (tax paid in kind) in 1925 was another measure taken by Kemalist nationalists in an effort to organize an internal market. Their goal was to commercialize small-producing farmers and strengthen the market position of large agriculturalists and commercial groups (Hershlag 1968: 45). The elimination of the tithe was particularly helpful in transforming the agricultural production of small farmers from household subsistence requirements to production directed to the market, giving farmers the cash needed to pay their taxes.

Small agricultural producers were dominant in grain production and responsible for approximately 90 per cent of agricultural activity. Most of this grain was consumed by the family who produced it. Because of the lack of transportation networks linking rural areas to urban centres, the grain that remained after family consumption was sold locally (Tekeli and Ilkin 1977: 37–8). The government based its wheat policy of the 1930s on this segment of small producers. By breaking the existing link between family subsistence food production and the peasantry, the government could institute another link between the peasantry, national markets, and export-agriculture. With the growth of agricultural production and the market involvement of small producers, Kemalists saw in the liberal economy a means to integrate Turkey into the world economy as an agrarian state.

The link between export-oriented agricultural production and a growing commercial bourgeoisie was instrumental in the creation of a Turkish industrial bourgeoisie. Agricultural export earnings were used to purchase machinery and other industrial inputs for the expansion of consumer goods-producing industries. Industrial input imports increased from 24 per cent to 35 per cent between 1924 and 1929, while textile, food, and other consumer goods imports declined from 66 per cent in 1924 to 51 per cent in 1929. The same trend in the import substitution of consumer goods continued in the 1930s: Total consumer goods imports declined from 42 per cent in 1930 to 22 per cent in 1938; intermediary industrial goods imports increased during the same period from 33 per cent to 40 per cent, and machinery and automobile imports increased from 10 per cent to 23 per cent (Tezel 1982: 107–10).

Despite the continuing rhetoric on imperialism and national independence, Kemalists did not oppose foreign capital. In fact, they supported foreign investment and encouraged joint ventures to stimulate Turkish industrial growth. Approximately one-third of the companies established between 1920 and 1930 were joint ventures, through which Kemalists hoped to replace the capital lost from banished Christian manufacturing and commercial groups. This would in turn foster the rise of Turkish capitalists and promote economic development in general. Once again, revenues necessary for industrial joint ventures were derived from export agriculture.

Industrialization was made synonymous with Turkish nationalism in the belief that this would lead the nation to economic independence. It is significant that between 1920 and 1930, 201 Turkish joint-stock companies were established, 66 of which were largely financed by foreign capital (Okcun 1971). These companies were particularly strong in textiles, food production, electricity production, and the cement industry.

Given the fact that there was virtually no Turkish presence in industry, civil-military bureaucrats transformed themselves into a national industrial bourgeoisie to fill the vacuum left by displaced non-Muslims. Many reputable deputies and high-level state bureaucrats participated in the founding of Turkish joint-stock companies. For example, in 1925 the Turkish Match Company was established as a joint venture, with a Belgium firm holding a 51 per cent share. Among the significant shareholders were Prime Minister Ismet Inonu, Finance Minister Celal Bayar, and deputy Cemal Husnu (Boratav 1982: 21).

The Business Bank (Is Bankasi), founded in August 1924, is another example. Mustafa Kemal himself founded the bank, often described as the 'bank of politicians'. The Finance Minister Celal Bayar was the bank director. Although it was established to provide credit for Turkish commercial and industrial groups, the bank gradually began to invest in the lumber industry, coal production, sugar, textiles, and glass. It also played an important role in developing exports by establishing export firms abroad (Hershlag 1968: 90–1).

State-ruling bureaucrats and politicians gained new capacities in relation to their involvement in the economy. Political struggles now centred more than ever on the questions of who had access to power, how decisions were made, and who benefited from the decisions. The repressive measures taken by state-ruling bureaucrats signalled that the state was the only agent responsible for the institution of the economy and the allocation of resources. It was also the sole representative of the nation. And the nation was unified in its struggle against both external and internal enemies of the state, including the foreign powers that occupied Turkey during the war, as well as the Kurds and Islamic groups who revolted against the secularizing policies of Mustafa Kemal. The Kemalist political regime underscored the dangers of Islam, ethnicity, and class conflict, while promoting the idea of national unity.

In the process of creating private Turkish commercial and industrial classes, bureaucrats emerged as the dominant group in society. With this development, an important question arises. Is this to be understood as a Turkish case of Polanyian dynamics, in which national protection came into conflict with the global free-trading regime? Or is this the case of a nationalist political reaction that ultimately stopped the destructive extension of market forces into the economy? I would argue that to portray the Kemalist movement as a Turkish response to a free-trade regime is misleading. Kemalism did not constitute a protective response to the institutions of laissez-faire, but placed Turkey on a trajectory where the general public came to recognize the state as the agent responsible for the creation of a national economy. This is a historical case of a 'peripheral state' embracing the global market economy at the very point when its global framework, centred on the gold standard, collapsed. Due to the displacement of non-Muslims and the absence of Turkish industrial capital, Kemalists adopted a policy of greater bureaucratic involvement in industry. That policy was clearly grounded in 'statism'. To appreciate how the collapse of the gold standard seriously affected Kemalists' attempt to create a national economy and a Turkish bourgeoisie, we must examine the rise of bureaucratic power in Turkey.

The untouchable bureaucracy

With the end of the Lausanne customs sanctions in 1928, and the establishment of government monopolies on the sale of tobacco, salt, alcohol, matches, sugar, oil, and gasoline, Turkish revenues increased, constituting approximately 23 per cent of total government income in 1929 (Hershlag 1968: 57; Tekeli and Ilkin 1977: 70). These policies had significant consequences for Turkey's international trading regime, and also affected its domestic social structure. The government reduced the importation of industrially produced consumer goods and gave priority to national production via an import-substitution industrialization programme. Shifts in state policy on national currency and relative pricing accompanied all these changes in trade and the organization of production.

Both paper and gold were used in Turkey. Paper money was used mostly in the western provinces while gold dominated in the rest of the country. During the war years the Ottoman government had printed some paper money. Only a small portion of it was convertible to gold, the rest had value only in relation to German state bonds. When Germany submitted its claim over the Ottoman debt to the Allied powers as part of its war indemnities, Turkish paper money lost its value because it was not backed by central bank gold reserves. Since it was not convertible into gold, the value of money was dependent on increases in exchange reserves from foreign capital imports and export revenues. Under the conditions of the Great Depression of 1929 there were significant fluctuations in exchange reserves. Consequently, the value of currency declined. Although it dropped only 5 per cent in 1929, the government imposed exchange controls in order to prevent future declines on reserves. It also passed legislation in 1930 on the Protection of the Value of Turkish Currency. This policy operated through central bank intervention (Tekeli and Ilkin 1981).

In 1930, the government founded the Central Bank as a national bank, thereby ending the Ottoman Bank's monopoly in issuing currency and controlling foreign exchange. The Central Bank's control allowed the credit available from state banks for commerce and private industrial activity to increase from 28 per cent in 1930 to 40 per cent in 1938 (Tezel 1982: 226). Because the government decided to avoid the depletion of its exchange and gold reserves, it stopped paying the Ottoman debt in 1930. The Lausanne Treaty did not require Turkey to pay war reparations, but it was supposed to pay Ottoman debts. In 1928, under the brokerage of the League of Nations, Turkey paid two-thirds of the Ottoman debt, in the amount of 84,597,495 gold lira. With the addition of interest, Turkey was required to pay 107,528,461 gold lira beginning in 1929 (Hershlag 1968: 21–3). This agreement was concluded with the understanding that Turkey reserved the right to cease payment if the value of Turkish money declined. With the 1929 economic crash, Turkey ceased payments on the Ottoman debt. No payment was made between 1930 and 1933.

In order to prevent the depletion of gold and exchange reserves bureaucrats showed no hesitation in applying even arbitrary controls to the trade structure. The Office for External Trade, instituted in 1934, reflected the political weight of bureaucrats in giving dominance to export agriculturalists and commercial groups. Importers and small producers were left to the good graces of government bureaucrats who imposed quotas and established bartering and clearing arrangements for individual traders (Kepenek 1984: 79–80). Bureaucratic intervention resulted in a surplus of exchange reserves, earned primarily from wheat exports to Germany between 1933 and 1938.

The state policy that worked to the disadvantage of importers and the advantage of exporters was mediated through shifts in government pricing policy. The price of imported items was raised to decrease their consumption. The world market price for sugar fell by 60 per cent between 1929 and 1935 but the price of imported sugar in Turkey only decreased between 19.3 and 27.3 per cent (Tekeli and Ilkin 1977: 85). This was complemented by decreases in the price of domestically produced export crops which had fallen in value by 60 to 75 per cent in the world market. The government wanted to increase exchange reserves by increasing earnings from export agriculture through a low-pricing policy. As a result, Turkey increased its exports by 40 per cent (Tekeli and Ilkin 1977: 89), while imports declined in 1933 to one-third of 1928 levels. There was also a decline in imported consumer goods, from 52 per cent of imports in 1928 to 25 per cent during the late 1930s (Tezel 1977: 201).

Government pricing policy was also disadvantageous for agricultural producers. The most disadvantaged group was small-producing family farmers, although large-producing farmers were also adversely affected. The government did not develop a policy to protect prices in agriculture. As a result, the living conditions of agricultural producers deteriorated. Wheat prices were allowed to decline in correspondence with a drop in world prices, while the price of imported goods was kept higher. Peasants had to exchange approximately eight kilos of wheat to purchase one kilo of sugar in 1931, while in 1929 they exchanged only three kilos of wheat for one kilo of sugar (Hatipoglu 1936: 52–7). However, the level of agricultural taxes, to be paid in cash after the abolition of the tithe tax, remained high. The discriminatory pricing policies of the government were also applied to industrial inputs imported for agricultural production. By keeping the price of imported oil and machinery higher than world market levels, the government encouraged the use of animal power in farming. This was intended to keep agricultural prices low and provide a greater incentive for export-agriculture.

Bureaucrats acquired the ability to hoard power due to the Great Depression and the absence of a commercial bourgeoisie. They became virtually untouchable. The more the state tightened its control over politics, the more bureaucrats appeared to be the embodiment of power. 'Statism', accepted as one of the founding principles of Mustafa Kemal's Republican People's Party in 1931, provided an avenue for bureaucrats to permeate the political system. It furnished them with the opportunity to decide whose taxes should be raised and whose benefits or social support programmes should be cut. As long as opposition parties were absent and popular resistance remained weak, bureaucratic domination of the economy persisted. This became very evident after the suppression of the Kurdish-Islamic revolt in 1925. Years of repression had reconciled the general population to the view that bureaucrats represented the interests of a supposedly unified nation.

The term 'statism' was not a well-defined concept in the 1930s and 1940s. Intellectuals writing in the Turkish magazine *Kadro* considered it a uniquely Turkish strategy for the constitution of an industrial economy. Celal Bayar, finance minister and director of the Business Bank at the time, claimed that statism was a strategy to bolster private enterprise. Sukru Saracoglu, prime minister from 1942 to 1946, defined statism as an 'advanced form of socialism' (Karpat 1959: 70). Nevertheless, Mustafa Kemal and his close associates believed in the eventual creation of industrial private capital via state regulation. During the 15 long years of a single-party regime statism served to consolidate the political and economic power of bureaucrats. Private industrialists only began to exploit significant opportunities during the 1960s.

Although there was a Law for the Encouragement of Industry, enacted in 1927 to assist private industrialists, in reality the law served the interests of large state-run industrial firms. Exchange reserves saved through restrictions on consumer goods imports and earnings from agricultural exports continued to be the main source of revenue for state industrial firms. Channelling resources to state firms sometimes took the form of governmental authorization of import quotas for selective exemptions on precious industrial raw materials. The Bank of Industry and Mines (1925), the State Office of Industry (1930), and the State Industrial Credit Bank (1930) were all effective in creating opportunities for bureaucrats to gain access to valuable resources. These institutions were formed to provide credit to state-run industries only. Given these circumstances, it is not surprising that more than 50 per cent of industrial enterprises were state owned by 1938 (Mardin 1980: 39). The textile industry was the only sector where private investment expanded (Hershlag 1968: 101–2), a fact of some significance for the later emergent industrial bourgeoisie.

With the transformation of bureaucrats into industrial capitalists, and, in the absence of opposition parties able to affect state policy, bureaucratic dominance was assumed. Moreover, bureaucratic power enabled state functionaries to exploit various ideological aspects of the Kemalist national project. Bureaucrats found the example of fascist Italy useful for widening labour repression and lowering costs, while Nazi Germany provided a major ideological influence (Kocak 1986). A legal framework for labour regulation was adopted from fascist Italy. In fact, the government's 1936 labour law was based on the 1935 Italian labour law (Yetkin 1983: 102). Workers were not permitted to strike or form unions. In 1938 the association law consolidated the labour law by denying both the existence of classes and the right to establish class-based organizations. Workers were told to live in 'harmony' in a society in which their interests would be looked after by the state.

Technical and financial assistance for the statist industrialization strategy came from the Soviet Union. Turkey used Soviet financial support to purchase the machinery and industrial equipment needed to build consumer goods industries. Workers selected for sugar and textile production travelled to the Soviet Union for training, while Soviet experts came to Turkey where they were employed in the government's preparation of the Second Five-Year Plan. They also participated in the implementation of the First Five-Year Industrial Plan as advisors and managers (Hershlag 1968: 64).

The Soviets were also very involved in the development of heavy industry, mining, and energy production in Turkey (Kuruc 1970: 19). The first and second five-year industrial development plans embraced in Turkey during the 1930s were similar to those already implemented in the Soviet Union.

Bureaucratic domination was realized through abusive state power, and, in general, state managers encountered little ideological opposition from the general population. Intellectuals of the period eloquently wove the Kemalist vision around the denial of conflicting class interests. An intellectual writing for *Kadro* magazine proclaimed: 'There is no mechanism invented to prevent class struggle in countries where private enterprise is dominant in the economy.

Statism is an obligatory strategy for Turkey to industrialize and prosper without becoming entangled in class struggles' (quoted in Atasoy 1998: 170). Statism, then, emerged as a mutually reinforcing assemblage of state power, bureaucratic control, and repression of labour and small producers.

Over and over again, the repressive legislation that outlawed labour unions and strikes and lowered industrial wages reinforced bureaucratic power and influenced a wide range of social processes. The government's low-agricultural-price policy combined with low-priced wheat exports kept industrial wages low. Real wages declined 25 per cent between 1934 and 1938, and another 40 per cent between 1938 and 1943. Although the cost of living went up by 247 per cent during the same period, wages increased by only 114 per cent (Keyder 1987: 104–5).

The industrial low-wage policy was closely linked to state control over the food supply and the ideological coercion of rural producers. In 1932 the Central Office for Soil Produce (TMO) was established. Wheat was purchased directly from small family farmers at a price below world market levels. The functions of the TMO were extended in 1939 to include the purchase and marketing of barley, oats, and other grains (Hershlag 1968: 109). Through the agency of the TMO the state was able to obtain grain cheaply enough to sustain its low-wage policy. Rural co-operatives, established in a manner similar to that of Soviet-style collectivization, extended the Kemalist statist vision into the countryside, complementing the policies of the TMO. The agricultural credit co-operatives instituted under the control of the Agricultural Bank had to finance programmes for the market expansion of wheat production and break the financial and political control of merchants over small-producing peasants. Furthermore, regional agricultural combines were legislated in 1937 (Ergil 1975: 479), concentrating rural settlements around 'centre' villages to which the government would supply all necessary infrastructure and social services. Around 1,000 agricultural combines were established during the late 1930s. They were later transformed into state farms during the Second World War. All of these innovations lent themselves to bureaucratic control over agricultural production. As a consequence, rural income was kept low while all other prices and taxes went up.

Small-producing peasants and industrial labour were both subject to state repression for the sake of establishing a relationship between state bureaucracy and national unity. The National Security Law of 1940 established obligatory paid work for small-producing peasants and wage labourers in mines, road construction, and industry. The peasantry was also subject to compulsory crop contributions and the confiscation of animals and household utensils (Pamuk 1988). In 1944, an amendment to the National Security Law created more severe penalties for violating compulsory labour legislation. Compulsory labour came to be viewed as a national duty comparable to military service, and security forces were authorized to return by force those workers who left their workplace (Bianchi 1984: 121).

The Kemalist attempt to create a national economy and industrial bourgeoisie through discriminatory price and wage policies and repressive laws, built into Turkish society what Tilly (1998) calls 'durable inequality'. State power became identified with vigilance over Turkey's transformation into a 'modern' nation-state. More precisely, the Kemalist trajectory of reproducing Western-style modernity took a repressive course in regard to the shape of domestic social structure, state power, and Islam. In the process, segments of private capital, large- and small-producing farmers, and commercial groups became thoroughly estranged from ruling bureaucrats.

Ethnicity also played an important role in the estrangement of private capital groups from the state. The Capital Tax of 1942 was particularly discriminatory against non-Muslim commercial groups of Armenian, Greek, and Jewish origin. It was designed to extract resources from large landowners, the private manufacturing bourgeoisie, building owners, and real estate brokers who had acquired their wealth during the war years (Aydemir 1983: 460–1). The estimated revenue from the capital tax was TL 465 million, 289 million of which was to be collected from minorities (Avcioglu 1978: 475–6). Those who could not pay the tax within 15 days were subject to forced labour until the completion of payment. According to then Prime Minister Refik Saydam, the state had an obligation to establish exclusive control over valued resources, and, when necessary, to exclude others from profit-making activities by setting up state monopolies (Avcioglu 1978: 475). Some minority merchants refused to pay the tax. Jews who did make large payments argued that the Turkish government was following a German-style, anti-Semitic policy (Aktar 1998). Allied Powers also accused Turkey of planning its post-war economy with the expectation of a German victory (Kocak 1986: 287–302). Under pressure from Allied Powers the government dropped the capital tax in 1944.

Throughout most of the single-party period, bureaucrats and private capital groups were involved in a love-hate relationship. State backing was essential for the creation of a commercial and industrial bourgeoisie, but capitalists also feared an image of the state as an embodiment of abusive and discriminatory bureaucratic practices. The widespread discontent of small-producing rural populations and workers was also an undeniable fact. These groups rightfully feared the deployment of coercive state powers. The national political space was fragmented between state ruling bureaucrats on the one hand, and peasants, wage earners, and various groups of private capital on the other. A closer look at the actual negotiations between ruling bureaucrats and these discontented groups over their repositioning in the state will clarify how Islam became an important element in the political life of Turkey. Chapter 3 examines the incorporation of Islam into the Turkish experience after the Second World War.

3

The Islamist Search for Selfhood

In the immediate aftermath of the Second World War Turkey experienced a shift from an exclusionary and authoritarian state to a more inclusive and liberal one. This change was reflected in political liberalization and the transition from a single-party political system to a multi-party system. However, political liberalization was not the result of societal opposition to an oppressive state. It entailed a more complex interaction between the state and civil society.

In the Cold War geopolitics that divided states into two antagonistic military blocs, anti-communist and anti-capitalist rhetoric dominated. During this period 'peripheral' areas were often considered testing sites for the Western ideal of modernity. The global rivalry between communism and capitalism also produced scepticism in the world about the replication of Western experience. In Turkey, the political twists and turns between liberal democracy and state-authoritarianism are rooted in this scepticism. During the transition to a multi-party system, both secular and Islamic projects questioned the universalism and replicability of Western ways. By highlighting differences in the daily cultural-political experience of individuals, we see how doubts about the pretensions of a Western vision yielded to political factionalism, one significant element of which was Islamic politics. At the same time, these doubts gave rise to state repression in an effort to preserve the strength and sanctity of Kemalism.

It makes little sense, therefore, to portray the relations between secular and Islamic politics in zero-sum terms. What was occurring was not an Islamist rejection of Kemalist secular principles per se. Rather, Islamists were expressing their wish to remain connected to the Islamic moral-spiritual universe which had long framed their fashioning of self and society.

The politics of 'cultural discontent' that emerged with the secularizing practices of the state helps explain what was happening during the early Cold War between 1945 and the 1960s. In this period Islamists and secularists could very well have been polarized into two rigid categories of cultural opposition. However, the transition to a multi-party system, along with the coming to power of the Democratic Party in 1950, allowed for the gradual incorporation of religious-moral sensibilities into the political system. In a unique way, the multi-party regime permitted political parties to mediate relations between various disenchanted groups. What is interesting about this mediation process is that the new regime permitted cultural discontent to be expressed within and through the legal-constitutional framework of the state. While firmly tying all citizens to the state, the Turkish political system also integrated Islamic culture into state-building. Islam was now acknowledged as an integral part of people's daily life experience, their family relations, neighbourhood ties, community solidarity, and customs. What made this a plausible cultural project was the inclusion of urban and rural small producers and lower classes into the state structure. While there is no natural connection between Islamic beliefs and the politics of cultural opposition, specific choices made by state managers and political elites framed the political space within which Islamic moral claims could be made.

The Cold War and the transition to a multi-party regime

It was Ismet Inonu who decided to establish a multi-party political system in Turkey. He was the second president of the republic, in office from the death of Mustafa Kemal in 1938 until the election of the Democratic Party (DP) in 1950. Inonu was motivated by the desire to position Turkey firmly within the anti-communist camp of the Cold War. The majority of Republican People's Party (RPP) members was opposed to competitive politics and a multi-party system. As one RPP member stated: 'I have always kept Ataturk's revolution and my leaders paramount in my life. Putting me in the situation of requiring the vote of the people means that I am for sale, doesn't it?' (Barutcu 1977: 277). However, Inonu believed it was vital that Turkey appear as a 'democratic' country if it wished to be accepted within the anti-communist Western camp (*Ulus Newspaper*, 2 November 1945). He expressed the desire to redirect Turkish politics onto a new trajectory that was different from single-party politics on a wide range of policy issues. This new trajectory included political liberalization and the forging of an alliance with the United States.

Inonu was well aware that political liberalization was a necessary condition for Turkey's inclusion in the Western alliance. What was crucial in this regard was whether or not the Soviet Union was seen as a danger to Turkey's security. Both during and after the war, the Soviet Union demanded the return of two Turkish provinces, Kars and Ardahan, which were located near Iran and the Caucasian oil fields in Baku and Batum. The Soviet Union wanted to control these provinces largely because of its anxiety over Iranian oil fields (Halliday 1979: 467–72). The Soviets also hoped for a revision of the Montreux Convention in order to establish a military base for light naval and land forces on the Turkish straits of the Dardanelles and Bosphorus (Kuniholm 1980: 136–43). Turkey was very alarmed that the US government could have easily accepted the Soviet proposal on the straits, especially with Roosevelt's sympathies towards Stalin at the time. Drawing an analogy with the US-

Canada border, Roosevelt stated: 'We have a frontier of over 3,000 miles with Canada and there is no fort and no armed forces. This situation has existed for over one hundred years. Other frontiers in the world will eventually be without forts and armed forces on their national boundaries' (US Department of State 1955: 903–5).

Moreover, the US government was proposing modifications in the Montreux Convention so that the straits would be open at all times to the warships of Black Sea powers—namely the Soviet Union (US Department of State 1947: 47). This was consistent with the Soviet proposal for a joint Soviet-Turkish defence of the straits (Kuniholm 1980: 256–7). Inonu was apprehensive and thought such changes would make Turkey easy prey for the Soviet Union. The US proposal did not make sense to Turkey. In the event of a military conflict between Turkey and the Soviet Union, Turkey could hardly wage a war with the Soviets while keeping the straits open to Soviet warships. Turkey warned the US administration that if Turkey decided to organize a joint defence with the Soviet Union the provisions of the Montreux Convention on more restricted rights for warships would also be extended to US warships.

Although we cannot know whether Stalin was actually interested in invading Turkey, there is evidence to support Inonu's fear that the Soviet Union posed a threat to Turkish interests (Hale 2000: 110–3). It is also evident that the Turkish government made strategic political use of the Soviet Union's land claims in eastern Turkey and their demand for a military base on the straits. Nonetheless, the US administration was not interested in a territorial dispute between the two countries (Kolko 1990: 586). In order to arouse US interest in Turkey and obtain a commitment to its territorial security, Turkish diplomats intensified their claims that the 'communist threat' to the Turkish straits and the Balkans was very real.

Turkey reminded the US administration of its strategic location interlocking the Balkans and the Middle East and its importance as a defensive shield against Soviet military expansion in the region. After lengthy hesitation (Kuniholm 1980: 109–18), the US government overtly acknowledged the strategic importance of Turkey, but not by suddenly deciding to protect its territorial security from the Soviet Union. Two factors played a decisive role in the reversal of US policy towards Turkey: first, the greater geopolitical need to protect US oil interests in the Middle East, and second, concern over the international balance of power in the emerging Cold War. Former Secretary of State, Cordell Hull, has stated: 'It was in the interest of the United States that no great power be established on the Persian Gulf opposite important American petroleum development in Saudi Arabia' (Kuniholm 1980: 160).

Increased US interest in the region was also tied to the particular colonial arrangements of the British-controlled oil regime in the Middle East. During the war, Middle Eastern oil production rose significantly, especially in Saudi Arabia and Iran. Saudi oil production increased from 0.5 million long tons in 1939 to 25.9 million long tons in 1950. During the same period Iranian production increased from 9.6 million long tons to 31.8 million long tons (Halliday 1979: 398–400). US company shares in Middle Eastern oil production increased from 16 per cent in 1939 to 31 per cent in 1946 (Armstrong et al 1991: 30). Despite their growing importance, US companies were excluded from many oil concessions. The British-controlled oil regime required non-British companies to obtain British consent for exploration rights in the previously untouched territories of the region (Venn 1986: 62–7). Under the influence of oil companies such as Cal-Tex, which eventually became the Arabian American Oil Company (ARAMCO), the US government redefined a broader strategic framework within which US interests could be firmly established (Kuniholm 1980: 179–80). This involved breaking pre-war colonial arrangements whereby the United States supported the decolonization process prescribed in the 1941 Atlantic Charter (Bromley 1991).

The reorganization of oil interests in the Middle East is best explained in relation to the specific timing of the extension of the nation-state system to the region. The question of whether 'communists' would be in a position to ensure the security of the territorial division of states determined US support for decolonization (Graebner 1970: 241). After some hesitation under the Roosevelt regime, the Truman Doctrine of 1947 established a US policy of 'stern containment' towards the Soviet Union (Ambrose 1983; Gaddis 1982). That said, the US policy of containment in the Middle East was not simply the result of successful Turkish diplomacy over Soviet territorial claims on Turkey. It was the 1946 Soviet-Iranian oil agreement which was decisive in mobilizing the US administration against the 'danger' to US oil interests posed by the Soviet Union.

From August 1941, Iran was under joint military occupation by the Soviet Union and Britain. The Soviet Union demanded that a joint Soviet-Iranian oil company be formed through which the Soviets would receive oil concessions and 51 per cent of the profits. In 1946, the Soviet Union agreed to withdraw its troops from Iran in exchange for oil concessions. However, under US pressure, the Iranian parliament refused to ratify the oil agreement. In May 1947, the US administration provided Iran with US$ 25 million in military supplies to help them expel Soviet troops (*The New York Times*, 31 May, 21 June, 22 October, 10 December 1947).

Also in 1947, the pro-British Hakimi became prime minister of Iran, replacing the pro-Soviet Quavam. The formation of a pro-Western government was crucial in determining whether the Soviets would be capable of exerting influence over Iranian oil policy. On the other hand, the US administration felt that the British could exclude US companies from oil concessions. Two

US companies, Socony Vacuum and Standard Oil of New Jersey, had been receiving oil concessions from Iran since 1943 (Elwell-Sutton 1955: 108). Their share was minimal though; the British-owned Anglo-Iranian Oil Company (AIOC) had a monopoly on Iranian oil production. Hence, for US companies to prosper, reliance on a pro-US government in Iran was crucial. When Mossadegh became prime minister in 1951 and sought to nationalize not only the AIOC but also US companies, the CIA engineered a coup against him. After the CIA-aided Iranian army overthrew Mossadegh and placed the Shah in power, US oil company shares in Iranian oil production increased from almost nil to 40 per cent (Keohane 1984:167–9).

The Truman Doctrine marked a turning point in the history of the Cold War and Turkey's position in it. As might be expected, Turkey, Greece, and Iran drew the international security boundaries of Soviet containment around the eastern Mediterranean. In the process, the strategic military position of Turkey was fully acknowledged, and, accordingly, it received US$ 100 million in aid. Greece received US$ 300 million.

Despite considerable controversy over the granting of aid to Turkey, Truman believed that US aid to Greece and Turkey was vital to prevent 'confusion and disorder' throughout the entire Middle East (Kuniholm 1980: 438). The importance of Turkey's primary strategic location was clear. It was a land and water bridge between Asia and Europe, between Europe and the Middle East, and between the Soviet Union and the Middle East. The Truman Doctrine was about 'keeping Russia from the sea' (*Herald Tribune*, 18 July 1947), and the Turkish straits were a vital element in accomplishing this task. In a speech to Congress on 12 March 1947, Truman explained:

> We can not realize our objectives unless we are willing to help free people to maintain their free institutions and their national integrity against aggressive movements that seek to impose upon them totalitarian regimes ... The time has come when nearly every nation must choose between alternative ways of life, one distinguished by free institutions and the other by terror and oppression ... Turkey now needs our support. Since the war Turkey has sought financial assistance from Great Britain and the United States for the purpose of effecting that modernization necessary for the maintenance of its national integrity. That integrity is essential to the preservation of order in the Middle East ... It must be the policy of the United States to support free peoples who are resisting attempted subjugation by armed minorities or by outside pressure (Kuniholm 1980: 434–9).

This shift in US foreign policy towards Turkey had several important implications. First, it marked the position of Turkey within the Western alliance as strategically crucial to the security of US interests. Second, the Turkish multi-party system began to consolidate when Inonu saw that US sponsorship went to governments which established 'free' institutions and opposed 'terror and oppression'. Still, it is very difficult to determine exactly how the emerging Cold War influenced Inonu's decision to support the multi-party system. Inonu was probably motivated more by territorial and security interests than by a firm commitment to 'democracy'. In dismantling the single-party regime he wanted to ensure Turkey's admission to the Western alliance structure. However, there is no proof that the US administration required Turkey to change its regime and adopt liberal democracy. Nonetheless, by presenting the world with only two choices, 'freedom' or 'oppression', Truman made it clear that Turkey had no alternative except to organize a new political regime. The signing of the US-Turkish Aid Agreement on 12 July 1947 was a key turning point. That same day President Inonu endorsed the opposition Democrat Party and silenced the hard-line statist faction within the RPP that opposed liberalization.

The resentment politics of state oppression

Although Inonu's decision to dismantle the single party system was primarily geopolitical, he was also unwittingly responding to those demanding greater liberalization in Turkey. Inonu channelled popular grievances in the direction of established institutional practices within the state structure in such a way that the Kemalist trajectory would not be endangered (Barutcu 1977: 306–8). He conceived of the multi-party system as a mechanism for the containment of political discontents within Kemalism. By choosing the multi-party system, Inonu largely pre-empted the possibility of a significant opposition movement. He turned to what he regarded as a 'loyal opposition': a non-communist and non-Islamist populist party that did not vie for power by making claims distinct from those of the RPP. The connection between Inonu's embrace of the Western alliance and the continuation of a Kemalist trajectory of social change is evident in the following statement: 'It never happened in my life that I haven't taken external problems into consideration as I was solving internal problems, or vice versa' (Barutcu 1977: 316).

Inonu believed the multi-party system would allow the domestic arrangements created during the 1930s to be accommodated within the emerging international order. As he explained on 1 November 1945:

> Freedom of expression, freedom of speech and writing, should
> not undo the limits imposed by the nation's own ability to support

> itself. [Otherwise] this nation would face the danger of anarchy and disorder. It is within our memory, we experienced it in the past, that this country can absolutely not sustain the weight of excessive and immoderate speeches which cause the rise of disorder in society (Inonu 1946: 397–400).

For Inonu, the state was unable to sustain a plurality of competing political claims for power. Therefore, there was an absolute need to keep the opposition party loyal to Kemalist principles as articulated by the RPP during the single-party regime. As Prime Minister Sukru Saracoglu indicated: 'Any kind of political activity can develop in our country, but only in a direction determined by the Republican People's Party' (*Vatan Newspaper*, 5 September 1945).

The establishment of the DP in 1946 was a rude awakening for Kemalist bureaucrats. It became clear that the emerging DP was a voice of opposition for those forced to bury their resentment of state oppression during the single-party era. Although a politics of discontent was definitely muted, the DP was toying with the idea of constructing an opposition movement against the bureaucratic control of the economy and militant secularism (Atasoy 1986).

In the economic realm, the most immediate inspiration for political opposition was the Land Reform Bill of 1945. The RPP government introduced the bill with the intention of redistributing all land worked by wage labour, tenancy, and sharecropping to the immediate tillers. It provided for all landed property in excess of 500 *donum* (123.5 acres) to be expropriated and redistributed to landless and land-short peasants (Selekler 1945). The Land Reform Bill was strongly opposed by large landowners, and after months of debate in parliament, the bill was modified to allow only for the redistribution of state-owned lands (Barkan 1945). The debate on the Land Reform Bill demonstrated the deeply rooted political conflict within the RPP. Large landowners who received the support of private industrial and commercial classes were disturbed by what they saw as 'arbitrary and unpredictable legislation' at the hands of RPP bureaucrats. Two examples of such legislation were the National Defence Law of 1940 and the Capital Tax of 1942.

Celal Bayar and Adnan Menderes, who represented the liberal wing of the RPP, were adamant in their opposition to the Land Reform Bill. Bayar was a businessman-banker and Menderes a cotton-growing landlord. Their criticism was based on two grounds: First, land reform would violate the principle of private property guaranteed by the constitution; and second, it would lead to a decline in production (Karpat 1959: 296–8).

Inonu's desire to situate Turkey within the Western alliance played a major role in shaping a liberal opposition in parliament. The government's acceptance of the Charter of the United Nations, for example, provided political opportunity. Bayar, Menderes, Koraltan, and Koprulu, who together represented the liberal element in the RPP, broadened their critique of the 'repressive' single-party system. Muhittin Baha Pars was the first parliamentarian to ask that the government be answerable to parliament. He also proposed that the government allow the press to be present in parliamentary discussions (*Ulus Newspaper*, 30 May 1945). Menderes accused the government of not acting in accordance with the constitution:

> We have accepted the Charter of the United Nations in accordance with our own constitution. This means that we cannot live in a political regime that is against the spirit of our constitution in the first place. We should work toward the elimination of the disharmony between actual political practice and constitutional requirements. (*Vatan Newspaper*, 16 August 1945).

The first act of the opposition was to present the joint motion (known as the *dortlu takrir*) to parliament on 7 June 1945. In the motion, Bayar, Menderes, Koprulu, and Koraltan demanded the restoration of individual and political rights for all citizens as stated in the constitution. They also demanded that the operation and control of government be returned to parliamentarians (Burcak 1979: 241–4). When the motion was rejected, the opposition used the press, particularly the *Vatan Newspaper*, to collectively argue against state repression.

Koprulu insisted on the separation of powers between parliament and government and accused the government of exerting dictatorial power over parliament. He exclaimed: 'I am ashamed of calling myself a representative of the nation in this parliament' (Barutcu 1977: 288). In an article entitled 'The Spirit of Democracy', published on 19 September 1945 in the *Vatan Newspaper*, Koprulu defined the single–party system as a dictatorship. He stated that the regime treated Turkish citizens like a flock of sheep who were expected to obey orders from bureaucrats on command. In another article, 'Enemies of Democracy', published on 25 September 1945, Koprulu went further and accused the RPP government of being an enemy of democracy:

> The primary objective of the government was [initially] to protect reforms from the possibility of [Islamic] reaction and to prevent the likelihood of any social disturbance in the country. This sort of reasoning led to the enactment of some very restrictive laws that were totally against the spirit of the constitution. As a result, it became impossible for the parliament to exercise its duty of controlling the government. The single party regime has totally damaged the spirit of democracy in Turkey. (*Vatan Newspaper*, 25 September 1945).

Because of their bitter and growing opposition, Menderes, Koprulu, and Koraltan were expelled from the RPP. Following Bayar's resignation from the RPP, the four men formed the DP on 7 January 1946, with Bayar as their leader. A close friend of Mustafa Kemal, Bayar was minister of the economy in 1924 and 1932, founder of the Business Bank in 1924, and prime minister in 1937.

Although the immediate reason for the establishment of the DP was opposition to the Land Reform Bill by large landowners, the DP was formed as a populist party. It mobilized not only large landowners and private industrial interests but also the small peasantry, wage earners, and various small commercial and manufacturing interests as well. All were strongly opposed to government economic policies.

The passion expressed by DP founders against the repressive centralized control of RPP bureaucrats was complemented by a vision that promoted the harmonization of popular grievances with the unifying principle of 'national interest' (DP Party Program, Article 6 and 7). This vision of inclusive citizenship was based on the Western liberal concept of individual rights and freedoms. The founders of the DP conceived of an opposition party as a vehicle for the political expression of popular discontent—in this particular case, against what Menderes called 'the tyranny of the RPP' (*Vatan Newspaper*, 1 April, 30 April, 19 May 1946).

The crucial question of the day was how to determine the normative grounds for expressing these rights and freedoms. Given that Inonu was committed to positioning Turkey as a 'democracy' in the Western alliance structure, the RPP made a number of changes in its by-laws to liberalize the regime (Atasoy 1986: 172–87). In fact, 'individual rights' became part of the political discourse. Another strategic question that arose was how to facilitate the expression of different types of political belonging. For example, at the Sixth Congress of 1946, the RPP recognized the existence of various social 'groups' in society. It acknowledged that these groups have different economic interests, yet it avoided using the concept of social class. This led, in June 1946, to the founding of the Turkish Socialist Workers' and Peasants' Party by Dr. Sefik Husnu Degmer. Bit by bit, the RPP adopted measures that acknowledged 'rights and freedoms' based on social class. At the Seventh Congress of 1947 the RPP advocated free enterprise in the economy and modified the Land Reform Bill to suit the interests of large landowners.

Changes in individual rights and freedoms were also understood in relation to popular claims of cultural belonging and discontent. At the Seventh Congress of 1947 the RPP decided to permit religious education in schools. This represented a shift in the RPP's understanding of an individual's relationship to the collectivity. The issue of religious education turned around a perceived need to strengthen the sense of belonging to a national culture. Nevertheless, Inonu was suspicious of dissent, the expression of diverse political interests, and the cultural contestation of secular principles, all of which he believed could undermine state power (*Vatan Newspaper*, 2 June 1946). Consequently, he formulated the concept of 'popular power among citizens', to be expressed with the consent of, and in harmony with, the national interest (Karpat 1957: 311). The notion of popular power helped to reinforce a common understanding of populism, which led the DP and the RPP to neutralize class-based differences and contentious cultural claims. This became most evident after the newly founded socialist political party was closed down in December 1946. The DP and RPP also shared the view that economic and cultural tensions should be situated within the state, rather than being rooted in collective struggles that challenge the state.

One way in which the RPP and DP tried to distinguish themselves was by accusing one another of being communist or soft on communism. RPP hardliners, for example, accused the DP of being 'in the pocket of Moscow' (Zurcher 1993: 223). Inonu brought a halt to the accusations and silenced RPP hardliners on the same day that the US-Turkish Aid Agreement was signed, 12 July 1947. In his declaration Inonu stated:

> The result I seek is the institution of confidence between the parties. This is necessary for the security of the country. The opposition will work without the fear of being closed down by the party in power; the government will be secure that the opposition demands nothing beyond its legal rights; the citizens will be confident in seeking the possibility of the transfer of power from one party to another. In order to overcome the obstacles to this end, I ask for genuine cooperation between the leaders of the opposition and government parties. (*Ulus Newspaper*, 12 July 1947)

The positioning of opposition within the state structure was a guarantee that the multi-party system would be instituted peacefully. In 1959 Inonu stated in an interview that there was an 'absolute need' to allow the opposition to form their own political parties (Erdemir 1962: 9). And in a speech delivered in parliament in December 1969, Inonu explained what he had meant: 'If we did not choose the multi-party democratic regime in 1945, there might have been a bloody revolution in society' (Burcak 1979: 55). Concerned with security and territorial interests, as well as domestic policy considerations, Inonu hoped to contain the contentious politics that flourished despite brutal repression by the civil-military bureaucratic cadres. In order not to exhaust the political framework of Kemalism, he needed the assistance of the DP and the cooperation of RPP hardliners (Barutcu 1977: 306–8, 316). Prime Minister Saracoglu also shared Inonu's hope for the containment of political dissent: 'We want only one thing. We should cooperate against a reactionary movement. We want unity in politics' (*Vatan Newspaper*, 7 March 1946).

Despite both parties' shared belief in the need to keep contentious politics within Kemalism, the DP was able to depict the political dominance of bureaucratic cadres as inimical to the interests of the general population. In doing so, the DP advanced competing claims for an oppositional politics. These claims involved large numbers of people whose values, interests, and way of life were excluded from the Kemalist reconstruction of Western modernity in Turkey. In recognizing the diverse and heterogeneous nature of people's daily experience, the DP provoked opposition by claiming entitlement for those in marginal or subordinate positions in society. The party took on the responsibility of constructing a moral programme of individual rights, freedoms, and cultural belonging out of the resentment of the general population.

According to DP leaders, the political conflict between the ruling bureaucratic elite, private capital groups, and the peasantry, was a political struggle between 'centre' and 'periphery'. The centre was embodied in ruling bureaucrats; the periphery was represented by a collection of people from various socio-economic categories. The DP saw the latter group as sharing a common interest in opposing the centre. Although the DP recognized class differences within the periphery, this did not distinguish the fundamental policy of the DP from the RPP. Rather, the DP fashioned a strategy to unify different class-based interests that viewed the periphery as constitutive of a community outside the state. The DP's notion of a peripheral identity involved a conception of morality that included judgements about justice, rights, and freedoms. It incorporated private capital groups, peasants, and the working class within a populist agenda mobilized against state-induced injustices. On the other hand, the RPP, in choosing to support the expression of discontent within the frame of national interest, advanced a conception of national security rights defined by the state ruling bureaucracy.

Cultural rights and freedoms: Islam within a secular state

The single-party era divided relations between the individual and the state in a hierarchical manner. It was essentially a division between the much larger population of the masses and a ruling bureaucratic elite. The RPP viewed the cultures of rural populations, the peasantry, the working class, and private capital groups as lacking the Kemalist prerequisites for state-making. Kemalist bureaucrats believed these groups had not acquired the norms and practices required for the secularization and westernization programme of Kemalism. Since they were seen as maintaining beliefs and behaviours consistent with Islamic tradition, these groups and their cultures were thought to be a source of reactionary political activity. In short, their 'backwardness' was detrimental to Turkey's westernization project. On this basis, Kemalism justified their exclusion from the political process. This in turn provided a moral foundation for the DP's reworking of relations between the Kemalist reproduction of Western ways and the development of a concept of justice that included the experience of marginalized groups.

The DP's understanding of personal rights and freedoms required the establishment of a link between access to rights and the creation of a sense of belonging. But the DP positioned marginal groups outside the state, as subjects of the periphery. This excluded the idea of class and class conflict from its conception of rights, freedoms, and justice. Consequently, members of the periphery were simply victims of the oppressed. As Bayar (1951: 124) stated: 'Our people have been punished in police stations and beaten up in the villages. These examples expose the police-state character of the existing regime ... Our peasants have been forced to pay taxes despite their inability to pay'. And in a speech delivered at a DP rally in Milas in November 1946, Menderes (1967: 35) announced: 'The national unity achieved under the single party regime is nothing but an encampment by the gendarmerie'. In another speech delivered at the Kutahya Provincial Congress of the DP in December 1949, Menderes (1967: 203) condemned RPP rule as equivalent to a 'dictatorship of intellectuals'— claiming to be doing good things for the people, but in fact doing things in spite of them.

According to DP leaders, the secular basis of Turkish nationalism would not be undermined by a more inclusive practice of citizenship. The masses were responsible enough to enjoy their democratic rights and freedoms without engaging in reactionary movements and rejecting the ideological foundation of the state. Koprulu (1964: xxx) declared: 'We should trust the unshakable determination and patriotism of our people. Their national and political comprehension is greater than that of those who claim to provide them with guardianship'.

For the DP, Islam was an important element of peripheral folk culture, capable of sustaining the sentiment of belonging to a national society. However, Islam was suppressed by the dominance of the secularizing 'high culture' of state-ruling urban bureaucrats. The DP argued that the high culture of the ruling elite had no relevance to the daily life experience of the people, while the social norms and practices of Islam represented something very real in their lives. The RPP was burdened by the social hierarchy and authority relations of the single-party system. They ruled without the support of the people. However, the DP was able to spread widely among rural populations and small producers in urban areas by creating a political framework that tolerated religious experience. This provided the DP with a cultural basis for shaping opposition against the RPP (Mardin 1957). Nevertheless, the DP's promotion of rights and freedoms remained connected to the secular practices and cultural ethos of

Kemalism. In other words, the DP was reshaping peripheral folk culture within the context of the Kemalist state-making project.

The religiously oriented conservative faction of the RPP also realized religion was an important element of peripheral folk culture. In this regard, both the DP and religious conservatives developed a sensitivity towards Islam that helped to promote feelings of cultural belonging. This strengthened the national consciousness of the younger generation in a way that the oppressive state actions of police, the military, and the courts could not (*Vatan Newspaper*, 25 December 1946). Tanriover, the most influential parliamentarian within the conservative faction of the RPP, stated that religion would provide good protection from the spread of communism and other 'divisive' foreign ideologies. Together with other members of the conservative faction, Tanriover demanded a change in state ideology that would reflect a synthesis between Islam and Turkish nationalism (Jaschke 1972: 83–100).

Although such a platform appealed to popular resentment of secular reforms, it did not constitute an Islamist reaction to the secular foundations of the state. According to Meeker (2002: 337), peripheral cultural practices were elements of the old state-society relations to be placed within the new state structure. Leading individuals and powerful families of the periphery were merely interested in repositioning themselves in the state and economy. For them, an Islamic political agenda was no more appealing than leftist politics. This was evident in the electoral failure of the Nation Party which tried to align religious issues and opposition politics.

The conservative faction of the RPP believed that secularism as practised during the single-party era was anti-democratic. It claimed that 'true' secularism had never been practised in Turkey. Bureaucratic cadres violated the freedom of conscience of the Muslim majority in the name of secularism and then used this as a means to keep people under their control. This was contrary to the very idea of secularism and to democracy as well (Basgil 1962: 145–50). Using a similar rationale, the DP proposed an end to the prohibition on the call to prayer and the reading of the Koran in Arabic. The DP believed these prohibitions prevented people from worshipping as they wished and therefore violated their freedom to act according to their conscience (Tunaya 1962: 226).

The RPP followed suit. At the RPP Seventh Party Congress in 1947, Inonu stated: 'We have to take national realities into account. We have to be responsive to the moral needs of the nation and relieve the people from a feeling of being neglected by the government' (Barutcu 1977: 326–7). As a result, the Seventh Party Congress amended the meaning of secularism to include a clause on respect for religion. Religious expression was now a matter of personal conscience. The RPP also undertook to protect worshippers from political threats and interference (Jaschke 1972: 85–6, 98, 100). Following this congress, RPP governments initiated a number of changes. These included the allocation of foreign currency for pilgrimages to Mecca, the restoration, in February 1949, of religious instruction for primary school students in their fourth and fifth year of education, the introduction of *imam-hatip* training courses for a period of three years by the ministry of education, and, the opening of the Faculty of Theology at Ankara University in January 1949 (Albayrak 1991: 258–73).

The DP came to power in the election of May 1950, winning a 53.4 per cent share of the vote and 408 seats against the RPP's 69. They strove to generate intense feelings of cultural belonging in the population, and also expressed an intention to connect the people to the state more firmly than ever. This was actually an attempt to complete the nationalization process that had been initiated by Mustafa Kemal. The DP aimed to integrate local popular cultures into the secular political state. The inclusion of religious courses in formal secular education was the first step taken in that direction.

In addition to lifting the ban on the recitation of the call to prayer in Arabic and permitting the reading of the Koran over state radio, efforts were made to increase the number of mosques and broaden the scope of religious education. During the 1950/1 academic year, elective courses on religion, which the RPP government had introduced in 1949, were included in the regular primary school curriculum for all students.

There was a significant increase in the number of *imam-hatip* schools as well. The Ministry of Education opened seven middle-level and lycée-level *imam-hatip* schools between 1951 and 1952. By 1958, there were 18, with 2,476 students. Most students in these schools were from the families of urban and rural small-producers (Gokce et al 1984: 123). Also of note, in 1959 the first Higher Islamic Institution was introduced.

In addition, the DP increased the budget of the Directorate of Religious Affairs from approximately 3 million Turkish lira in 1950 to approximately 40 million lira in 1960. Between 1950 and 1960, the years in which the DP ruled, 15,000 new mosques were built. Between 1951 and 1954, a total of 616 mosques and historical shrines were repaired. More than 5.5 million Turkish lira were allotted to the Directorate-General of Pious Foundations for the repair of mosques and shrines (Toprak 1981: 80–1).

Although the changes undertaken by the DP had already been initiated by the former RPP government, the DP's most significant contribution was to create a tolerant political environment for religious education (Reed 1954: 281). The DP government enabled Islam to be taught in a way that would allow the state to extend its rural influence, provided Islamic institutions remained within the state structure (Dodd 1979: 76). The programme of religious education forged a link between religion and the state by offering a blend of Islamic and secular courses. The state maintained strict control over all religious education. Students who became prayer leaders and preachers were employed exclusively by the state.

Islamist moorings and the self

The specific historical conjuncture of the Cold War not only undermined the single-party political system, it also made it possible to envision different ways of thinking about morality. A multi-party system provided the requisite political space for the articulation of contested projects. Frey offers an interesting metaphor to suggest that the rise of Islamic politics was also a distinct possibility in the expression of contentious politics. '(One) might merely propose that the lid which had been put on the pot was lifted at this time and that some people were surprised and alarmed to see certain parts of the stew still bubbling' (Frey 1964: 223). According to Frey, the stew's ingredients were Islamic cultural practices and social arrangements, and the bubbles were the religious orders and Islamist intellectuals who survived state repression, working underground outside of state control.

The Sufi orders, which had gone underground after the suppression of the Sheikh Said Revolt of 1925, experienced significant growth from 1950 to 1960. While the DP was in power, there was also an increase in the number of private Koran schools and organizations formed to oversee the construction of new mosques (Robinson 1971). The number of private organizations established by the religious orders increased from 95 in 1949 to 251 in 1951, reaching 5,104 by 1960. The ratio of private religious organizations to all other private organizations increased from 5.5 per cent in 1949 to 10 per cent in 1951, and to 29.7 per cent by 1960 (Yucekok 1971: 133). This growth was partly a result of the DP's tolerance for religious orders. In return, Said Nursi and his followers supported the DP in the 1954 and 1957 elections.

Although Said Nursi had in the past described Menderes as 'the champion of Islam' (Kisakurek 1990: 148–51), Menderes, who was prime minister from 1950 to 1960, was not about to permit the rise of anything resembling an Islamic counter-revolution against secular Kemalist principles. In 1951 the DP passed a law (PL 5816) making it a crime to attack the personality of Ataturk and Ataturkism (meaning Mustafa Kemal and Kemalism respectively) (Tarhanli 1993: 28). On the basis of this law, members of the Ticani order were handed severe jail sentences. Pilavoglu, the sheikh of the order, was sentenced to 15 years' imprisonment and exiled to an Aegean island for the rest of his life (Tunaya 1962: 231). Necip Fazil Kisakurek, an Islamic intellectual, was imprisoned for nine months because of an article he published in the *Buyuk Dogu* (Great East) periodical that was deemed offensive to secularism.

Said Nursi, who had been accused many times of establishing a politically motivated secret religious order (Algar 1979; Mardin 1989), was arrested in 1952 for the fourth time. The charges against him were based on the publication and distribution of a section of the *Risale-I Nur* entitled 'Guide for Youth' (Algar 1979: 321–3). His support for women's veiling and religious instruction at all school levels was seen as a direct threat to secularism. He also argued that an Islamic dress code was better suited to the dignity and modesty of Muslim women than imported Western fashion. In his court defence Said Nursi asked the prosecution whether it was necessary for women to expose their bodies and for children to grow up ignorant of religion in order to preserve the state. If the answer was yes, then did such a state deserve preservation? He declared that the trial was an indication of how secularism was being used to mask hostility towards religion (Algar 1979: 323). Said Nursi was acquitted, but he was also forced to take up residence in Emirdag in western Anatolia. A ban continued on the publication and distribution of his work, collected under the title of the *Risale-I Nur.* Possession of the collection was an offence until 1965 because it was written in Arabic script. During this time, its distribution was restricted to handwritten and mimeographed copies (Algar 1979: 323; Mardin 1989: 101). After 1956 it was possible to distribute the *Risale-I Nur* on a wider scale than ever before. Dr. Tahsin Tola, a follower of Said Nursi and a parliamentarian for the DP, managed to lift the ban on printing the book in Latin script.

Both the RPP and DP governments helped shape an emergent politics of discontent. In the process, public politics became more inclusive, largely due to the multi-party system initiated at the beginning of the Cold War. A range of ideological positions grew out of this more mature political environment, including a desire on the part of Islamists to be moored to an Islamic moral-spiritual foundation. Islamists sought a place in society with secure rights, freedoms, and principles of justice. They were also searching for a discourse drawn from their daily social lives that would engender feelings of meaningful attachment and belonging—feelings not generated by Kemalism.

The quest for a uniquely Islamic moral outlook has roots going back to the beginning of the Ottoman accession to Western modernity in the nineteenth century – a period that stimulated cultural dualism in intellectual activity between secularists and Islamists (Bulac 1983). In contrast to the secularist wholesale adoption of Western cultural values, Islamists advocated the adoption of Western science and technology but not its culture. For them, Western cultural practices and social arrangements were embedded in an integrated system of meaning, perception, and ontology. The Kemalist practice of emulating Western ways ignored the true nature of cultural experience, according to Islamists who viewed culture as a unified whole. Islamists examined the notion of modernity by insisting on the need to fully explore its conceptual content. For them, a nation that turned its back on its own culture could only reproduce a rootless imitation. Of utmost importance was the need to chart a path based on a world-view embedded in day-to-day cultural meanings. This path had to be consistent with the morally inspired rights and freedoms required to counter the dominance of bureaucrats and repression of the periphery. Among these

Islamists was Necip Fazil Kisakurek (1904—83), one of the most outstanding Turkish poets.

Necip Fazil Kisakurek: an Islamist poet

Kisakurek was born into a highly educated family in Istanbul. His father and grandfather were high-level bureaucrats in the Ottoman judiciary. Kisakurek was educated in the Ottoman school system, which offered courses on both religion and the modern sciences. After graduating from the Ottoman Naval Academy (the Mekteb-I Funun), he studied literature in Paris in 1924 and 1925, where he enjoyed a bohemian lifestyle (Kisakurek 1978). Kisakurek's grandmother had already exposed him to French literature during his childhood. After returning from Paris, he worked in the Business Bank (Is Bankasi) until 1938. Between 1938 and 1941 he taught literature at the French School; the School of Fine Arts in Istanbul; Ankara Conservatorie; the American Robert College; and the Faculty of Languages, History, and Geography at Ankara University. Kisakurek established his own periodical, the *Buyuk Dogu* (Great East), where he published his essays and literary work. The *Buyuk Dogu* was shut down several times between its founding in 1943 and the military coup of 1971. For more than a quarter of a century it served as an effective vehicle for transmitting an Islamic message to a large, anonymous audience of readers.

Kisakurek was a nationalist who believed that Islam was an indispensable element in the shaping of a national identity. He assigned Islam a political role, arguing that it could produce a coherent cultural orientation and strengthen the emotional attachment of individual citizens to the Turkish nation-state.

Kisakurek formulated his Islamic message against the background of increased anxiety over the meaninglessness of a state-imposed secular culture in Turkey (Kisakurek 1976; 1979). He insisted that the complete moral development of an individual required a coherent cultural orientation within a community, strong interpersonal relations, and adherence to a strict moral code. However, Turkish accession to Western ways had broken the integrated pattern of cultural practices in Turkey. This process, which started with the Tanzimat, reached its peak during Kemalist secularization. The westernization project undermined the emotional connection between the self and the moral community, producing rootlessness within the general population. Kisakurek's poems reflect the sense of cultural dislocation created by the major social changes experienced in Turkey since the Tanzimat. A meeting with Sheikh Arvasi of the Naqshbandi religious order in 1934 was pivotal in forming Kisakurek's view of cultural derangement. He identified Sheik Arvasi as his 'saviour'. Kisakurek described his life before meeting Arvasi: 'For the whole thirty years my watch moved, I stopped; Unaware of the sky, I flew my kite' (quoted in Dogan 1983: 43).

The early poems written by Kisakurek, before his meeting with Sheikh Arvasi, were secularly oriented. Among them were 'Spider Web' (1925), 'Sidewalks' (1928), and 'I and Beyond' (1932). His later poetry, 'Caravan to Eternity' (1955), 'Suffering' (1979/1962), and 'My Poems' (1969) reveal his Islamist orientation more clearly. *Suffering (Cile)* in particular occupies a special place in terms of its Islamic message. In the work, Kisakurek publicly rejects all his earlier poems, believing them unworthy for not clearly demonstrating his attachment to God. In the preface to *Suffering*, Kisakurek (1979: 7) writes:

> If I am the owner of the property, it must be known that I neither want them nor recognize them. I now throw them into the trash ... This [*Suffering*] is my book of poetry, this is all; none of the other poems that I have written before this book can be attributed to me, to my name, and my soul.

Kisakurek's writings focus on the meaninglessness and emptiness of the secularization discourse in Turkey. Through his poetry he urged readers to create the climate for a meaningful connection between self and society. In 'Suffering' Kisakurek (1979: 14–6) writes:

> I moved around for months, shattered and perplexed,
> My soul is a cauldron and my intellect a ladle,
> Within ear-shot of the village of lunatics,
> Each and every idea is a pair of handcuffs within me.
>
> Time and time again the scorpion stung my soul,
> I moved from season to season in that way.
> I realized neither in fire nor in the gouging of flesh
> Is there a greater torture than the suffering of the mind.
>
> Dictionary, give a name to describe me;
> A name that everybody will recognize!
> My old clothes hold my hand;
> Mirrors tell me who I am. (My translation)

Kisakurek's poetry expresses the deep pain caused by an absence of cultural belonging and the rejection of Islam as a way of life. He writes: 'My brain has become the shelter of deep anxiety about the "absolute truth" ... My soul is like an aching tooth ... Even if the Oceans were made of ink, if all the trees constituted only one pen, they would still not suffice to express my suffering in depth' (quoted in Atasoy 2003b: 68). For him, this emotional and intellectual pain born of the secularization process was commonly experienced throughout Turkey. In *Ahsap Konak* (wooden mansion), Kisakurek expresses his feelings of moral derangement through the image of a deplorable house. The *konak* is where he spent his childhood during the later years of the Ottoman Empire. It symbolizes the moral disintegration experienced under the influence of social change in Turkey. Kisakurek writes:

> Every floor of this three story *Ahsap Konak* is a different world:
> Top floor: my grandmother crying while holding prayer beats
> Middle floor: my mother dancing with her lovers
> Downstairs: My sister screaming at the tom-tom beats.
> Like the maggoty cheese that I cut through from the middle,
> Please come and see it through its floors, here, my home!
> What kind of a pathetic tree that is, surrounding my entire vision.
> Its roots are honesty, its branches are imitation, its fruits are prostitution (quoted in Kabakli 1983: 4). (My translation)

The *Ahsap Konak* illustrates a world fundamentally shaped by dissonant social context. The home represents a fragmented social space and the cognitive emptiness in the minds of individuals. This disorientation was created by the forerunners of the westernization project whom Kisakurek called 'spurious heroes'. According to him, all Western-oriented intellectuals and rulers from the Tanzimat period of the Ottoman Empire to present-day Turkey are spurious heroes, Mustafa Kemal included. The scholastic, overly formalistic, and *sharia*-influenced structure of the Islamic educational system was also responsible for the spiritual estrangement that, according to Kisakurek, led the religious establishment into inertia during the Western challenge to the Ottoman Empire.

Kisakurek's writings cannot be classified as 'fundamentalist' in any religious sense. Rather, his work reflects a desire to reclaim a sense of spiritual resonance in the cultural lives of individuals. His goal was to create a new type of self and a new type of society in the process. Hence, the title of one of his plays is *To Create a Self*, and the title of his manifesto written for youth is *The Web of Ideology* (*Ideolocya Orgusu*).

The incongruity between the individual self and society which Kisakurek understood to be caused by the westernization project underscores a view of cognition that stresses a highly self-contained individual still very much influenced by social context. George Herbert Mead (1934) has suggested that the I and the Me are two interrelated aspects of the self united within an individual. Similarly, Kisakurek points to the significance of social interaction for a complete understanding of the self as an entity situated within a broader context. The context in this case is oppositional, created by the tension between the subjects of the oppressed and the oppressing cadres of the westernization project. The asymmetric power relations shape the cognitive reactions of subordinate subjects. These subjects view themselves as being outside the Kemalist representation of cultural belonging. Kisakurek (1976) thus locates the Islamic configuration of an integrated self in the reconstitution of society.

Said Nursi and the reconstitution of society

In a manner akin to that of Kisakurek, Said Nursi promoted the strengthening of individual morality within a framework of faith set out in the Koran. He was not interested in establishing a religious order but in cultivating an Islamic cultural community through a 'return to the Koran' movement. His writings reveal an interpretation of the Koran which he hoped would serve as a guide for the personal development of his followers. Said Nursi used the print media to deliver his message and strengthen the resolve of the faithful, but he did not wish his followers to focus on himself as 'the master'. His emphasis on the use of printed books for guidance underscores the importance he gave to reinterpreting the Koran as a means of finding 'solutions' to contemporary political and economic concerns.

Said Nursi's writings focus on political demands for justice, equality, and freedom. The lack of social justice and democratic principles he described was symptomatic of the disintegrating moral framework caused by the replication of Western ways in a Muslim society. He firmly believed in the cultural-symbolic opposites of Islam and the West. The 'immorality' he ascribed to the social arrangements of the West is very evident in his work. He writes:

> [The West's] support is founded on force and aggression; its aim is benefit and self interest; its principle of life is conflict; its tie between communities is racism and negative nationalism; its fruits are stimulation of the appetites of the soul and increasing the needs of human kind ... It is because of its founding principles as such that Western culture has negated the happiness of human kind. Because, [it] has brought bad consequences for human kind such as wastefulness, poverty, idleness, and egoism, it has cast the great majority, some 80 per cent of humanity into wretchedness (quoted in Atasoy 2003b: 69–70).

He believed that individuals should reflect upon the social structure of the society in which they live. He was convinced that Western cultural patterns negate principles of social justice because they are embedded in the perpetual creation of social hierarchies of domination.

Western civilization as it stands today has acted contrary to divine law. Consequently, its evils have been greater than its benefits. The real goal of civilization, which should be understood as the general well being and happiness of everyone in this world, has been undermined. Wastefulness and vice have predominated over frugality and contentment, and laziness and comfort have prevailed over work and service. This has made humankind wretched both in body and spirit (quoted in Atasoy 2003b: 70).

Said Nursi argued that Western ways were not congruent with human happiness and were therefore unsustainable. The collapse of Western culture was inevitable and would result from the awakening of humankind and the realization that an alternative cultural ground could be created through Islam (Said Nursi 1990a). He held firmly to his belief that Islam should be the central element of a cultural framework for enhancing social justice and democracy. He identified westernization as the chief source of injustice and moral decay in society and believed that the proliferation of conspicuous consumption was clear evidence of humanity's regression. He states:

While in the primitive state of nomadism, people needed only three or four things. And those who could not obtain these three or four things were two out of ten. The present tyrannical Western civilization has encouraged consumption, abuse and wastefulness. Ceaseless appetites have made nonessentials into essentials. This so-called civilized person is now in need of twenty things instead of four. Yet he can only obtain two of these twenty. He still needs eighteen. Therefore, Western civilization impoverishes humankind (quoted in Atasoy 2003b: 70).

In this binary view of Islam and the West, morality appears as the fundamental source of cultural conflict. To counter the moral hegemony of Western culture on the self, Said Nursi proposed the reconstitution of Muslim society. This could only be achieved by cultivating individual faith through the reading of the Koran and interpretative writings such as the *Risale-I Nur*.

According to Said Nursi, faith at the individual level was the first prerequisite for realizing social justice in a moral community. The establishment of *sharia* law was the second requirement for reconstituting Islam as a way of life. The third requirement was the unification of all Muslims against the 'moral regression' of the West. This final requirement referred to the global integration of Muslims as a *cemaat* (*ummah*) beyond the territorial limits of nation-states. However, unless the first task of strengthening faith was successfully completed, the second and third tasks could not be undertaken.

Political parties of the centre-right which emphasized the importance of religious education received the support of Said Nursi's followers. In the 1950s the DP was one of these parties. Their incorporation of Islam into the state educational system was helpful over the long term in bolstering Muslim faith. In the 1960s and 1970s, the Justice Party, which in 1961 became the successor to the DP, enjoyed the support of the *Nurcu cemaati*.

Said Nursi tried to link the idea of an 'internal *jihad*' to an external one. Internal *jihad* involves the development of a moral self through knowledge of the Koran, and the practice of Islamic morality in everyday life. The concept of 'external *jihad*' refers to the collective struggle of Muslims against the domination of morally corrupt values from the West. For Said Nursi, internal and external *jihads* were interrelated; both were essential for the integration of self and society. Interestingly, it seems that Said Nursi developed his view of the social at the same time that he came to appreciate the importance of reversing Turkey's peripheral location within the capitalist world economy.

Although Said Nursi was opposed to the westernization project, he was unable to explain the high-level of industrialization achieved by western European states and the United States without reference to culture as being constitutive of the economy. In conformity with the modernist Islamic view that developed in India and Egypt (Moaddel 2001; Cooper et al 2000), Said Nursi tried to show the congruity of Islam with rationalist thinking and modern science. He argued that the Koran reveals the laws of nature as the work of God, and that their discovery is to be made through a rationalist interpretation. For Said Nursi, then, Western progress ideology, formal rationality, and faith in modern science and technology were not only acceptable but in complete conformity with the Koran. The task for Muslims was to gain scientific knowledge by using the sole authority of the Koran, and to then link that knowledge to, amongst other things, the reorganization of the economy. In short, Said Nursi sought to realize his vision of 'progress' through the implementation of Islamic principles. He offered a rationalist interpretation of the Koran through the *Risale-I Nur* in order to counter the Kemalist view that westernization was the route to scientific advancement. Somewhat reminiscent of Weber (1971), Said Nursi assumed that an existing cultural opening was necessary for the development of industrial capitalism. Unlike Weber, however, he believed that Islam represented just such an opening for the cultivation of rational thought and growth of modern scientific technology.

The Naqshbandi order

After the abolition of religious orders in 1925, Naqshbandi sheikhs were unable to revive them. It was only in the 1930s that Sheikh Abdulhakim Arvasi emerged as a successor worthy of the great Ottoman Naqshbandi Sheikh Gumushanevi. Although Arvasi was highly influential among his followers, the Naqshbandi order experienced a break from active political engagement between 1925 and 1950. When the harsh secular measures of the single-party era were moderated by DP rule between 1950 and 1960, the Naqshbandi order, along with the *Nurcu cemaati*, became more assertive in the shaping of an Islamist agenda in Turkey.

There are hundreds of branches of the Naqshbandi order throughout the world. Although some are loosely connected, there is no overarching structure of global Naqshbandi governance or 'supreme' leadership. Most branches operate independently. Among the hundreds of minor branches, there are three major strands of the Naqshbandi in Turkey. These evolved during the 1950s after the death of Arvasi. An important branch of the Naqshbandi that followed the Gumushanevi line was founded by Mehmet Zahid Kotku, who became the sheikh of the order in 1952. Another strand of the Naqshandi emerged from the followers of two sheiks: Arvasi (1865–1943) and Suleyman Hilmi Tunahan (1888–1959). This strand was founded in the 1940s and known as the *Suleymancilar*, after its founder Suleyman Hilmi Tunahan. Kemal Kacar, Tunahan's son-in-law, is the current leader of the *Suleymancilar*. The *Isikcilar* constitute the third strand of the Naqshbandi. It was named after its founder, Sheik Huseyin Hilmi Isik, a follower of Sheikh Arvasi. The current leader of the *Isikcilar* is Enver Oren, Isik's son-in-law.

Mehment Zahid Kotku became the Naqshbandi sheikh while he was the *imam* of the Ummugulsum Mosque in Istanbul. He was appointed to the position by the Directorate of Religious Affairs. In 1958 he was transferred to the Iskenderpasha Mosque in Istanbul and worked there as a state employee until his death in 1980. The mosque where he had officially worked as a prayer leader became the Naqshbandi centre for his teachings (Mardin 1991). Kotku became what one might call a 'grand sheikh' in Turkey. He emphasized the role of *sohbet* (oral teaching) in building an Islamic society from small-scale community-based networks. His followers, who strove to embody Islamic principles, were students, university professors, educated professionals, and members of the bureaucracy. Among those in his inner circle were Professor Necmettin Erbakan, who later became leader of the pro-Islamic party and prime minister of Turkey; Turgut Ozal, former prime minister and president of Turkey; and Korkut Ozal, Hasan Aksay, and Fehmi Adak, ministers of various coalition governments during the 1970s.

Sheikh Kotku encouraged his followers to take advantage of the moderate ideological climate under a multi-party regime. He rallied his supporters to promote Islamic education and establish Koran schools in Turkey, believing that both were essential for strengthening Islamic faith. He also showed remarkable success in following the 'economic development' discourse of secular intellectuals. Faith, according to Kotku, needed to be held in tandem with a cultural openness to rational thought and scientific innovation. Consistent with Said Nursi, Kotku displayed a modernist Islamist stand in regard to technological progress.

Kotku also believed that a devout Muslim should develop an active interest in national problems and assist in the industrialization of the country. For example, he encouraged Professor Necmettin Erbakan to design a model industrial plant and establish it on a national level (Mardin 1991: 134). National industrial development was necessary to counter peripheralization, which Kotku (1984a) referred to as 'colonial status'—something Turkey had experienced since the Tanzimat era. Kotku's followers, who worked in the State Planning Organization during the 1960s and 1970s, devised heavy industrialization strategies for Turkey. In the 1980s and 1990s Kotku's enthusiastic support for technological development was taken up by his successor, Professor Cosan, from the Faculty of Theology at Ankara University.

Kotku's view of national industrialization stressed Islamically defined consumption norms. Islamic education, he reasoned, especially for the younger generation, must be sensitive to the importance of teaching students to avoid Western consumer goods, particularly food and clothing. It is significant that Islamist industrialists and commercial groups of the 1980s and 1990s adopted Kotku's idea of linking industrial production to an Islamic lifestyle. Today in Turkey, Islamist capitalists are making cultural claims by distinguishing their products from those that reflect the prevailing consumption norms embedded in a Western lifestyle (Navaro-Yashin 2002). As will be seen in later chapters, these capital groups are struggling to reposition themselves in the highly competitive relations of a capitalist market economy. In this struggle they appeal to Islamic cultural standards and practices to create Islamically defined consumption patterns for devout Muslims.

The *Suleymancilar* branch of the Naqshbandi order focuses on religious education. The founder of the branch, Suleyman Hilmi Tunahan, was educated in the Suleymaniye Theological School, and worked as a preacher in Istanbul in the early 1920s. During the 1930s he quit his work as a preacher and began to offer private instruction on the Koran at his farm. Although Koran schools were outlawed, Tunahan continued to operate them in all kinds of places, including shops and barns. He took it upon himself to build a network of Koran schools throughout Turkey. His followers continue to extend the network in Turkey and abroad, particularly for Turkish migrants living in Germany. These schools oppose the state-led religious education found in *imam-hatip* schools. The *Suleymancilar* believe that *imam-hatip* schools are designed to secularize the minds of the younger generation, thereby providing an abridged and 'subverted' version of Islam. Despite their opposition to secularism, the *Suleymancilar* have supported centre-right political parties since the 1950s.

The *Isikcilar* branch of the Naqshbandi order opposes secularism and Islamic modernism. It hopes to restore the works of classical scholars on Sunni

Islam to a position of unquestioned authority (Algar 1983). Followers of the *Isikcilar* adhere strictly to Sunni beliefs and oppose any reform of Islam. This group is currently composed of some of the wealthiest Islamist business groups, including the Ihlas Holding Co. established by Enver Oren.

The political liberalization experienced in Turkey after 1945 opened up a political space for the emergence of intellectual activity from writers such as Necip Fazil Kisakurek, movements like the *Risale-I Nur*, and religious orders such as the Naqshbandi. There also emerged an Islamic political agenda that was supportive of Western progress ideology and worked to strengthen Islamic faith among Muslims. An overview of the history of the Islamist agenda helps to explain why Islam became a salient political symbol in the 1970s. As the development strategies of the period generated new sources of conflict, concerns over rights, freedom, and justice became closely tied to Islam.

4

The Cold War and the Creation
of a National Bourgeoisie

lthough the post-war era has generally been seen as a period of
divergence from the Kemalist trajectory of state-led economic growth,
it was actually part of a single historical development of Turkish
accession to Western ways set out by the Tanzimat. The programme established
in Turkey during the Great Depression to build a national economy and create
a national bourgeoisie accelerated in the Cold War political environment of
the world economy. In effect the Cold War presented new opportunities for
furthering the industrialization process that had begun in the 1930s. The policy
debate of the post-war years alternated between the liberal market economy
and state-led growth models, but the positions converged around the 'mixed
economy' in regard to state regulation of the national economy. The mixed
economy combined the market principle with state intervention in such a way
that these two seemingly disparate models were compatible. In contrast to the
statist trajectory of Kemalism which embraced the collapse of the international
economy, post-war state intervention integrated domestic programmes into the
reconstruction of an international system around the Cold War, thus keeping
open the road to westernization.

In relation to political support, the connection between the mixed
economy model and the political formula chosen to accommodate the model
was riddled with tension. An analysis of the twists and turns of Turkey's
industrialization policy helps explain the shift in the political response to the
effects of the world economy on the inequalities that emerged during the period.
Two parties dominated: the Republican People's Party (RPP), in power from
1961 to 1965, and the Justice Party (JP), which rose to power in the 1965 general
election. The JP ruled Turkey either alone or in coalition for most of the 1970s.
Turkish disillusionment with the United States over the Cuban-Turkish missile
crisis and Cyprus led both parties to adopt a stronger nationalist stance and
to follow a policy of partial disengagement from US Cold War politics. There
was great demand for a 'national approach' to the constraints of the Cold War
world economy on specific governmental policies. For example, Turkey pursued
a foreign policy agenda that included closer ties with the European Economic
Community. It was believed that such a policy could facilitate the strengthening
of a national bourgeoisie. The 1950s and 1960s were a muted period in Islamist

politics. But, as will be seen in the next chapter, the pro-Islamic party grew out of a political disillusionment with the economic development projects of the period.

A market economy and the development ideal

The primary political objective of the United States in the immediate aftermath of the Second World War was to organize an open, multilateral trading system under its control. However, there is clearly some diversity in national economies, social structures, and political systems. There is a multiplicity of ways to organize a particular form of national economy, depending on the social-political context of the national space. This presented the United States with a considerable challenge in its efforts to organize a specific international order. The US policy goal at the end of the war was to link each state within a new international framework. This required a plan whereby various aspects of labour, production, and finance would be coordinated to evolve along complementary lines. To that end, a vital institution was created in 1944 based on the convertibility of the US dollar to gold at a fixed price—the Bretton Woods monetary system. National currencies could then be converted into US dollars at a set exchange rate (Block 1977).

It is well known that at the end of the war European countries (and most of the world, for that matter) had neither gold nor dollar reserves. The European dollar shortage could have been remedied by maintaining old bilateral trading arrangements and other forms of national-protectionist planning (Milward 1984). However, US policy-makers believed that once an open, multilateral system was restored, Europe would be able to export its way out of the dollar shortage (Eichengreen 1996: 99). The International Monetary Fund (IMF), the International Trade Organization (ITO), and the General Agreement on Trade and Tariffs (GATT) were negotiated, and, with the exception of the ITO, created in order to establish non-discriminatory trade practices through a general reduction in tariffs. They also aimed to restore exchange stability around the Bretton Woods monetary system. Multilateralism required that the United States and Europe open their protected domestic markets.

Despite these developments, the process of restoring a liberal principle in the world economy was not an easy one. It was subject to conflict and contradiction. European states and the US administration were unwilling to reduce their own tariff barriers. For their part, US policy-makers were more interested in opening up new markets, both to export US surplus products and to increase private investment by US corporations abroad. They also wanted to protect their own domestic market from imports. This was very evident in food production (Friedmann 1993).

Not only the recovery of western European economies was of concern to the US government, but the form this recovery would take—whether it would be co-operative or competitive with the US economy (Kolko and Kolko 1972: 337–8). In his speech at Baylor University on 6 March 1947, Truman made it clear that US firms must not be forced into competing with state-owned or state-planned economies. There was no place in the world for a diversity of economic systems; it was either communism or free-enterprise capitalism (Fleming 1961: 436–7). The granting of military and economic aid through the Marshall Plan was a first step in the project of linking economic recovery programmes to a policy of anti-communism (Truman 1955). Within this framework, US efforts to liberalize trade were coordinated with the national policies of other states (van der Pijl 1984).

The Marshall Plan envisaged two different strategies for the economic restructuring of western Europe and states of the emergent 'Third World' (Wood 1986). For western Europe, the strategy was to restore industrial productive capacity through a Fordist economic model based on mass production and mass consumption. This was to be mediated by full employment and a high-wage policy (Aglietta 1979; Lipietz 1987). For states of the emergent 'Third World', the Marshall Plan adopted a strategy that grounded the reorganization of their economies in the ideology of 'development'.

The term 'Third World' was not used officially in the Marshall Plan, nor was the concept of 'underdeveloped' or 'undeveloped' (Sachs 1992). Nevertheless, the concept of 'Third World' was used to describe those states that were either European colonies, mandates in Asia and Africa, or newly founded independent nation-states. These states were all situated within the European sphere of trading arrangements to some degree. The creation of a political category known as Third World (Escobar 1995) coincided with the invention of 'underdevelopment', as poverty was 'discovered' and came to be seen as a defining feature of colonial, post-colonial, and newly founded states of the Third World. According to Esteva (1992: 6–7), the era of development began on 20 January 1949 when Truman became president of the United States. In his inauguration speech Truman declared: 'We must embark on a bold program for making the benefits of our scientific advances and industrial progress available for the improvement and growth of underdeveloped areas' (Cowen and Shenton 1996: 7).

The post-1945 understanding of underdevelopment implied a failure of the capitalist industrial economy to reproduce itself in the Third World. As Shanin (1997: 65) has explained, the appeal of development is rooted in the expectation of an irreversible advance from an endless diversity of nations towards a world unified around a single-market economy credo. The ideological impetus behind this movement is a belief in the cultural capacity to apply the ideas of progress, science, and technology (Esteva and Prakash 1998). In explaining the construction of the nineteenth-century market economy, Polanyi (1944) highlights the importance of deliberate political intervention. Markets exist by virtue of state-made rules and state-enforced agreements that create the impression that they are self-regulating (Atasoy 2003c).

The European, linear perception of time imposed a fixed pattern on history, expressing a belief in progress toward a greater good (Shanin 1997). The idea of progressive historical change fostered an image of development as a necessary process in which traditional societies move on to more advanced stages of growth. This idea was most evident in the writings of US development studies scholars (Leys 1996). Parallel with the worldwide expansion of the market economy, development scholarship presented the values of democracy and freedom as key to bridging the gap between the 'developed' West and the 'underdeveloped' non-West. During the Cold War these values were identified as both virtuous and consistent with the aims of US foreign policy—a policy which at the time was largely directed at combating communism (Gendzier 1985).

What is significant about Truman's speech of 1949, according to Cowen and Shenton (1996: 7), is that he tied the idea of development to state sovereignty. Decolonization was necessary for the completion of the nation-state system and the constitution of an open world economy because it provided greater assurance that old economic ties between western European states and the colonies would be broken. Yet, in their support for national independence movements, US policy-makers had to contain emergent nationalist regimes so that US dominance would not be threatened. Much of this was dependent on whether a free-enterprise capitalist system or a communist economic model prevailed in national economic policy decisions.

Turkey had already established itself as an independent state. The government's main concern was building a national economy and an industrial bourgeoisie. Given the lack of private and public investment capital on a large scale, the inflow of foreign capital was considered vital for industrial development. Then President Inonu was willing to liberalize the economy and commit Turkey to the Western security structure as a 'democratic' country if foreign capital could be attracted. These were the economic and political circumstances that determined Turkey's place in an integrated post-1945 world economy.

Having become part of the 'free world' after the transition to a multi-party political system, Turkey became eligible for US aid. The first agreement on aid was signed by the RPP government on 12 July 1947 and was military related. In the agreement, based on the Truman doctrine of containment, Turkey promised that US aid would be used to contain the 'communist threat' in Turkey. In return, the United States guaranteed that it would provide military protection to Turkish territories, including the straits, from the Soviet threat. The most controversial aspect of the agreement was Article 4, which gave the

US administration complete control over the Turkish government's use of aid for the national armed forces (Sander 1979: 27).

Turkey hoped that US aid would reduce its military expenses, thereby allowing Turkey to use its wartime savings for national industrialization (Aydemir 1979: 397–419). However, the US government was not willing to extend Marshall economic aid if Turkey planned to use it for state-planned industrial development projects rather than contribute to the European recovery plan. To be considered for aid, Turkey was advised to change its economic policy towards producing foodstuffs for European markets (*Ulus Newspaper*, 16 January 1948). A report written at the Paris Conference, convened on 27 June 1947, tied conditions for the distribution of US aid to the elimination of nationalist planning programmes. It became obvious at the Paris Conference that the distribution of Marshall aid would divide Europe into military blocs. The Soviet Union, a participant in the conference, withdrew from the proceedings on 2 July 1947, forcing all east European states to withdraw as well. The Soviets claimed that economic integration under the Marshall Plan would strengthen the position of pro-Western capital groups in eastern Europe (Smith 1963: 31). After withdrawing from the Paris Conference, the Soviet Union called on all communist parties to oppose the Marshall Plan and establish a formal organization known as the Cominform (Communist Information Bureau). A special conference of eastern European communist parties held on 22–23 September 1947 became the foundation for communist unity under Soviet leadership. The United States responded by founding NATO in 1948. Cominform and NATO came to personify the antagonistic relationship between capitalist and socialist systems.

The Turkish government considered its inclusion in the Marshall Plan aid programme an important step in confirming Turkey's status as a 'democratic' country. On 18 March 1947, the *Ulus Newspaper* stated that 'for Turkey, Europe is not only a geographical area of interest, but a symbol of liberal democracy in the new world order'. On 19 April 1948, the same newspaper claimed that 'to not be included in the Marshall Plan will leave Turkey alone and isolated in European politics'. Security concerns and geopolitical positioning within a Euro-American alliance became paramount for Turkey; national control over the industrialization process became secondary.

During the 1930s Turkey achieved significant industrialization under the ideological guidance of statist-nationalist planning. Nevertheless, by virtue of its incorporation into the US aid programme in 1948, it was required to adopt an agriculture-based development strategy (US ECA 1949: 2–3). With the silencing of the hardline faction within the RPP, which insisted on state-led heavy industrialization programmes, the RPP and the DP turned their attention to agricultural development. Both parties wanted agriculture to be structured along the lines suggested by development economists who saw

Turkey's comparative advantage in the growth of agricultural production. A World Bank report written in 1949 argued that the industrialization effort did not improve the general well-being of Turkish citizens. Alternatively, the report argued, Turkey should increase its productive agricultural capacity and invest in road construction, infrastructure, and agriculture-based industrial projects (Thornburg et al 1949: 91, 141–2). The report reinforced the economic policy position of the DP, and was entirely consistent with the development plan of 1947 formulated by the RPP government, as well as the recommendations of the Istanbul Economic Congress of 1948.

Peasants and rural migrants: the new players in coalition politics

The DP government's primary task in the 1950s was to build and manage a national economy. Starting with a policy shift away from state-led heavy industrialization to export-oriented agricultural production, the DP government proceeded to implement economic liberalization policies. Any serious industrialization programme would have to start with capital accumulation through market-oriented agricultural production. The political implication of this was that the 'development' project was linked to the mobilization of rural producers.

A very complex set of geopolitical and world economic dynamics mediated state management of the national economy and the rural communities of agricultural producers. US military and economic aid played an intervening role in the creation of a new interest structure by directly determining Turkey's economic policy, thereby reframing political alliances in the state structure. The RPP's earlier adherence to the development ideal of US experts in relation to Turkey's agricultural policy, in exchange for aid, determined the domestic political framework within which the DP was able to mobilize rural voters against the RPP government and subsequently win the 1950 elections. The new partners in DP coalition politics were the large- and small-producing farmers from rural areas.

Under the DP government, market-oriented agricultural production resulted in differentiation within the countryside based on the amount of land cultivated, tractor ownership, and access to credits and loans. Large landowners expanded their production and export earnings, yet this differentiation did not produce class polarization, nor did it increase the power position of large landowners against small-producing farmers. The DP was supportive of both large- and small-producing farmers.

The DP established massive state subsidies and cheap credits to farmers as well as a high-price policy for agricultural products. The party also expanded land under cultivation, and increased mechanization in agriculture. The DP considered investment in agriculture to be a matter of correcting the social 'injustice' previously perpetrated by the RPP against rural populations (Pamuk 1988). Undoing this social injustice, Prime Minister Menderes (1967: 116) argued, did not only involve government support for agricultural growth; it also required the incorporation of rural producers into the 'development' process and the recomposition of social life in village communities. Menderes outlined his vision in a speech delivered in 1950:

> Whatever needs to be done by a civilized nation, we will do it. No roads? We will build them! The land is not fertile? We will make it fertile! We will distribute land to the landless villagers. No houses? No cement, factories or food? Inadequate clothing? No electricity? No schools? We will build them! We will make them available to our villagers! (Aydemir 1969: 228–9).

Supported by Marshall aid funds that lasted until 1952, the DP government imported a large number of tractors from the United States. The government's cheap-credit policy allowed these to be purchased on credit. By 1957, 44,144 tractors had been imported, up from only 1,750 in 1948 (Hale 1981: 95). The introduction of tractors to Turkey resulted in the release of sharecroppers from large farms - more than 79,000 by 1960 (Singer 1977: 206). In contrast to the massive displacement of peasants which occurred throughout the Third World (McMichael 2000: 43–76), the introduction of tractors in Turkey did not result in the development of large-scale capitalist farms nor in the deterioration of the peasant economy. Under the DP government, independent small-producing family farmers consolidated their position in Turkish agriculture.

Even though the DP was opposed to land reform, it was responsive to the demands of peasants who held little or no land (Pamuk 1988). Its resettlement programme included carving out additional lands for agriculture from state-owned communal properties. The government redistributed state lands to the landless and least-propertied small producers. In this manner the amount of land under cultivation increased approximately 67 per cent (Margulies and Yildizoglu 1987: 281). Farm land was also increased through deforestation by burning. This common strategy for increasing arable land accounted for 22 per cent of total cultivated land in 1948 (Tekeli 1977: 30). Between 1950 and 1960 the proportion of landless families decreased from 16 to 10 per cent. And between 1950 and 1963 the number of small-producing family farms increased 30 per cent from 2.3 million to 3.1 million (Keyder 1987: 131).

In the distribution of government credits, small loans made up 88 per cent of all loans and represented 42 per cent of total credit distributed by the Agricultural Bank. Large loans constituted 15 per cent of total credits and were given to only 0.48 per cent of farmers (Koksal 1971: 499–528). What is most important about the distribution of these credits is that through them agricultural machinery was made available to a wider group of producers, not just large landowners. This was the case despite the fact that land cultivated by the use of animals on small family farms increased 40 per cent during the 1950s (Tekeli 1977: 15). All of these changes were complemented by a 16 per cent increase in the government purchase price of wheat (Avcioglu 1979: 620).

In addition to increasing land under cultivation and extending the mechanization of agriculture, the DP endeavoured to increase yields as well. High-yield seed varieties and chemical fertilizers were imported under the Marshall aid plan, factors that enabled Turkey to significantly increase its food and cash crop production. Between 1950 and 1953 the country experienced a phenomenal economic growth rate of 13 per cent a year.

Turkey's export earnings reached a peak in 1953, when agricultural exports rose approximately 50 per cent (Keyder 1987: 294). By the early 1950s, Turkey was a grain exporter with three-quarters of the increase in production occurring in central Anatolia (Mann 1980: 198).

The DP's rural and agricultural development strategy worked well until 1954. Falling wheat prices in world markets and a sudden 20 per cent drop in overall agricultural production in 1954 undermined this strategy (Krueger 1974: 8). Although poor climatic conditions were the immediate cause for the drop in Turkish production, the fall in world-wheat prices was the primary reason Turkey became a wheat importer again after 1954. The price decline was due to subsidized US exports in the form of food aid to the 'Third World' under Public Law 480 (Friedmann 1982). Combined with the decreased level of foreign capital inflow after the end of the Marshall Plan in 1952, falling grain prices signalled the end of the DP's development ideal based on capital generation from agricultural export production.

Dependence on wheat imports was not unique to Turkey but experienced by all states throughout the Third World (Friedmann 1992). This dependency was accompanied by a change in the organization of the world economy with a shift in economic policy from agricultural growth to import-substitution industrialization (ISI). The reorganization of the world economy that accompanied the crisis in agriculture prompted the rise of new social classes through a massive relocation of labour from rural to urban areas. Turkey's agricultural crisis was also linked to an industrialization process that was mediated by the movement of large numbers of rural labourers to urban areas. For example, the percentage of people living in villages declined from 81.5 per cent in 1950 to 74.8 per cent in 1960 (Yasa 1966: 25). Between 1950 and 1960 the population of the four largest cities in Turkey increased by 75 per cent, as one out of every ten villagers migrated to urban areas.

Not surprisingly, this process created cultural 'fragmentation' in urban areas. During the early 1950s the emphasis given to agricultural growth by

DP policies facilitated the emergence of rural producers as coalition partners in politics. These producers were very aware of their cultural difference from urban dwellers. Interestingly, this cultural 'divide' was reinforced by the government's road-building efforts in the 1950s. Between 1950 and 1954 there was a 255 per cent increase in capital investment in Turkey and road construction was a key element of this (Zurcher 1993: 235). The DP government increased hard-surfaced roads from 1,600 km to 7,500 km, and expanded the loose-surfaced road network from 3,500 km to 61,000 km, all within a ten-year period (Hale 1981: 90). Road construction was followed by a mushrooming of bus and transportation companies. The DP's road development projects opened up the villages of Anatolia for the first time in Turkish history, bringing rural and urban populations closer together. Paradoxically, the expansion of the road network gave rise to tensions related to class and culture. With the large-scale migration from rural to urban areas, rural migrants and urban dwellers came to discover significant differences in their lifestyles.

By the second half of the 1950s it was clear that Turkish cities were not equipped to receive large numbers of villagers in permanent residential settlements. Migrants began to build their own houses on unused public or private lands on the outskirts of the city. These emerging settlements were essentially shantytowns, or as they are commonly referred to in Turkish, *gecekondus,* which literally means 'built at night'. In these sprawling *gecekondu* neighbourhoods, migrants imitated village life by growing fruits and vegetables, and raising chickens, sheep, and cows in their backyards. They kept close ties with their villages, receiving most of their staple food (wheat flour, beans, chickpeas, lentils, and rice) from family members who remained behind. Although the *gecekondus* lacked an infrastructure—they had no water, electricity, roads, or sewers—their inhabitants were resourceful. And despite being marginalized and impoverished, *gecekondu* dwellers did not present an image of powerlessness. They maintained and upgraded their neighbourhoods by investing their earnings and agricultural savings in the improvement of their houses.

Gecekondu inhabitants soon realized that the development ideal had overlooked their interests in relation to municipal services, health, education, wages, and employment possibilities. In time, *gecekondu* dwellers emerged as a distinct faction in the coalition politics of the development project. They demanded that the government deliver municipal services, civic amenities, and land entitlements. As the *gecekondu* population of large cities swelled, it became a political force that no politician could afford to ignore.

The *gecekondus* of Turkey reflect the tense encounter between middle-class urbanites and lower-class rural migrants. However, this encounter has been largely misconstrued. For example, Ozyegin (2001) presents it in terms of a conceptual dichotomy between the 'modernity' of urban professionals or bureaucratic groups and the 'tradition' of rural migrants. Karpat (1976) defines *gecekondu* dwellers as 'un-urbanized peasants'. These views ignore the fact that the inhabitants of *gecekondus* are neither silent nor passive and uninvolved in urban affairs. Rather, they are actively engaged in efforts to render their city life more meaningful. The story of *gecekondu* residents transcends urban and rural as cultural opposites and refocuses our attention on the conjunction between class and culture.

I was born and raised in a *gecekondu* neighbourhood in Ankara, Turkey, and I have had the opportunity to observe these migrants first-hand. My parents are among them. My observations strongly suggest that *gecekondu* inhabitants have been in a constant, committed struggle to reposition themselves in the city and establish a sense of belonging.

I cannot envision a more dramatic example of this process of building a new life in the city than that of my mother. In 1986 I was a research assistant at the Middle East Technical University (METU) in Ankara, working for Professor Sencer Ayata. He was conducting a study on *gecekondus* in the Ata district of Dikmen, Ankara. My family and I lived in this neighbourhood of 150,000 people, and I interviewed 250 men and women there for the study. As my parents and grandparents were among the first people in the neighbourhood, almost everyone I interviewed knew of my family. One of the questions I asked my respondents was how the Ata *gecekondu* district of Dikmen received its municipal services. Many of them told me that I needed to ask my mother this question because she was the person primarily responsible for organizing residents to put pressure on the city to provide services—in this case, running water. This was the first time I had heard of my mother's involvement in neighbourhood politics. She confirmed the story, but indicated modestly that she did not do much. 'Some men were already employed by the city doing this kind of work', she said. 'I just asked them to get a move on and help their neighbours'. 'We need to have access to running water', my mother told them. 'Everybody else in the city has it. What is wrong with us? Aren't we also citizens? Isn't it our right to have what others have?' My mother convinced the men to dig the trenches necessary for laying the water pipes. Once the digging was finished, she organized the neighbourhood women to petition the mayor to send the pipes, and then, after some effort, to get the water turned on.

This can hardly be characterized as a conflict between urban modernity and traditional ways of life. It represents a sustained effort on the part of active, informed men and women seeking full citizenship rights.

A private industrial bourgeoisie

Although priority was given to agricultural growth projects, the DP government proceeded with the idea of creating a private industrial bourgeoisie. By imposing import restrictions on consumer goods, the government acted to support the establishment of private industrial firms that produced consumer goods domestically. A 1960 survey on the history of 126 private industrial companies in Turkey reveals that approximately 60 per cent of them were founded between 1946 and 1960 (Bugra 1999: 69). Another survey of the 405 largest private industrial firms presently operating in Turkey shows that 49 of these firms were established between 1950 and 1959. Only nine were founded between 1940 and 1949 and only four between 1930 and 1939 (TUSIAD 1989).

The founders of many of these private firms had their roots in the state bureaucracy. Merchants were the second largest group involved in the expansion of private industry. Those who previously held positions in the state bureaucracy made up 24.41 per cent of private industrialists; merchants constituted 20.83 per cent. Only 3.14 per cent of these industrialists were large landowners (Bugra 1999: 72), most of them involved in the textile industry due to their success in cotton production (Serin 1963: 228–30). To a large extent, private industrialists were of Turkish-Muslim origin (83 per cent), while Jews made up 9 per cent and Greeks 7 per cent (Payaslioglu 1961: 19–22).

Most of the newly founded consumer goods–producing industries were funded by the Industrial Development Bank of Turkey, established under the auspices of the IBDR and the World Bank (IDBT) (Rozaliyev 1978: 294–307). The Industrial Development Bank was created as a joint venture between Turkish and foreign financial firms to supervise and fund private industrial investment projects. By 1956 it allocated US$ 145 million of credit to 131 new industrial investment firms. About a third of this credit came from IMF loans (Sanayi Odasi Bulteni, 15 April 1956). Most of the bank credits were allocated to the largest consumer goods- producing private industries. The textile industry received 22.6 per cent of bank funds, the cement and glass industry 20.6 per cent, the chemical industry 17.2 per cent, and food industries 13.1 per cent (Uyguner 1959).

Turkey's export performance had declined after the 1954 crisis, so the government had limited resources for industry. Direct foreign investment was also very limited. No more than 30 foreign firms invested in Turkey and they never exceeded 1 per cent of total private investment (Zurcher 1993: 235). As a result, the government decided to rely heavily on foreign loans and grants, the most important source of capital being the United States (Bulutoglu 1974: 118–9; Harris 1972: 182). After the end of the Marshall Plan, the main source of US aid to Turkey was food aid under PL 480. Between 1954 and 1962, US$ 351.2 million was obtained through the PL 480 (Kepenek 1983: 103). The Turkish lira equivalent of the US subsidized wheat shipped to Turkey was deposited in the Central Bank and the government used this money to support industrial investment.

Although the DP focussed on private industrial investment, it also supported state-owned industries (SEEs) through foreign funds. SEEs were intended to produce capital and intermediary goods so that private industry could produce finished consumer goods. The government adopted this strategy to make up for the lack of private sector investments. Between 1950 and 1960, the share of the state sector in total industrial investment increased from 57 per cent to 60 per cent. It reached 78 per cent in 1962 (Kepenek 1983: 115–6). State-led enterprises established by the DP as the backbone of its industrialization strategy included iron and steel production, the machine and chemistry industry, the fertilizer industry, the cement and nitrogen industries, and the pulp and paper industry.

With government support, industry's share in the gross national product after 1955 increased from an average of 10 per cent to 14 per cent, with agriculture's share dropping from 49 to 43 per cent (Keyder 1987: 134). During the 1950s, overall industrial production increased 77 per cent, at an annual rate of 7.7 per cent (Ozgur 1976: 192). This strengthened the political position of private industrialists vis-à-vis the bureaucratic cadres. However, it did not signify a fundamental change in the coalition politics of the development project. Most of these private industrialists were former bureaucrats who held high positions in the state bureaucracy and had no intention of weakening their ties to the state (Yalman 2002: 34). The government also continued with the Kemalist economic position established during the 1930s by strengthening the linkage between statist policies and a liberal orientation.

The DP's support for industrial projects was fraught with difficulty. In addition to limited direct foreign investment and a lack of domestic investment capital, foreign aid was not enough to meet the DP's capital demands for industrialization. Imports and exports had both declined since 1954. In order to increase its import capacity the DP government followed an inflationary finance policy. The DP could have solved at least some of its financial problems by taxing rich landowners, who earned more than one-fifth of the GDP yet paid only 2 per cent of total tax revenue. However, this was not a policy option for the DP. Instead, it borrowed money from the Central Bank of Turkey, which meant printing more money. As a result, inflation rose from 3 per cent in 1950 to 20 per cent in 1958 (Zurcher 1993: 239). Economic growth fell from 13 per cent to around 4 per cent, and Turkey experienced a huge balance of payment deficits (World Bank 1975: 345).

The DP also borrowed money from foreign governments. The consequence of this was a 410 per cent increase in foreign debt between 1950 and 1960. In 1960, Turkey's total debt, including interest, was 33 per cent of exports (Kepenek 1983: 103). The DP's strategy was to exchange military concessions within the international framework of the Cold War for much-needed US capital. The DP promoted Turkey's new strategic position in NATO to increase the government's bargaining power for more aid. In the process, the DP made it clear that they would serve US interests in the region. In addition to sending troops to Korea and becoming a member of NATO in 1952, the government used the Suez crisis of 1956 to highlight Turkey's military importance to US interests in the Middle East.

The 1956 Suez crisis

With the outbreak of the Korean War in 1950, the US government began to view Western security interests on a global level. The US administration had initially thought of Turkey's post-war international position within a Middle Eastern context. Turkey's application for NATO membership was therefore rejected in 1950. However, the outbreak of the Korean War, which increased the US defence budget to US\$ 50 billion in 1950/1 (Hale 2000: 117), prompted the US administration to recognize that Turkey's strategic location was vital to Western security interests. The DP government confirmed Turkey's loyalty to the West by sending 25,000 troops to Korea. In return, Turkey secured US support for NATO membership in 1952.

The DP government saw Turkey's NATO membership not only as insurance against Soviet aggression but also 'as guaranteeing the flow of Western aid and loans' (Celik 1999: 37). According to Prime Minister Menderes, Turkey, for strategic and military reasons, was of primary importance to NATO and the defence of the Middle East—so much so that the US administration was bound to provide Turkey with economic assistance (Okyar 1962: 16). This strategy of exchanging military concessions for 'aid' became well established during the Suez crisis of 1956.

Although it is difficult to completely differentiate military aid from economic aid, Hale (2000: 123) estimates that between 1948 and 1964 Turkey received close to US\$ 2,271 million in military aid, plus US\$ 328 million in surplus equipment. Combined with approximately US\$ 2,080 million in economic aid, the Turkish government was able to sustain its industrial growth projects, even though its export earnings declined after the 1954 economic crisis.

It is not accurate, however, to link Turkey's integration with the United States-led Western defence structure solely to the government's desire for financial aid. The government also wanted to establish an image of Turkey as a European state. Although Britain and France were reluctant to view Turkey as European, the United States was willing to do so as long as Turkey served US interests in the region.

The British considered the Suez Canal, and hence Egypt, as vital to the integrity of the British Empire (Bromley 1994: 46–86, 106–7). With the accelerating Cold War, Britain wanted to form a counterweight to the Soviet

Union in the Middle East that was independent of US power (Gorst and Johnman 1997: 9–27). Britain assumed that Arab governments would regard their major interests as identical to those of Britain (Hourani 1991: 357). This assumption proved to be unfounded, because US and Soviet opposition to colonialism had already given nationalist movements an impetus towards independence. The Egyptian Revolution in 1952 and Mossadeq's rise to power in Iran in the early 1950s made it clear that growing nationalism in the Middle East would not make it easy for these states to back Britain. Rather, the nationalists wanted to throw off Western control and consolidate their rule internally. Britain therefore saw growing nationalism in the Middle East as the central problem, especially Egyptian antagonism to British domination in the Arab Middle East.

Britain wanted to organize a Middle East Defence Organization (MEDO) to contain nationalist movements. The US government was more interested in organizing a northern chain of defence in the immediate southern frontier of the Soviet Union. Despite its decolonization rhetoric, the United States also opposed indigenous nationalist forces contesting British and French colonial control. In response to Nasser securing power in Egypt and growing nationalism in Iran, the US government supported a monarchy in Saudi Arabia, the Shah's regime in Iran, and Hashemite rule in Iraq. However, the United States did not need to become involved in the British-led MEDO. They shifted their emphasis to the 'northern tier' concept, assembling Turkey, Iran, Iraq, and Pakistan into a defence pact. Turkey played a significant role in the formation of this pact, but the United States was not a member. After the British entered, this alliance came to be known as the Baghdad Pact (1955). Turkey's role was to extend US military influence in the Middle East, but the Arab world, especially Egypt, resisted the pact because it was seen as the continuation of Western imperialism in the region.

The tripartite aggression of Britain, France, and Israel against Egypt in 1956 confirmed that the Baghdad Pact was an instrument of Western imperialism. As a result, Egypt and Syria were pushed into a closer alliance with the Soviet bloc. The Soviet Union did not care much about indigenous nationalist movements and was more supportive of pro-communist movements that presented alternative models to Arab nationalism (Bromley 1994).

In 1957 the Eisenhower Doctrine was developed to contain the 'communist campaign of indirect aggression' against conservative regimes in the Middle East. It was based on a US commitment to provide economic aid and military protection to any state in the region that might be under direct or 'indirect communist aggression' (Gonlubol et al 1987: 287–90). The notion of 'indirect communist aggression', although imprecise, was used to include any nationalist and leftist movements. In practical terms, the 'indirect communist aggression' clause allowed the US military to intervene in the internal politics of any state for the purpose of suppressing opposition movements—as in the case of Lebanon and Jordan in 1958.

The Soviet delivery of arms to Egypt and Syria after the Suez crisis and the Syrian destruction of the IPC oil pipeline intensified Turkey's fear of communist penetration in the Middle East (Fleming 1961: 815–28). Consequently, Turkey placed 50,000 troops on the Syrian borders (Petran 1978: 123). The US government backed Turkey's military move. Secretary of State Dulles declared that a Soviet attack on Turkey would trigger US retaliation (Fleming 1961: 890). In response, Khrushchev threatened Turkey by saying that the Soviet Union was prepared to use military force if necessary: 'When the guns begin to fire, the rockets will begin flying and then it will be too late to think about it' (*The New York Times*, 10 October 1957). Although Khrushchev did not persist in his threats, the Turkish-American Mutual Security Act, signed in 1959, contained a clause of assurance that the United States would come to Turkey's defence even in the case of 'indirect communist aggression'.

This caused heated debate in the Turkish Parliament, centred on the suppression of leftist political movements and the possibility of US military intervention in Turkey. The manner in which the Turkish state was engaged in the US-led Western security alliance underscored the fact that both factors represented a threat to national independence (*Ulus Newspaper*, 18, 23, 27, 30 July 1958 and 1, 3 August 1958). The US military had intervened in Lebanon and Jordan using the Incirlik air base in Turkey without the consent of the Turkish government (Harris 1972: 67). The so-called U-2 crisis and the placement of nuclear weapons in Turkey in the form of 15 Jupiter missiles also reinforced the belief that state power had diminished. On 1 May 1960, an American U-2 intelligence plane flying from Incirlik carried out a reconnaissance mission all the way from Pakistan, across the Soviet Union, to Norway. It took photographs of industrial centres, airfields, missile bases and other military installations in the Soviet Union. On 9 May Khrushchev warned Turkey and other neighbours of the Soviet Union that 'if they allow others to fly from their bases to our territory we shall hit those bases' (Fleming 1961: 1003). The opposition party (RPP) accused the DP of making Turkey an immediate target of Soviet missile attacks (*Cumhuriyet Newspaper*, 18 May 1960).

The Turkish development ideal: a historical account

Prime Minister Menderes's primary concern was to encourage industrial development. He was less concerned with the implications of exchanging military concessions for foreign aid. The military-strategic conditions under which Turkey experienced its industrialization resulted in the subversion of the national independence principle implicit in the post-war 'development' project spelled out by President Truman himself in his inauguration speech of 20 January 1949.

The IMF-imposed economic stabilization programme of 1958 was another indication of the subversion of national independence. The IMF made the continuation of foreign aid conditional on the government's acceptance of a stabilization programme that devalued the Turkish lira, reduced budget deficits, restricted monetary growth, increased the price of SEE products, decreased government spending, curtailed the role of the state in economy, and liberalized imports. The inflow of foreign aid was also conditional upon the government's support of industrialization based on private investment (Szyliowicz 1991: 76). Moreover, IMF experts urged the Turkish government to adopt more planning in order to bring some degree of control over public spending and the allocation of foreign exchange. Although a planning board was formed in 1959, the transition to a planned industrialization strategy did not begin until the military coup in 1960 ended DP governance.

The DP was popular among rural producers and urban industrial and working classes. Menderes was a well-respected charismatic leader, but he could not gain full control over the military bureaucracy. His inability to secure the loyalty of high-level military bureaucrats contributed to his overthrow in the coup of 27 May 1960. After the coup, the DP was shut down and Menderes was executed, along with his ministers of finance, internal affairs, and external affairs. With the overthrow of the government, military bureaucrats hoped to regain control over the course of the development process. The type of populist alliance that the DP cultivated among rural producers and private industrialists had clearly broken the bureaucratic tradition of governance in Turkey.

In the process of realizing development goals, national policy-making was increasingly locked into the complex bargaining process of Cold War diplomacy. Bureaucratic cadres questioned the soundness of the government submitting to an international institutional and ideological framework that was expressed in the very policies and procedures of national policy-making. In the view of military bureaucrats, successful industrialization necessitated a return to strong bureaucratic supervision of the economy. Military coup bureaucrats instituted a centrally planned industrialization policy to be supervised by the State Planning Organization (SPO). This opened up possibilities for the emergence of new political alliances, but the focus on state-planned industrialization carried with it a bias against agriculture. The result was a novel historical compromise based on a coalition between bureaucrats and large private industrial capital.

The stability of the political coalition between bureaucrats and large private industrial capitalists depended on the international conjuncture of growing rivalries in NATO between western Europe and the United States on the one hand, and Greece and Turkey on the other. Economic and political ties with the European Economic Community (EEC) allowed Turkey to follow a state-led industrialization policy. The political-strategic conflict between Turkey and the United States over the Cuban-Turkish missile crisis and Cyprus brought

Turkey closer to the EEC. On the economic front, the increasing competitiveness of European economies with the United States created positive conditions for industrialization efforts in Turkey. Migration from rural to urban areas, both nationally and internationally, also facilitated the process of industrialization. In addition, Turkey benefited from the export of labour abroad and the inflow of workers' remittances. Labour migration aided the Turkish economy by easing the internal political problems caused by urban unemployment.

Planned industrialization: Turkey, the United States, and the EEC

In the 1950s the Marshall Plan facilitated co-operation between the United States and western European states. The 1960s saw this relationship become one of competition and rivalry as these countries adjusted to their changed positions in the world. In order to integrate Europe into the Atlantic capitalist economy, US policy-makers encouraged western European unification around a trading bloc (Block 1977). In 1958 the European Economic Community (EEC) was formed to increase the volume of intra-European trade. In 1993 this organization became known as the European Union (EU). US policy-makers thought of the EEC as an instrument for the flow of goods and capital between Europe and the United States, and between them and the Third World.

How did Turkish governments reconcile domestic policy objectives with shifting patterns in the world economy? It became clear that Turkey contained a powerful political faction that favoured heavy industrialization. But, however strong their support for industrialization on domestic grounds, heavy industrialization compelled governments to play out transatlantic tensions between the United States and the EEC over economic and military relations.

The US administration placed a high priority on the economic integration of the Third World into the Atlantic economy through private industrial investment by transnational companies. At the same time, nationalism was spreading throughout the Third World. Notable examples include pan-Arabism in the Middle East, especially after the Suez crisis, and South Asian revolutionary movements, particularly in Vietnam, Indonesia, the Philippines, and Malaya (Goodwin 2001). US policy-makers were then faced with a 'Third World problem', resulting from the difficulty of balancing global economic integration with political nationalism. Turkey's situation involved a highly complicated interplay of economic, political, and military factors. By virtue of its geopolitical location, Turkey was able to cultivate close relations with the EEC, the Soviet Union, and Muslim countries of the Middle East. It also allied itself with the United States while promoting nationalism.

Turkey was an ideal ally during the 1950s, but in the face of rising US criticism against the government's public spending, and the IMF-imposed stabilization programme, Prime Minister Menderes decided to seek Soviet economic assistance (Kucuk 1984: 536). Nevertheless, the government's effort to establish closer relations with the Soviet Union was thwarted by the military coup of 27 May 1960. Turkish generals declared that they were not interested in improving relations with the Soviet Union. In fact, the leader of the coup, General Gursel, rejected Khrushchev's offer of US\$ 500 million in economic and technical aid (Gonlubol 1971: 336).

The military coup was actually instrumental in paving the way for the political coalition of bureaucratic cadres and an industrial bourgeoisie around a planned industrialization strategy. The State Planning Organization (SPO) was created three months after the coup in September 1960. Planned industrialization became a constitutional requirement in 1961. Given that the industrial bourgeoisie carried little weight in the Turkish economy and that organized labour was yet to be discovered, the goal of the SPO was to prepare them to become dominant players in society. The key principle of this political economy model was to manage industrialization through political compromise—an accommodation between private industrialists, agricultural groups, commercial capital, and bureaucratic cadres—such that private industrialists would eventually emerge as the leading group.

Coup leaders tried to transfer political power to development planners out of a conviction that bureaucratic control and supervision of the economy was necessary for industrialization. However, there was no consensus between bureaucrats and private industrialists on a concrete plan for industrialization. Moreover, industrialization plans did not conform to the interests of small producers. This new period witnessed constant political and ideological tension between political parties over the allocation of scarce resources and income distribution. I will return to this argument later.

The State Planning Organization prepared three consecutive development plans, each of them for a five-year period. All were part of two 15-year timetables. The first and second plans were part of the first strategy of import-substitution industrialization. The third plan was an application of the second strategy to be followed over the next 15 years. The first plan covered the period between 1963 and 1967, the second plan between 1968 and 1972, and the third plan between 1973 and 1977. There was also a fourth plan to be followed between 1979 and 1983. Due to the IMF-imposed structural adjustment programme of 1979, it was not applied. In fact, after the third plan, the very idea of planned development in Turkey lost its importance.

All economic development plans aimed to achieve a complete system of national industry through protection from international competition. National industry consisted of three main branches—consumer goods, intermediate goods, and investment goods production. The first and second plans required the government to assist the private sector in project preparation and the granting of sizable investment and export incentives. Industrial projects which private industry did not find attractive were to be undertaken in the public sector. For large projects, which could not be undertaken by the private sector alone, the mixed enterprise approach was preferred over wholly state-owned enterprise. The third plan gave priority to investment in intermediate- and capital-goods producing industries such as metallurgy, petrochemicals, iron, steel, and machinery. This plan emphasized more vigorous state participation in industry. Developers of the plans determined that the growth rate of the gross national product should be 7 per cent per year.

The growth rate in manufacturing was calculated at more than 10 per cent. Since non-durable producing textile and processed food industries had already been developed, and given that consumer markets had grown with the participation of small-producing peasants, the first and second plans targeted the production of consumer durables for domestic consumption. This included cars and household appliances. Most of the foreign exchange necessary for industrial investment would be obtained through the OECD and EEC in the form of loans.

The implementation of the SPO plans became a major source of contention between the United States and Turkey. The US government used a report prepared by the economist Kenneth Berril from Cambridge to argue that a 7 per cent growth rate in gross national product was too high and unrealistic for Turkey. More importantly, the US government wanted Turkish planners to give priority to private investment in consumer goods–producing industries. They also insisted on the elimination of state economic enterprises (Kepenek 1984: 330–1). It should be noted that Turkish-US relations could not be limited exclusively to economic policy, since political, diplomatic, and military issues were also implicated. In fact, the distinction between economic, political, and military concerns was an illusion. The Cuban missile crisis of 1962 and the Cyprus question of 1964 provided ample evidence to convince Turkish governments that the United States was not a reliable ally. Convinced that the United States was more interested in its own national interests than the national security of its NATO allies, Turkey began to cultivate closer relations with the EEC and to shift its foreign policy from a unidimensional NATO policy to a multidimensional one.

The 1962 Cuban-Turkish missile crisis

The Cuban missile crisis and subsequent Soviet-US strategic dialogue over the future of nuclear-headed missiles in Cuba and Turkey led to a rapprochement between the US and Soviet governments. Khrushchev sent a letter to Kennedy on 27 October 1962, stating that the Soviet Union would remove Soviet missiles from Cuba and respect the national sovereignty of Turkey if the United States would guarantee the same for Cuba and remove Jupiter missiles from Turkey (Council on Foreign Relations 1962: 396–7). In the event of a US invasion of Cuba, on the other hand, the Soviet Union would retaliate by invading Turkey and attacking their NATO military bases. In response, the US government decided to abandon its Jupiter nuclear missile project in Turkey in exchange for Soviet withdrawal of missiles from Cuba.

Despite the fact that Turkey refused (Vali 1971: 128–9), the US government proceeded to remove the missiles from Turkey. Turkey was not included in Soviet-US negotiations and interpreted this as a direct US violation of its sovereignty rights. It was suddenly confronted with the question of what NATO membership meant. The reality was that NATO evolved from a transatlantic mutual assistance treaty into an integrated military alliance run by the United States. The decisive weapons for NATO's defence were not subject to integration, but were under direct US control (Calleo 1970: 28). Turkey interpreted the US handling of the missile crisis as the assertion of US national self-interest over Turkey. Consequently, the restoration of national principles outside of US military control became an urgent concern (Sander 1979: 198-203).

US unilateralism in NATO reduced Turkey's strategic importance for US Cold War policy in the Middle East, while Saudi Arabia and Iran became more important. Turkey proceeded to increase its bargaining power with the United States by improving political and economic relations with the EEC, the Soviet Union, and Muslim states in the Middle East. The tension within NATO between Turkey and Greece over Cyprus became another issue that illustrated the importance for Turkey of maintaining the national sovereignty principle.

The Cyprus question

Until its independence was granted in 1960, Cyprus had been a formal British colony—a status accepted by both Turkey and Greece as part of the 1925 Lausanne Peace Treaty. During the 1950s, Greece shifted its policy and began to campaign for the end of British rule in Cyprus and the unification of Cyprus and Greece. The Greek ideal of uniting Cyprus with Greece is known as *enosis* (Couloumbis 1983).

Under the strong political influence of US and British diplomacy, the UN decided in 1957 that the Cyprus problem should be solved by negotiations between Britain, Turkey, and Greece (Adams and Conttrell 1964: 72–83). In 1959, through NATO mediation, the Zurich and London agreements were negotiated between Greece, Turkey, Britain, and the leaders of Greek and Turkish communities in Cyprus. Following these agreements an independent

Cyprus state was established in 1960 (Ehrlich 1974: 37–8). As a NATO policy compromise, Greece was to give up the idea of *enosis* and Britain was to renounce colonial control of Cyprus. Both Greece and Turkey accepted the principle of an independent Cyprus in which Greek and Turkish communities would share power (Hale 2000: 131).

The 1960 Treaty of Guarantee made Turkey, Greece, and Britain guarantor powers with the responsibility of prohibiting all activity that directly or indirectly promoted union with Greece or partitioning of the island. In the event of a breach of treaty, guarantor powers reserved the right to take action after consultation with each other. According to the Treaty of Alliance, Greek and Turkish governments were empowered to protect Cyprus militarily. This included the establishment of a permanent military headquarters stationed with 950 Greek and 650 Turkish troops. The Treaty of Establishment, on the other hand, stipulated that Britain would retain sovereignty over two military bases— an area totalling 99 square miles (Hart 1990: 143–58).

The Johnson letter and the Acheson plan

The Cyprus question re-emerged in 1963 when the Greek leader and President of Cyprus, Makarios, suspended the Zurich-London agreements and decided to revise the constitution. His intention was to pursue the independence of Cyprus under exclusive Greek rule. For this, he sought support from the Soviet Union and the non-aligned states of the Bandung Conference (Hitchens 1984: 57–60).

The US and Turkish governments were not supportive of an independent Cyprus. The US government was unhappy with Makarios's close relations with the Soviet Union and Egypt, as well as his collaboration with the communist AKEL party in Cyprus (US Congress 1980). According to US Undersecretary of State George W. Ball, Cyprus had important strategic implications for NATO defence. However, because of the ethnic ties of Cypriots to Greece and Turkey, and the complicated treaty structure of the Zurich-London agreements, the Cyprus conflict had the potential to undermine the stability of NATO's southern flank defences. The US government was worried that the Cyprus conflict could bring the Soviet Union into the strategic eastern Mediterranean (Adams and Conttrell 1968: 4).

Concerned with the fate of Turkish Cypriots, the Turkish government, led by the RPP, decided to intervene militarily in Cyprus to prevent the abolition of all partnership rights and protect the autonomy of the Turkish minority (Celik 1999: 48). Prime Minister Inonu informed the US government of his intention. The US response was spelled out in a letter written by President Johnson on 5 June 1964 (Hart 1990: 163–75). President Johnson told Inonu that Turkish intervention in Cyprus would lead to a war between Turkey and Greece. A war between NATO countries was 'literally unthinkable'. Johnson was blunt in his assertion that NATO and the United States would not be obliged to protect Turkey, since they 'have not had a chance to consider whether they have an obligation to protect Turkey against the Soviet Union if Turkey takes a step which results in Soviet intervention' (Hale 2000: 149). President Johnson also told Inonu that Turkey was not to use any US-supplied military equipment for purposes other than those involving NATO interests without US consent. Johnson's ultimatum-like letter caused bitter parliamentary debate and deep concern over the US and NATO commitment to Turkey's security. For Inonu, an alliance that ignored its contractual obligations and its commitment to members' security was unimaginable (Hart 1990: 163–72).

The Johnson letter was interpreted as an abandonment and betrayal of Turkey. As a result, anti-American sentiments grew and helped to foster nationalist fervour in Turkey. Inonu announced that 'our friends and our enemies have joined hands against us' (Vali 1971: 132). Ecevit, the RPP Secretary General, declared that NATO membership 'would be useless for Turkey if [our] allies changed their commitments to the defence of member states' (Ecevit 1965). The Turkish press started to call for a revision of Turkey's foreign policy. For example, Cetin Altan urged the government to follow a non-alignment policy (Milliyet Newspaper, 11 July 1964). Abdi Ipekci called for an improvement in relations with the Soviet Union (Milliyet Newspaper, 5 August 1964), and the Workers' Party of Turkey became highly vocal in expressing anti-American sentiments, calling for Turkey's withdrawal from NATO.

Rising anti-Americanism was further intensified by a proposal from former US Secretary of State Dean Acheson in 1964 to partition Cyprus (Hitchens 1984: 58–60). Turkey and Greece both rejected the plan. Johnson's response to Greece's rejection of the plan was to withdraw NATO aid from Greece. Prime Minister George Papandreou, in turn, decided to rethink Greek membership in NATO. Johnson replied with a blatant threat to Greek sovereignty:

> Fuck your parliament and your constitution. America is an elephant. Cyprus is a flea. Greece is a flea. If these two fellows continue itching the elephant, they may just get whacked by the elephant's trunk, whacked good ... If your Prime Minister gives me talk about democracy, parliament and the constitution, he, his parliament and his constitution may not last very long (Hitchens 1984: 61–2).

The Turkish response to US belligerence was also one of dismay and disillusionment, leading to a more independent foreign policy that would allow Turkey greater flexibility. The search for independence brought with it closer ties to the EEC.

Turkey and the EEC

There was general consensus among political parties that it was in Turkey's best interest to maintain a balance in relations between Europe and the United States in order to maximize flexibility within NATO. The DP government applied for EEC membership on 31 July 1959. Greece had applied two weeks earlier and Turkey did not want to be left behind (Birand 2000). Although disrupted by the military coup, membership negotiations resulted in the Ankara Treaty of Association being signed in 1963. Greece had signed its association agreement in 1961.

The period during which Turkey's membership in the EEC was negotiated coincides with the period when industrialization plans were conceived and subsequently applied. The Ankara Treaty and the subsequent Brussels Supplementary Protocol of 1970 shaped the first two industrialization plans of Turkey (Balkir 1993). Both the Ankara Treaty and the supplementary protocol stipulated a schedule for a 'preparatory period' (1964–73), to be followed by a 'transitional period' (1973–95). A gradual reduction of trade barriers and the elimination of tariffs would culminate in a customs union for Turkey by 1995, thus creating the possibility of Turkish accession to the EEC (Hale 2000: 175). Turkish industrialization plans were designed to prepare Turkey for free trade within the customs union.

Turkish planners accepted import substitution as the most suitable strategy for industrialization. It was assumed that capital goods imports would grow with industrial development. Exports of agricultural goods were expected to increase very slowly, and industrial exports, it was believed, would emerge only with great difficulty. Pessimism regarding exports was based on the limited world demand for Turkish agricultural goods. Therefore, economic plans of the period did not include programmes for agricultural growth (Kepenek 1984: 159). Planners hoped that the import substitution strategy would eventually limit the trade deficit resulting from high import and low export levels. Having thus acknowledged the continuation of large gaps in trade balance, Turkish planners relied on the flow of foreign capital to fill the trade gap. With the Ankara Agreement, the EEC committed itself to providing Turkey with financial aid from the European Investment Bank (EIB). Between 1964 and 1969 Turkey obtained 175 million ECU to finance project investment. In 1970 the EEC agreed to provide Turkey with another 220 million in credit, to be used between 1973 and 1976 (Karluk 1990: 248–51). The bulk of EEC aid was allocated to public sector investments in intermediary and capital goods production, as well as energy related investments. Turkish planners hoped that import-substitution industrialization would produce a balanced trade regime that would eventually result in a reduced need for foreign financing.

The EEC was founded to increase the volume of intra-European trade through tariff cuts. Therefore, Turkey's integration with the EEC required changes in the state planning of industrial growth and a move away from protective import-substitution industrialization. However, the statist faction within the RPP, along with SPO bureaucrats and newly emerging Islamist groups, were opposed to reductions in tariffs and other trade barriers. The period between 1964 and 1979 in Turkey was therefore marked by political tension between protectionism and trade liberalization. As successive JP governments of the period implemented policies for the gradual removal of trade barriers, opposition to the JP became more vociferous.

Although EEC countries reduced customs duties on a number of commodities imported from Turkey, agricultural concessions were limited. Tariffs did not disappear and the EEC Common Agricultural Policy (CAP) kept agricultural import prices very low. Turkey's chances of increasing exports to the EEC were very limited. Nonetheless, Turkey's imports from the EEC increased from 29 per cent in 1963 to 42 per cent in 1972 (Karluk 1990: 213–4, 234–8). Consequently, the foreign trade deficit increased from US$ 147.5 million in 1960 to US$ 3,338 million in 1975 (Hatipoglu 1978: 114). This was largely due to the fact that the CAP and the free movement of agricultural products among EEC member states involved the diversion of imports away from other countries to full members. In addition, other Mediterranean countries such as Spain, Portugal, and Greece, whose products were similar to those of Turkey, and an increasing number of countries from Europe's former Mediterranean colonies, were also used to import substitute Turkish exports (Kazgan 1976: 331–41). The consequence of this trade regime was that un-exportable agricultural commodities were dumped in domestic markets at low prices while foreign exchange earned from agricultural exports remained low.

Agriculture

Despite the limited opportunities for increasing agricultural exports, Turkish governments of the period continued to support agriculture, just as the DP had in the 1950s. These governments aimed to achieve self-sufficiency in food production and to increase the production of agricultural export items. By 1977 the value of support extended to farmers was equivalent to 22 per cent of that year's total agricultural output (Keyder 1987: 158). Governments also regularly increased their purchase prices. In the case of wheat, government purchase prices increased from 4.5 per cent in 1972 to 34.6 per cent in 1977. Cotton prices rose from 7.9 per cent in 1967 to 19.8 per cent in 1977. Government credits to agriculture also increased, from 10.74 per cent in 1963 to 62.16 per cent in 1975 (Kepenek 1984: 243, 254). In 1979, subsidies for fertilizers amounted to between

60 and 80 per cent of product cost (World Bank 1982: 302). As a result, the terms of internal trade continually improved in favour of agriculture.

In the 1950s production increases were due to the expansion of the area under cultivation. Growth in agricultural production in the 1960s and 1970s was a result of increases in yield. This was achieved through the introduction of improved methods of cultivation, expansion of the area under irrigation, increased use of chemical fertilizers, improved pest and disease control, and the development of an efficient marketing system. In 1973, 57.8 per cent of family farmers used insecticides, 30 per cent of the total irrigable land was irrigated, and 85 per cent of farmers used a combination of industrial inputs in their production (Kepenek 1984: 242–9). The number of tractors also increased more than tenfold, reaching a ratio of one tractor per 37 hectares. The capital-output ratio in agriculture rose from 1.9 per cent between 1966 and 1968 to 4 per cent between 1973 and 1978 (World Bank 1982: 29).

The rapid expansion of commercial activity in agriculture did not result in class polarization among rural producers. In fact, peasant ownership was consolidated. Governments refrained from imposing any direct taxes on agricultural property and income. They also continued to subsidize agricultural inputs and increase support prices for most crops. With government support, peasants constituted an important consuming segment for domestic industry. They consumed domestically produced textiles, clothing, processed food, fertilizers, TV sets, cars, and tractors. Although the level of migration from rural to urban areas was high, this was not because of the rural push factor resulting from landlessness and poverty. It was state policy in order to create cheap labour for industry.

Industry

The cornerstone of the development strategy was to transform the productive structure from consumer goods–producing industries to investment and intermediary goods–producing industries. Planners hoped that the structural changes in industry would reduce Turkey's dependence on foreign borrowing and facilitate the country's full integration with the EEC in relation to trade.

However, the Ankara Agreement of 1964 and the Brussels Supplementary Protocol of 1970 anticipated gradual reductions in protective measures for domestic industry. Tariff reductions were to take place according to a 12-year and 22-year timetable. For consumer goods, 69 per cent of the value of production was subject to 22 years of protection, while 31 per cent was protected for 12 years. For intermediate goods, the figures were 58 per cent and 42 per cent, and for capital goods 63 per cent and 37 per cent respectively (Okyar 1976: 38). In the course of meeting the requirements of the supplementary protocol,

Turkey reduced tariffs on imports. The average import tax rate was reduced to 55 per cent in 1970 and then to 40 per cent in 1973. The tariff rate was at its lowest in 1974, at approximately 30 per cent (Korum 1976: 192).

The five-year development plans and integration with the EEC constituted aspects of the official industrialization strategy of Turkey. The question of whether or not they were compatible underpinned the political tension between protectionism and trade liberalization as expressed by the RPP and pro-Islamists of the period. In 1976, the RPP government stopped tariff reductions and froze Turkish-EEC relations until after 1987. This decision was made out of a conviction that EEC integration was incompatible with Turkey's development plans.

The difficulty of financing imports for industrial growth was behind the government's decision to freeze relations with the EEC. Export purchasing power was lowest between 1970 and 1977 (World Bank 1980a: 46). The economic recession in Europe during the 1970s, which resulted from the oil price shock and collapse of the Bretton Woods monetary system, further weakened the export purchasing power of Turkey. As explained below, the recession in Europe ended the Turkish export of labour and reduced the inflow of workers' remittances. The resulting labour surplus in Turkey placed an enormous financial burden on the government, which was unable to create enough jobs to absorb urban unemployment. In the context of the unfolding financial crisis, the government recognized that trade liberalization was unsustainable. It therefore suspended Turkey's tariff reduction obligations.

The export of labour to EEC countries

In the course of rapid post-war economic growth Europe experienced significant labour shortages. Japan also faced a similar problem. While Japanese firms chose to invest in the Third World, European capitalists systematically recruited workers from the Third World. With the participation of migrant labour, European countries restructured their economies and achieved strong economic growth rates. They were also able to increase their export capacity and accumulate capital at a faster rate than the United States (Armstrong et al 1991). Europe imported labour temporarily with the understanding that migrants would return to their country of origin after this period had elapsed. In West Germany, the migrants were defined as guest workers. They were men under the age of 40 working on 12-month contracts and living in dormitories and hostels on a short-term, rotating basis (Kolinsky 1996: 80).

Europe met its labour needs by importing workers from North African, southern European, and other Mediterranean countries. France received migrant labour from its North African colonies of Algeria and Tunisia. Germany recruited workers from Turkey, Greece, Yugoslavia, Portugal, Spain, and Italy. The labour shortage was especially acute in West Germany when the Berlin Wall shut off the labour supply from East Germany. During the 1960s and early 1970s at least 15 million workers migrated from southern Europe and the Mediterranean to Europe. In Germany, migrant workers comprised 10.3 per cent of the total labour force. In France in 1974 the figure was 10.8 per cent (Atasoy 2003b: 61).

Although Turkey was a late starter in exporting labour compared to other countries of the Mediterranean (Krane 1979: 146–220), high-levels of rural migration to the cities produced a significant number of potential migrants. Development managers encouraged rural migration and adopted an urban high-wage policy to create an industrial working class. The 1961 constitution, adopted after the military coup, granted workers the right to form unions and to strike. These rights were introduced to allow workers to bargain for higher wages through collective bargaining. As a result, real wages in the organized sector of large import substituting industries rose by 5 to 7 per cent annually between 1963 and 1971. This further stimulated migration to urban areas, especially for those released from farming by agricultural mechanization. However, industrial job creation was not as successful as development managers hoped. The first development plan forecast 7 per cent growth in industrial employment, but the actual increase amounted to only 58 per cent of the target (Paine 1974: 33). The second development plan also produced considerably less industrial employment than expected. In 1972 the unemployment rate reached 13.3 per cent of an economically active population of 15 million. It appears that the state-planned high-wage policy that encouraged high-levels of rural migration was producing a wage-earning class in urban labour markets that was potentially unemployable.

Exporting excess urban labour abroad was thus an attractive policy for reducing urban unemployment and easing potential political problems. This was in addition to the economic benefits resulting from the inflow of export workers savings and remittances. Turkey's unemployment figures also remained lower than they would have otherwise. The increase in employment abroad was slightly more than one-third of the increase in domestic non-agricultural employment— about the same as the number of jobs created by Turkey's industrial sector (TUSIAD 1982). In the early 1970s Germany absorbed nearly 100,000 Turkish workers a year (Atasoy 2003b: 60). By 1976 there were 600,000 Turkish workers abroad, in addition to approximately one million family members. The inflow of remittances from these workers increased foreign exchange earnings so that Turkey could import capital goods and raw materials for its industry without entering into a debt crisis. By the early 1970s, workers' remittances added 1 per cent to the annual growth of the GNP (Paine 1974). The inflow of remittances to Turkey amounted to US$ 1 billion annually (Hale 2000: 176).

The energy crisis of 1973 and the economic recession that followed directly affected Europe's capacity to absorb migrant labour. Beginning in 1973, EEC countries terminated further recruitment of foreign labour. The labour recruitment ban was accompanied by a programme of financial incentives to encourage workers to return to their country of origin. Between 1974 and 1975 the number of foreign workers employed in industry fell by more than 20 per cent (Leithauser 1988: 179). With labour migration coming to an end, Turkey experienced a threefold increase in unemployment between 1974 and 1978. By the end of the 1970s the unemployment rate was almost 16 per cent (Atasoy 2003b: 61). The decline in European demand for migrant labour during the mid-1970s resulted in a significant decline in Turkey's foreign exchange earnings from workers' remittances. Remittances dropped from US$ 1.4 billion in 1974 to US$ 982 million in 1977. This seriously constrained the external financing of industrialization plans in Turkey.

Table 2: Exports, Imports, Trade Balance, and Workers' Remittances (Million US$)

	Exports	Manufacturing Exports	Imports	Trade Balance	Exports/ Imports (%)	Workers' Remittances	Overall Balance
1963	368	65	688	-320	53.5	-	-30
1964	411	76	537	-126	76.5	9	40
1965	464	82	572	-108	81.2	70	82
1966	490	79	718	-228	68.2	115	8
1967	523	75	685	-162	76.4	93	55
1968	496	66	764	-268	64.9	107	-16
1969	537	99	801	-264	67.0	141	28
1970	588	109	948	-360	62.0	273	144
1971	677	149	1171	-494	57.8	471	223
1972	885	243	1563	-678	56.6	740	267
1973	1313	443	2086	-769	63.1	1133	917
1974	1532	600	3777	-2245	40.6	1462	-461
1975	1401	503	4730	-3329	29.6	1312	-1301
1976	1960	596	5129	-3169	38.2	982	-1766
1977	1753	586	5797	-4044	30.2	982	-1908
1978	2288	621	4599	-2311	49.7	983	-388

Source: Hale 1981: 230; OECD 1983: 69

A deteriorating trade balance and declining workers' remittances pushed Turkey into a foreign exchange crisis between 1975 and 1979. In 1978, then Prime Minister Demirel announced that the Central Bank's disposable cash reserves for financing industrial imports amounted to only US$ 30 million, sufficient for just two days (Colasan 1983: 25–7). With the reduced capacity to finance industry, Turkey experienced a dramatic slowdown in job creation. This became a serious political problem as an increasing number of 'un-exportable' workers joined the informal sector of the economy. Regardless of political affiliation, governments of the period responded by increasing industrial investment in the public sector. Their hope was to create sufficient employment to offset that lost from labour exports. With declining remittances and an increasing trade deficit, state investment in industry was maintained only by draining foreign exchange reserves and borrowing in short-term credit markets from private banks.

State economic enterprises (SEEs) undertook a significant portion of industrial production (Szyliowicz 1991). Despite the fact that they were consistently in a trade deficit situation, governments subsidized SEEs with higher credit rates from the Central Bank at very low interest. Meanwhile, SEEs were protected from international competition by protective tariffs and an overvalued Turkish lira. The Central Bank compensated for the foreign exchange losses of state enterprises by printing more money. This produced a record high inflation rate in Turkey, rising from 10.1 per cent in 1975 to 85 per cent in 1979 (US Congress 1980: 33).

Government support for investment in the state sector did not succeed in creating jobs for the urban unemployed. This problem was further compounded by a substantial drop in private sector manufacturing investments—down 10.2 per cent between 1979 and 1980. Public sector investment also fell, from 17.7 per cent in 1963 to 4.7 per cent in 1977 (TUSIAD 1982: 13). These declines in investment resulted in a drastically reduced capacity for government to create jobs for those who could not be exported abroad or kept in rural areas.

As workers' remittances declined and the trade deficit increased, governments in Turkey borrowed from private banks on a short-term basis to gain access to foreign exchange for job creation. This policy was unsustainable and resulted in a debt crisis. Between 1975 and 1978 medium- and long-term debts were three times higher than they were between 1970 and 1975. Short-term borrowing, which was almost non-existent in the early 1970s, amounted to 60 per cent of the total debt in 1977. The term structure of medium- and long-term debts also worsened. Consequently, Turkey was unable to repay its debt. The debt-service ratio increased from 7 per cent in 1975 to 20.2 per cent in 1977, reaching 26.7 per cent in 1978. Although the debt-service ratio does not reflect the build-up of arrears on the short-term debt, it does reveal that post-war development projects in Turkey entered into crisis in the late 1970s.

Table 3: External Debt (Million US$)

	1970	1972	1975	1977	1978
Debt outstanding and disbursed	1911	2538	4724	11405	14126
Medium and long-term	1896	2519	3336	4805	6657
Public sector	1854	2450	3176	4326	6100
Private sector	42	69	160	478	557
Short term	15	19	1398	6600	7469
Trade financing	-	-	-	2433	2209
Banks	15	19	1011	2500	3671
Others	-	-	387	1275	1589
Terms of borrowing on loans to the public sector					
Average interest (%)	3.6	4.4	7.3	7.6	6.9
Average maturity (years)	18.0	22.1	13.4	12.7	14.8
Grant element (%)	18.3				
Debt/service ratio	18.8	13.1	7.0	20.2	26.7

Source: World Bank 1980a: 31; World Bank 1980b: 161

The enormous price increases in oil in 1974 and again in 1978 further intensified Turkey's debt crisis. Turkey's oil bill increased from US$ 124 million in 1972 to US$ 1.2 billion in 1977 and then to US$ 3.86 billion in 1980. It was financed largely by increasing short-term external debt. As a direct result, the cost of all imports doubled between 1977 and 1980. This in turn triggered a 40 per cent drop in Turkey's importing capacity (TUSIAD 1981: 138). It also contributed to a sharp decline in government job creation efforts.

The debt crisis of the late 1970s led governments to give priority to capital-intensive and technologically advanced industrialization projects. Nevertheless, in the context of the world economic crisis of the 1970s, the political and military conjuncture of détente, and Turkey's conflicts with Greece over Cyprus, Turkey became a marginal state in its relations with the United States and the EEC. Unable to mobilize its geopolitical importance to solve its economic difficulties, Turkey sought a solution from another source. A policy of rapprochement with the Soviet Union and Muslim countries in the Middle East aroused domestic political passion for the creation of a national approach, one that would turn old 'foes' into new friends. As I will demonstrate in the next chapter, the appeal for a national approach came, in particular, from the Islamists.

5

The Islamist National View

Throughout the 1970s politics in Turkey was marked by two opposing voices: one expressed the nationalist imaginings of Turkish development, the other conveyed imperialist images of Western dominance in the world economy. After a long period of rather muted politics in the 1950s and 1960s, Islamists had become vocal in their demand for a nationalist orientation in government policy. The pro-Islamic party, founded in 1970, promoted a national view ideology that stimulated debate on the erosion of national sovereignty. The party offered a critique of the relationship between Turkey's adoption of Western modernity and the historical relations of poverty and wealth creation. The national view was formulated to problematize the power relations constructed in the creation of a national bourgeoisie. This view also spurred moral claims for social justice, rights, and freedoms by those adversely affected by the underlying economic relations.

The pro-Islamic party argued that Turkey's economic and political activities were maladjusted to the idea of national development. The existing economic arrangements allowed large industrial capitalists privileged access to scarce resources. However, governments could not sustain the political ground necessary for large industrialists to become dominant players in the economy. Moreover, this was not in the interests of rural and urban small producers and medium-sized capital groups. Thus, the entire period of the 1970s witnessed sharpened grievances among social classes and the fragmentation of multi-class populist alliances in the industrialization project. The pro-Islamic party built on the idea that the overall development trajectory required a major readjustment.

Protesting against the inefficiency of existing strategies, the pro-Islamic party argued that national development might still be achieved if the nation could control its own destiny. It popularized the theme of 'Western imperialism' and questioned the presumed universality of a Western model. It also revived the debate over culture and technology that had been advanced by Ottoman pan-Islamists. Finally, the national view was developed to redirect the country's national history by reinterpreting the relationship between Muslim cultural values and the economy.

This chapter outlines the argument that political Islam in Turkey emerged as an expression of opposition to the ways in which Western modernity was imposed and the domestic imbalances generated by the Cold War world economy. Its objective was to reconstitute Turkey's socio-political terrain. This required realigning political opposition around the complex relations created by Turkey's economic and political-military rapprochements with the Soviet Union and Muslim states in the Middle East. This was a multi-tiered transnational process that also integrated Turkish migrant labour in Germany into the construction and reinforcement of a national view ideology.

Conflicts between regions and capital groups

The private sector consisted of five major groups: agricultural interests, commercial interests, commodity brokers, industrialists, and small artisans and shopkeepers. These groups were organized into quasi-public organizations. The Union of Agricultural Chambers organized agricultural interests, while the Confederation of Tradesmen and Artisans organized artisans and shopkeepers. The Turkish Union of Chambers (TOB) organized regional chambers of commerce, industry, and commodity exchanges (Bianchi 1984: 134–8). Founded in 1950 as an umbrella organization, the TOB was responsible for administering government economic policy within the private sector. In 1971 large capital groups founded the Turkish Industrialists and Businessmen Association (TUSIAD) to represent, together with the Turkish Confederation of Employers' Union (TISK), the largest industrial and commercial interests.

The TOB remained an organization for small- and medium-sized private industrial and commercial firms. It connected development managers from the State Planning Organization with private capital groups involved in import-substitution industrialization. In the 1970s when the availability of foreign currency was extremely tight, government allocation of foreign exchange generated intense competition among various private-sector groups seeking to influence government policy (Eralp 1990). Industrialists were in favour of continuing state protection, although there was a divergence of interests within this group. Anatolian industrialists who advocated intermediate and capital goods production were supportive of protection, while those involved in consumer durables production in the assembly plants of the Istanbul region were not (Zeytinoglu 1981: 31). Commercial groups were also divided in relation to the continuation of state protection in the economy. The small- and medium-sized commercial firms from small Anatolian cities engaged in domestic commerce welcomed a protective strategy. Their main competitors were importers whose interests were closely aligned with consumer durables producing large industrialists (TOB 1978). As most importers were located in Istanbul, their opposition to protectionist state policy was centred there.

Anatolian commercial groups and industrialists were the strongest supporters of state protection. Concerned with the adverse effects of a customs union with the EEC, they argued that the Turkish economy would not survive European competition without such state protection (Barkey 1990: 115). The Eskisehir Chamber of Commerce stated that it would do everything in its power to prevent a customs union between Turkey and the EEC. Anatolian-based chambers of commerce reacted by strenuously lobbying against the removal of import restrictions and customs duties required by the 1970 Brussels Protocol.

Large industrialists from the Istanbul region who were involved in the assembly production of consumer durables for domestic markets favoured a more open import regime. A substantial portion of their investment capital was foreign. A 1973 survey of 89 industrial firms in the assembly industry shows that 42 per cent of the total capital of these firms belonged to foreign capital groups. The ratio of imported goods in their production process was a very high 38 per cent. Although only 3 per cent of their production value came from exports, the number of government credits allocated to them was equal to 44 per cent of their total capital (Akgul 1976: 13). Anatolian industrialists viewed government support of assembly production as support for foreign firms through joint ventures with large industrialists. This practice was considered discriminatory against smaller Turkish firms.

Changes in the banking system further intensified the divergence of interests within private capital. Prior to 1973, banking laws prohibited banks from lending more than 10 per cent of their capital to any single firm. By the mid-1970s, however, banks were allowed to lend unlimited sums to firms that owned more than 25 per cent of their equity (Oncu 1980: 472). This change was initiated by the Istanbul Chamber of Industry (ISO), which claimed that banks provided its members with only a small number of credits at high interest, whereas public economic activity received the majority of bank credits (Gevgili 1973: 462). Changes in the banking system allowed large industrialists and holding corporations to control the banking industry, while small- and medium-sized industrial companies had limited or no access to bank credits (Tekeli and Mentes 1978: 16–45).

Small firms received only 2.7 per cent of total bank credits in 1974, although they were responsible for 25 per cent of total industrial production and 88.3 per cent of the total manufacture of footwear, other apparel, and textile goods. This represented only a 1.5 per cent increase in credits allocated to small firms from the 1963 level. The credit rate increase for other industrial firms was 11 per cent, rising from 18 per cent in 1963 to 29 per cent in 1974. Agricultural and commercial credits either declined or remained stagnant over the same period (TIB 1978: 112, 117–9).

The diversification of interests among large-holding corporations and small- to medium-sized industrial firms was played out through regional conflicts between the Istanbul and Anatolian chambers of commerce. As Table 4 illustrates, the Marmara region contained the greatest percentage of large industrial corporations and the largest percentage of corporate turnovers in Turkey. Istanbul held the most privileged position in this area and received the lion's share of foreign exchange and credits. This became the major source of conflict between Anatolian and Istanbul industrialists.

Table 4: Distribution by Region of the Largest Private Industrial Corporations, 1980

	No of Firms	% of Firms	% of Turnover
Marmara	283	67.2	70.3
Istanbul	253	60.1	61.7
Aegean	65	15.4	11.6
Mediterranean	29	6.9	10.3
North Central	34	8.1	6.5
South Central	9	2.1	1.4
Black Sea	1	0.2	0.0
East Central	-	-	-
Northeast	-	-	-
Southeast	-	-	-

Source: Istanbul Chamber of Industry 1981

The TOB became the focus of political struggles over the state allocation of funds. The TOB's official role was to prepare and distribute government-set import quotas for industrialists and commercial importers via its constitutive chambers of commerce and industry. It was also responsible for monitoring and verifying the import prices claimed by importers. Governments allocated foreign currency and credits on the basis of information obtained from TOB reports. These reports indicated the capacity figures and import needs of individual enterprises. Among TOB members, small- and medium-sized firms were on the losing end, as governments supported large industrialists and commercial groups. The smaller cities of Anatolia containing more modest industrial and commercial interests also experienced discrimination.

Despite evidence to the contrary, large industrialists and commercial groups held the view that the TOB supported smaller firms. This perception was rooted in the increasing overall number of smaller firms in Turkey and the number of small firms holding TOB membership. The number of small firms employing fewer than 50 workers rose from 93 per cent of the total in 1963 to 98.1 per cent in 1968. The number of large industrial firms employing more than 100 workers comprised only 1.9 per cent of total manufacturing corporations (National Productivity Center 1973: 12–3). Large firms interpreted the increasing number of small firms as a sign that their position in the TOB would eventually be weakened.

To defend their own class interests more effectively, large industrialists and commercial groups broke away from the TOB and established TUSIAD in 1971. The establishment of TUSIAD had far-reaching effects, not only on the government allocation of foreign exchange but on the general economic policy of Turkey. TUSIAD advocated a move away from protectionism in favour of export promotion, in contrast to Anatolian industrialists who continued to support protectionism (*Cumhuriyet Newspaper*, 8, 11, 19 April 1979). Export promotion remained a highly contentious issue given that the interests of large-holding firms were fragmented between importers and exporters (Oncu 1980). Those producing for domestic markets favoured protection, while others producing for export favoured openness in the trade regime.

These conflicts of interest resulted in contradictory approaches to a customs union with the EEC. For example, the Aegean Chamber of Industry President, Sinasi Ertan, supported a customs union with the EEC to increase Turkey's foreign currency earning capacity. Industrialists in the Aegean Chamber of Industry hoped to benefit from the export of textiles, leather, hide products, and processed food. Ertan was therefore critical of the distribution of bank credits to importing industrialists who were not earning foreign exchange from exports (*Cumhuriyet Newspaper*, 28 May 1969). On the other hand, Vehbi Koc, the leading import substituting industrialist in Turkey, argued for the distribution of credits in favour of those industrialists who produced for domestic markets. Although Koc was not against EEC membership, he supported protectionism and defended the credit distribution system. He made the claim that 'KOC Holding saves a lot of foreign exchange by producing FIAT cars in this country' (Barkey 1990: 117).

When Prime Minister Bulent Ecevit froze relations with the EEC in 1976, he was responding to political pressure from the State Planning Organization, the Anatolian-based chambers of industry, and the Istanbul Chamber of Industry. TUSIAD called this decision foolish and declared the government incapable of defending Turkey's national interests. The organization became highly political and publicly criticized the government's actions. In 1979, TUSIAD placed an editorial in a number of leading daily newspapers, defending free trade and stating that excessive state intervention was the source of Turkey's economic problems.

TUSIAD and TISK began to see working-class wage demands as a threat to economic growth. Both blamed the government for not doing enough to support private industrialists. According to TISK, the increasing power of trade unions was responsible for inflation and the political instability in the country.

The organization further argued that a high-wage policy hindered private sector profits and prevented investment in industry. TUSIAD and TISK demanded substantial wage decreases.

Until the 1980 military coup, which drastically curtailed trade union activities in Turkey, public sector wages consistently increased in contrast to those in the private sector. Within the private sector, wages in large private industrial firms were higher than in smaller firms (Bademli 1978: 17–27). The catalyst for wage increases was unionization, which rose from 10.8 per cent in 1963 to 46 per cent in 1977 (State Planning Organization 1977: 323). In smaller firms employing ten workers or fewer, where unionization was low, the average wage was approximately 40 per cent of that in large unionized firms employing 100 workers or more. The average wage in firms with less than 50 workers was 50 per cent higher than in firms with less than ten workers (Keyder 1987: 175).

As far as TUSIAD and TISK were concerned, high wages in state-owned and large private firms were diverting state funds from private industry and inhibiting the competitiveness of large industrialists. Large industrialists blamed the government for not preventing labour disputes. According to the Turkish Confederation of Employers Association, there were 51 strikes and 3 million workdays lost to strikes in 1977 (World Bank 1980a: 142). The number of workdays lost between 1977 and 1980 was three times greater than the days lost between 1973 and 1976 (Keyder 1987: 191–2).

The large capital groups that became highly vocal through TUSIAD were the first to leave the social coalition of the national industrialization programme. However, no capital group emerged as politically dominant from this fragmentation of class alliances.

The break-up of political alliances

Under the leadership of Suleyman Demirel, the JP became the leading centre-right party between 1961 and 1980. It was founded in 1961 to replace the DP, which was shut down after the 1960 military coup. The very name of the party came to symbolize the undoing of 'injustices' brought by the military upon Menderes and the DP. Demirel was a 'development politician' who promised to deliver the benefits of industrial development without fear of accumulating a large foreign debt (Mango 1994: 18). The JP's populist agenda presented the image of 'a party of the people' and claimed to incorporate all sectors of private capital, small-producing peasants, and working classes into a national platform. However, in the context of the 1970s economic crisis, the JP could no longer subsume the diversity of interests within a popular national unity agenda. Interest cleavages between small, medium, and large firms, between importers and exporters, and between Istanbul-based and Anatolian-based commercial groups and industrialists resulted in the near disintegration of the JP.

The stage was now set for the realignment of coalition politics in Turkey. A national view framework grew out of the JP's inability to contain opposing forces in the economy. It presented an Islamist programme for reconfiguring social classes and reformulating industrial policy, one that appealed to Islamic moral principles of justice and equality and equipped smaller capital groups with a sense of entitlement to state resources and incentives.

Necmettin Erbakan, elected leader of the TOB in 1968, was instrumental in widening the crack within the populist ideology of the JP. According to Erbakan, who became leader of the pro-Islamic National Order Party in 1970, the TOB had represented the class interests of a non-Muslim 'comprador-Masonic minority' centred in Istanbul, to the detriment of smaller Anatolian industrial firms and commercial groups. Erbakan wanted the TOB to favour the interests of these smaller Anatolian firms (Saribay 1985: 98–9).

Erbakan (1972) was opposed to a customs union with the EEC. He argued that large industrial and commercial interests in the Istanbul region would benefit from a customs union, as their class interests would be integrated with European capital groups. Small capital groups, however, according to Erbakan, required state protection to gain access to the new technology and state credits necessary for their success. Erbakan's insistence on a coherent national view in government policy also concealed his desire to promote closer economic and political ties with Muslim countries in the Middle East.

Social democrats shared Erbakan's call to support smaller Anatolian interests. According to Eskisehir Chamber of Industry President Zeytinoglu (1981: 121), the difference between Istanbul and Anatolian industrial capital groups was the former group's direct ties with western European capitalists and the latter group's dependence on the merchants of Istanbul for their production and consumption. In their own way, both social democratic and pro-Islamic groups advanced an economic strategy that would support and reposition smaller industrial and commercial groups in the economy. This strategy involved opposition to a customs union with the EEC.

In the unfolding history of Turkey's marginalization within NATO, no government was politically strong enough to contain the opposing interests of private capitalists and various social classes in relation to economic policy and the issue of customs union. Within this context, the pro-Islamic party began to question the desirability of a single orientation to Western ways. It raised the possibility of another path—of cultivating ties with Muslim states in the Middle East. Such an alternative emerged as an ideology that could mediate the different interests of class and capital fractions and build a multi-class populist alliance based on an Islamic moral framework.

The Islamist national view

Following the 1964 Cyprus crisis, when the government adopted a multifaceted foreign policy approach, Turkish politics experienced an ideological polarization between centre-left and centre-right. While the RPP identified itself as left-of-centre, the JP adopted a centre-right stance. The Left positioned itself within a strong Kemalist orientation (Culhaoglu 2002: 179), thereby gaining the reputation of being anti-religious, bureaucratic, and elitist (Cakir and Cinemre 1991). The JP, on the other hand, established itself as a protector of religious freedoms and guardian of Muslim beliefs and practices in Turkey.

While the RPP found itself entangled in the single-party era legacy of state oppression, the JP sought to ground its political power base in the struggle for moral rights and freedoms—a struggle by 'the people' against bureaucratic oppression. Although in the 1970s the RPP adopted a democratic leftist orientation and came to view Islam as an important part of national culture, the party continued to be tainted by allegations that it was anti-religious.

Suspicion over the RPP's motives intensified after the JP deployed a propaganda campaign designed to associate the RPP with 'communism' and 'anti-religiosity'. The RPP was definitely populist, but hardly communist or anti-religious. Although there was an illegal Turkish Communist Party (TCP), with its headquarters in East Berlin, the TCP's role in Turkish politics was negligible and not connected to the RPP. Since the founding of the Directorate of Religious Affairs in 1924, a state-interpreted 'official Islam' has been part of Turkey's secular identity. The RPP continued to support a state-controlled version of Islam.

All variants of the Left were subject to an 'anti-religious communist' propaganda campaign. They drew support from the newly organized urban working class and *gecekondu* dwellers, enjoying their strongest moment when the Workers' Party of Turkey (TIP) was founded in 1961 (Culhaoglu 2002). The establishment of the Confederation of Revolutionary Labour Unions (DISK) in 1967 also contributed to increased leftist political activism. The Revolutionary Youth (*Dev-Genc*) movement of the late 1960s and the Revolutionary Path (*Dev-Yol*) of the 1970s were also highly influential in stimulating leftist activity.

In addition to the 1971 military coup in which coercive power was used to persecute leftists, a number of state sponsored organizations launched anti-leftist campaigns. They included the Association for the Struggle Against Communism, the Turkish Nationalist Youth Society, and the National Youth Foundation. The number of such organizations increased from only nine in 1963 to 141 in the early 1970s (Yucekok 1972: 150). Together with the ultra-right Idealist Youth (*Ulkuculer*), these organizations were highly influential in promoting Muslim beliefs and practices and directing them against the Left.

It would be incorrect, however, to associate Islam solely with an anti-leftist politics. In the 1970s, political Islam emerged to reorganize the existing social, political, and cultural arrangements in Turkey. Islamists began to give a particular political and ideological content to Islam. Most notably, they criticized the oppressive and inegalitarian nature of the industrialization project and the conditions under which Western modernity was imposed.

The National Order Party (NOP), founded in 1970, was Turkey's first pro-Islamic party. Its political programme was known as the National View (*Milli Gorus*). The Constitutional Court banned the NOP from politics after the 1971 military coup, but the national view continued to define the ideological framework of pro-Islamic political parties. These included the National Salvation Party (NSP), founded in 1972; the Welfare Party (WP), founded in 1983 (after the NSP was banned by the 1980 military coup); and the Virtue Party (VP), founded in 1997 (with the expectation that the WP would be banned, which occurred in 1998). In 2001, the Constitutional Court closed down the VP. Erbakan was the leader of all these political parties until 1998, at which time the Constitutional Court banned him from running for office. After the VP was banned, the pro-Islamic party movement split into two political entities, the Prosperity Party (PP) led by Recai Kutan, but actually controlled by Erbakan from behind the scenes, and the Justice and Development Party (AKP), led by Recep Tayyip Erdogan. While the PP continues to be situated within the national view programme of the NOP, the AKP adds a globalist twist. After the AKP came to power in November 2002, winning 35 per cent of the popular vote and 365 seats in parliament, the PP and national view ideology seem to have lost ground. The AKP has now departed from the national view, which fashioned pro-Islamic party ideology in Turkey for more than 30 years (Cakir and Calmuk 2001). It now views Islam as a moral-cultural value in the competitive relations of the global economy (Atasoy 2003a).

For the NOP and its successor, the NSP, Islam was a social project intended to stimulate industrial development. The national view was an antidote to both the Left and liberalism (Landau 1976: 2), which, as variants of Western developmentalist ideology, according to Erbakan, were ineffectual in bringing about national development. An Islamist emphasis on the 'national' involved the re-evaluation of culture and the role of the state, and a rethinking of the possibilities for reorganizing life from a non-Western standpoint.

Erbakan promoted himself as the sole representative of the national view. He denounced Demirel, leader of the JP, as a liberal 'freemason' working for large business interests. And he condemned Ecevit, the leader of the RPP, as a communist upholding an unjust state over a 'silenced Muslim majority'. Erbakan wanted to spread ideological doubts about the possibility of achieving equality and justice within the existing relations of the economy. His ideas found support among the small- and medium-sized fractions of private capital groups who were adversely affected by the world economic crisis of the 1970s. The urban *gecekondu* neighbourhoods in particular proved to be a fertile ground for the growth of national view ideology (Toprak 1981: 104–21). The anti-imperialist and anti-Western stand of the national view also became popular among marginal urban and rural populations, as well as university students who were children of modest lower-middle-class families in small Anatolian cities and villages.

In the 1973 national elections the NSP obtained 11.8 per cent of the popular vote and 10.6 per cent of seats in parliament, with much of its support coming from smaller cities in central and eastern Anatolia. In the 1977 elections it received 8.5 per cent of the popular vote and 5.5 per cent of seats in parliament (Bugra 2002: 111). Although its support declined, the NSP emerged as a real power broker with parliamentary representation throughout the 1970s, when no political party was able to win a clear majority in parliament. There was a succession of no less than ten coalition and minority governments from the 1973 elections to the military coup of 1980. At first, the NSP formed a coalition government with the left-of-centre RPP. Ecevit was prime minister and Erbakan his deputy. Later, the NSP formed right-of-centre coalitions with the JP and a number of other smaller parties, with Demirel as prime minister.

The *Nurcu cemaati* and the Naqshbandi order supported the NOP and the NSP (Cakir 1990: 214-22; Genc 1971: 230-307). Husret Hoca, then leader of the *Nurcu cemaati*, actively participated in their founding. The NSP's secretary general, Sevilgen, was an open follower of the *Risale-I Nur* movement of Said Nursi. However, the support of the *Nurcu cemaati* was shortlived. Husret Hoca withdrew his support when the NSP formed a coalition government with the RPP. A group of *Nurcu* parliamentarians then resigned from the NSP to protest the government's legislation on an amnesty that the Constitutional Court extended to all prisoners of conscience convicted under PL 141 and 142 of the Penal Code (Sevilgen 1980: 109–54). The *Nurcu* faction of the NSP interpreted the amnesty as a concession to alleged communists convicted under the martial law administration set up after the 1971 military coup. After the parliamentary resignations, the *Nurcu cemaati* gave its support to the centre-right JP (Demirel et al 1977), leaving the NSP to be supported by the Naqshbandi order.

Some of the most influential members of the NSP were Naqshbandi affiliates. Among them were Necmettin Erbakan, leader of the party; Korkut Ozal, minister of agriculture in various coalition governments between 1973 and 1980; Abdulkadir Paksu, minister of labour; and Salih Ozcan, a parliamentarian.

The Naqshbandi Sheikh Kotku played a significant role in the formulation of the national view. Sheikh Kotku's *sohbets* (oral teachings) contributed to the Islamist rethinking of social experience by referring to secular cultural meanings and daily life practices. There is no evidence to suggest that Kotku promoted a theologically centred politics, but he did long to refashion secularism by injecting social life with greater moral strength.

Kotku was convinced that secularism had devalued the moral-ethical dimension of social existence. Ersin Gurdogan (1991: 11) has defined Kotku's teachings as an invisible university, the purpose of which was to ground individual life in Islam through a process of self-purification. According to Kotku, this process should take place away from the negative moral and cultural influences engendered by the state's secular educational institutions.

Kotku (1995: 17–46) claimed that achieving moral-spiritual maturity is the most difficult task for an individual, requiring a total redefinition of life. For him, unless 'faith in God' and a 'willingness to work for the well-being of Muslims' are combined in the moral make-up of the self, a social life in need of transformation cannot even be imagined. Kotku located his politics in the creation and dissemination of an Islamic moral discourse through the Naqshbandi practices of *sohbet* and *dhikr,* as well as in the study of the Koran. For him, the Koran is the ultimate educational tool available to humanity. Kotku (1995: 110) states: 'We look at the mirror and try to beautify ourselves. We arrange our cloths accordingly. We wash our bodies to be clean. But our bodies are the property of the earth. It is the soul that ultimately must be beautified.'

Kotku (1994) appreciated the difficulty of resisting and escaping from immorality, given that Muslims were living under an unrestrained capitalist social system. Kotku (1995: 85–101) argued that cultivation of the appropriate conditions for an Islamic life requires Muslims to insulate themselves from secular orientations and pressures, and depart from un-Islamic ways. This is reminiscent of the ideological politics of the Muslim Brotherhood, founded in Egypt in 1928 (Esposito 1987: 130–42), and the Jama'at-I Islami, founded in Pakistan in 1941 (Nasr 1993). These groups call for the eradication of un-Islamic governments and secular lifestyles through an organized political movement. Until that goal is realized, Muslims in non-Islamic contexts must isolate themselves by living in Islamic enclaves. Kotku (1994) argues that Islamic education is key to the embodiment of Islamic morality and essential for avoiding the moral distress induced by the unfolding history of capitalist development.

Kotku cautioned his followers about the conspicuous display of wealth found in consumerism, which he believed to be the source of this moral distress. Kotku warns:

> Don't love this world! The world is arable land for the afterworld. Whatever you sow here you will reap it there. Be generous, charitable, and benevolent. Don't waste your money for sinful things. Don't become lost in loose and dissolute ways of living. But you should love this world. Why? [Because] We will go to heaven from here. We will earn money here. We will look after the poor

and needy with this money. We will live here in accordance with the knowledge [of the Koran], and educate others. Don't care much for amusement. Don't take delight in voluptuousness. Engage in practices that will lead you to heaven (Kotku 1995: 73–4).

Kotku believed that Muslims could bring about social change and he encouraged those in his *sohbet* circles to engage in politics. He argued that if the correct state policies were pursued, it was possible to awaken a broader social consciousness and steer development towards a truly Muslim society (Kotku 1994: 119–34). But for this to take place, political leaders must possess high moral standing if they are going to create effective social policy on human rights and justice.

To that end, the national view programme summoned the emotions and sentiments surrounding a moral, religious conception of 'national' thought. In his book *Milli Gorus* (The National View) (1975), Erbakan also underlined the role of the state in managing morality and de-linking society from the imitation of Western themes. This required changes in both national education policy and the mass media. The national view, then, presented a moral critique of dominant social norms, and an assertion of Islamic cultural meanings as crucial to human character formation.

Kotku (1984a) associated the term 'development' with 'corruption'. This finds its ideological basis in the Muslim Brotherhood of Egypt and the Jama'at-I Islami of the Indian subcontinent. According to Sayyid Qutb, the major theoretician for the Muslim Brotherhood, there are only two choices open to humanity in constituting a society. These are *jahiliyya* (ignorance) and Islam (Atasoy 2003e). Qutb argues that Muslims can either imitate Western models or embrace Islam. He defines the condition in which Muslims turn away from Islam as *jahiliyya*, and promotes Islam as the superior choice in all respects for righteous living. Mawdudi, of the Jama'at-I Islami, was deeply committed to the doctrine of *tawhid* (unity)—'One God, One Prophet, and One Book'. He saw Islam as a universal ideology not subject to territorial nationalism. He also held that the acceptance of inappropriate foreign innovations by many Muslims, and consequent deviation from Islam, was the primary cause of their exploitation by Western imperialist states. The Muslim Brotherhood and Jama'at-I Islami popularized the ideological schism between Islam and the West as a civilizational divide. The defeat of Nasser in the 1967 Arab-Israeli War contributed greatly to the rise in popularity of this idea of Muslim unity against Western imperialism. Wallerstein (2000: 359) describes the current institutional incarnation of this imperialist power as US hegemony.

Proponents of the national view in Turkey espoused the spiritual transformation of individuals through Islamic principles, regardless of whether or not there was an Islamic state within Turkey. Further, the national view's conception of development included the cultivation of a moral ethos of scientific discovery and technological innovation. This negated the dominant development ideology based on the imitation of Western cultural norms. In an effort to steer Turkey away from a century-long pattern of imitating Western ways, the pro-Islamic party planned to decentre the Western model. In its place, Islam was to be positioned as a moral-cultural value in the technological and industrial advancement of Turkey.

The development idea would draw from the public ethos of Islamic morality. It would not involve an authoritarian embodiment of Islam but would use democratic principles. The pro-Islamic party imagined 'democracy' to be a political system that would lead to the election of those most capable of installing a 'rights and justice' discourse in the social realm. As for the means to inculcate the moral principles necessary to sustain such a discourse, the party believed that only the national educational system could maintain the required moral framework for future generations. In short, a national educational system could create the conditions for nurturing a correspondence between Islamic culture and economic development.

Erbakan (1975: 51–6) argued that the doctrine of imitation relegated Islam to a position of obscurantism and backwardness, having failed in relating itself to the modern techno-scientific world. Secularism became an instrument of state bureaucrats for undermining the public ethos of Muslims through a systematic 'oppression of believers'. As a result, Turkey lacked the necessary moral foundation from which it could draw inspiration and creativity to develop in the technological and cultural realms (Erbakan 1975: 29–40). Erbakan believed the state itself must take responsibility for individual moral regeneration and the reconstitution of justice in society.

The national view focus of the pro-Islamic party was essentially a revival of the nineteenth-century pan-Islamic philosophy that rejected wholesale westernization during the Ottoman Empire. In order to re-establish a strong position in the state system, as the Ottoman Empire had during its classical era, Turkey would have to regain its consciousness as a Muslim nation. For this, the state would be required to establish the primacy of Muslim moral culture and spirituality in the national consciousness as well as in the character of individuals (Karahasanoglu 1975: 114). It would fall to the state educational system to rejuvenate the 'glorious past of one thousand years' (Tanju 1978: 112). Erbakan, therefore, gave the state a pivotal role in managing the economy, in order to re-embed it in a network of social relations governed by Islamic morality.

Pro-Islamic sensitivity to Islamic moral and cultural practices linked the economy to the state regulation of production and consumption norms. Sheikh Kotku encouraged the development of Islamically regulated patterns of consumption as a way of restoring Muslim morality. He argued that the

Islamic shaping of the economy depended on the forging of political alliances between the state bureaucracy and private industrialists. While the development managers of the state bureaucracy would take care of the establishment of large capital goods–producing industrial plants, private firms would produce consumer goods (Gurdogan 1991: 57–9, 88, 93–130). However, it was important that consumer goods production be regulated by the state, to ensure that Islamic normative standards prevailed. The relationship between the economy and Islamic morality was to be mediated by extensive state control over both production and consumption norms. It would therefore be the responsibility of a politically strong state to reconfigure the socio-cultural realm, regulate relations among various segments of society, and reorganize Turkey's relations with other states in the state system. However, according to Kotku, a powerful state could only materialize if morally upright individuals ruled.

Kotku viewed 'corruption' as a sign of the state's diminished capacity to formulate and implement policies in accordance with the interests of society as a whole. Turkey's integration into Western security alliances disempowered the state and undermined its capacity to introduce effective social policy for the welfare of peasants, working classes, and small producers. Kotku believed that Western dominance in the world economy was inducing powerlessness in the Turkish state—the result of structural imbalances created by the world capitalist economy between 'core' Western states and 'peripheral' states of the Third World. The national view linked the problem of class inequality and social injustice to the operation of the world economy. Consequently, it promoted a national orientation in economic and social policy. Kotku insisted that the successful rearrangement of the economy and society required a decoupling from Western models and rapprochement with Muslim states.

The national view: transcending state territory

Erbakan's reference to an Islamic global project also involved changing the structural position of Turkey in the world economy from a peripheral to a primary location. He argued for a common market with Muslim states in which Turkey could strengthen its industrial capacity and also emerge as a stronger state. For Erbakan, a strong state would assure the market power of its national bourgeoisie. He stated: 'As opposed to struggling with the EEC to be able to sell some parsley ... We should sell our agricultural and manufactured goods to Muslim states [and] build their industries [and] their roads' (Erbakan 1975: 266–8). Erbakan's national view is reminiscent of the 'dependency' theory of the 1970s, which imagined that national development requires de-linking from the world capitalist system (Amin 1976), but Erbakan departs from this theory. He does not argue that development should be confined within national boundaries. Rather, he believes in strengthening Turkey's market position by forging a Muslim common market. According to Erbakan, a Muslim common market would counterbalance the 'conditioning situation' within the world economy in which political and military relations are governed by the United States. The foreign policy implications of the Cyprus War are a case in point, a subject to which I now return.

The Cyprus War

Turkey invaded Cyprus in 1974. The US government, already weakened by the Vietnam War and the Watergate scandal, was unable to mediate between Turkey and Greece. It was also preoccupied with Middle East peace negotiations after the 1973 Arab–Israeli War. On 15 July 1974, a Greek junta engineered a coup d'état and removed Makarios from power in an attempt to unify Cyprus and Greece (Bolukbasi 1988: 167–9). When negotiations to restore political stability and prevent *enosis* failed, Turkish military forces landed in northern Cyprus on 20 July 1974, capturing 7 per cent of the island. The Soviet Union did not contest the Turkish military intervention (Ecevit 1976: 65) but the US administration viewed it as a clear indication of Turkey's defiance.

The Greek junta, quite unprepared for the Turkish military operation, collapsed on 23 July 1974. This also led to the failure of the coup in Cyprus (Hale 2000: 157). Although the de facto existence of autonomous Greek and Turkish administrations was agreed upon in the peace declaration of 30 July 1974 (Couloumbis 1983: 96), Greeks and Greek Cypriots were not eager to accept the Turkish proposal for a loose bizonal or a multicantonal federation in Cyprus. Turkish troops carried out a second military operation on 12 August 1974 in order to forcibly implement this proposal. The military operation was actually symptomatic of political tension within the government of Turkey between the centre-left RPP and the pro-Islamic NSP. Social democrat Ecevit (1976: 83, 95) wanted to have a territorial federation within the independent Republic of Cyprus. Pro-Islamic Erbakan (1975: 389) favoured its partitioning. Unable to contain this difference of opinion within the government, Ecevit resigned, thereby triggering a collapse of the coalition government on 7 November 1974.

The Cyprus crisis had important long-term consequences for Turkey's relations with the United States. Prime Minister Karamanlis withdrew Greece from the military command of NATO, accusing both NATO and the US government of being unwilling to react to the Turkish use of force in Cyprus. In order to bring Greece back into the NATO military command, and largely due to the efforts of a strong Greek lobby in the US Congress, the US government imposed an embargo on military aid to Turkey on 5 February 1975 (US Congress 1980, 1981, 1983). The Turkish government responded by closing a number of US military bases in Turkey. The US arms embargo lasted until 1978, with the start of the Islamic Revolution in Iran and the Soviet-engineered coup in Afghanistan. Both of these events increased Turkey's strategic importance in the region.

Supporters of the embargo used a combination of legal and strategic arguments. The basis of the legal argument was that Turkey had used US arms and equipment to invade Cyprus, which was contrary to the US Foreign Assistance Act of 1961 (PL 87-195), and the Military Sales Act of 1968 (PL 90-629). These acts stipulated that any arms or services provided to a country were to be used only for internal security and self-defence purposes (US Congress 1981). The further strategic argument was that the Soviet Union did not represent an immediate threat to Turkey and that the eastern Mediterranean and Turkey were secondary to NATO's overall military planning (US Congress 1977).

The arms embargo resulted in a dramatic shift in US military aid policy towards Turkey. From the days of the Marshall Plan until the arms embargo, US military aid to Turkey was mostly in the form of grants. With the introduction of the embargo, military grants were discontinued and loans became the only form of US aid available to Turkey.

Table 5: US Military Assistance, 1950-1980 (Million US$)

	Grant	Loan	Total
1950 to 1970	3,406.6	-	3,406.6
1971	204.0	-	204.0
1972	164.4	15.0	179.4
1973	186.7	20.0	206.7
1974	117.7	75.0	192.7
1975	20.4	75.0	95.4
1976	-	125.0	125.0
1977	-	125.0	125.0
1978	.2	175.0	175.2
1979	5.3	175.0	180.3
1980	3.4	250.0	253.4
Total	4,108.7	1,035.0	5,143.7

Source: US Congress 1980: 17

After the United States, Turkey had the largest standing army in NATO. During the 1960s Turkey ranked sixth among all aid recipients (Tuncer 1975: 206-24). In 1979, Turkey spent US$ 2.6 billion on its active armed forces of

566,000 men, which amounted to 5.1 per cent of its GNP (US Congress 1980: 15). The embargo forced Turkey to purchase military equipment, weapons, and spare parts with hard currency payments. Combined with the decline in workers' remittances and economic isolation within the EEC, the arms embargo pushed the economy into an even deeper crisis.

Greece's application for EEC membership also adversely affected the Turkish governments' ability to receive long-term loans from Europe. After withdrawing from NATO's military command in 1975, Greece applied for full EEC membership. There was unanimous acceptance of the Greek application in 1976 and Greece became a full EEC member in January 1980 (Featherstone 1989: 188–90). It is well known that Greek diplomacy was successful in isolating Turkey in Europe by linking the Cyprus problem to Turkey's status vis-à-vis the EEC. Eralp (1993) suggests that Turkey's inability to extricate itself from the Cyprus problem provided Europe with an excuse for refusing to provide Turkey with financial assistance.

Financial problems, diplomatic tension, and the arms embargo all reflected the powerlessness of the Turkish state. Together, these factors reinforced the perception that Turkey was unable to maintain control over its internal and external spheres of national sovereignty. This prompted Turkish policy-makers to develop closer relations with the Soviet Union and Muslim states in the Middle East. The Islamic national view programme based the empowerment of the Turkish state on a general Muslim disengagement from the West. The process of empowerment itself was to take place in the midst of changes in Soviet-Middle East relations which culminated in the gradual re-forming of global Islamic ties.

Turkish-Soviet rapprochement

The Soviet Union presented offers of economic aid to Turkey from the early 1960s in exchange for Turkey's neutrality in the region. In 1961 an offer of US$ 500 million was extended to the military government, which President General Gursel refused (Gonlubol et al 1987: 336). Another US$ 400 million was offered to Inonu when he became prime minister of the civilian coalition government in 1961. Inonu also refused. Demirel was the first to accept Soviet economic aid, worth US$ 200 million in 1967 (Arcayurek 1984: 262–7). By the end of the 1970s Turkey had become one of the largest recipients of Soviet aid outside the Warsaw Pact bloc (Rubinstein 1979). This included US$ 280 million for the Iskenderun iron and steel plant under a ten-year economic agreement involving a sum of US$ 1.3 billion by 1977 (Golan 1990: 253). Another agreement in 1979 worth US$ 3.8 billion was for the construction of mostly energy-related projects (Norton 1992: 106). By the beginning of 1980 Moscow was providing financial support for 44 different development projects in Turkey, in addition to supplying approximately 7 million barrels of crude oil annually (Boll 1979: 623). Soviet economic assistance was to be paid back by agricultural exports on barter terms (Golan 1990: 253).

Joint investment projects included the Orhaneli thermal power station (with a capacity to produce 200 million watts of electricity) and the Can thermal power station (with a capacity of 600 million watts) (*Milliyet Newspaper*, 27 October 1978). The Soviet Union also committed itself to building a number of large industrial facilities including the Iskenderun Iron and Steel Mill, the Seydisehir Aluminum Smelter, and the Izmir Aliaga Oil Refinery (Rubinstein 1982: 27). The oil refinery, iron and steel complex, and aluminium smelter were completed with Soviet credits worth US$ 1 billion.

Turkey and the Soviet Union had already established closer ties in 1964 after President Johnson warned Turkey not to expect NATO assistance if Turkish intervention in Cyprus provoked a Soviet military response. Late in 1964 the Turkish Minister of Foreign Affairs and a group of parliamentarians visited Moscow. Prime Minister Urguplu also made a trip to Moscow in 1965 (Ulman and Dekmejian 1967: 779). Soviet President Podgorny reciprocated with a visit to Turkey, followed by a visit from Gromyko, Soviet Minister of Foreign Affairs, in May 1965. Prime Minister Kosygin visited in January 1967 (Rubinstein 1982: 20).

These visits resulted in a decidedly lower level of Cold War rhetoric between the two countries. Turkey cancelled its participation in a NATO multilateral nuclear force and banned American U-2 flights from Turkey in December 1965 (Arcayurek 1984: 309–10). The government also refused an US request in 1966 to dispatch Turkish troops to Vietnam (*Yon*, 25 February 1966). Most significant of all was Turkey's demand that NATO agreements be modified to include an explicit statement on the organization's defensive character (Ulman and Dekmejian 1967: 780). During the 1967 and 1973 Arab-Israeli wars, Turkey did not allow the United States to use NATO military bases in Turkey for refuelling, reconnaissance, direct combat or logistical support (Rubinstein 1982: 38). However, the Soviet Union was allowed to carry out naval transit and military deployments, as well as flights over Turkish airspace and the straits (Golan 1990: 251–4).

As Turkish and Soviet relations warmed, a Turkish military delegation was permitted to observe Georgian and Armenian military manoeuvres in 1976 (*Gunaydin Newspaper*, 28 February 1978). A second military delegation toured ground, naval, and air units in Moscow, Leningrad, and Volgograd military districts (*Milliyet Newspaper*, 4 June 1976). A Soviet military delegation visited Turkey in the company of General Ogarkov, Soviet First Deputy Defense Minister and Chief of Staff. The purpose of the visit was to discuss possible military aid to Turkey. Discussions included plans for the building of an arms plant in Turkey that could produce spare parts for the aeroplanes and tanks previously supplied by the US government (*Gunaydin Newspaper*, 28 April 1978).

In 1978, Turkey and the Soviet Union also signed a 'Treaty on the Principles of Good Neighbourly and Friendly Cooperation'. Although it was not a non-aggression pact, the treaty was a breakthrough for Soviet relations with a NATO country. The agreement included a mutual prohibition clause on the use of their territories for aggressive or subversive actions against each other. The literal interpretation of this clause would preclude US surveillance facilities along the strategically important Turkish-Soviet border (Boll 1979: 621). From the Soviet point of view, the treaty was meant to prevent Turkey's high-level involvement in NATO. From the Turkish perspective, it represented a diversification of foreign policy and Turkey's disengagement from the Western alliance (Hale 2000: 162). It was only after the US government lifted the arms embargo and resumed economic assistance to Turkey in the wake of the Islamic Revolution in Iran and events in Afghanistan that Turkish foreign policy entered a new phase of re-engagement with the Western alliance.

Turkish–Middle East relations

From the founding of the republic in 1923 until the Cyprus crisis of 1964, governments in Turkey all wanted to break away from the cultural and political traditions of the Muslim Middle East. As the only NATO country situated between the Middle East and Europe, Turkey chose to promote Western interests in the region and link Arab states of the Middle East into a Western military alliance. When the Cyprus crisis revealed the limitations of Turkey's pro-Western alignment, Turkey's Middle East policy ceased to be a function of competitive East-West Cold War politics. To institute a friendlier approach towards the Arabs, Turkey began to support Arab resolutions at the UN. For example, it voted for UN Resolution 242, which prescribed the withdrawal of Israeli forces from territory occupied during the Arab-Israeli War of 1967 (Robins 1991: 74–9). In 1975, Turkey also recognized the PLO as the exclusive representative of Palestinians and in 1979 permitted the PLO to open an office in Ankara.

By establishing friendly relations with Muslim states in the Middle East, Turkey hoped to ease its economic difficulties. The 1973 oil shock had increased the price of Turkish oil imports fivefold from US$ 207 million in 1973 to US$ 1.2 billion in 1977. As a result, the trade deficit, which was a manageable US$ 45 million in 1973, skyrocketed to US$ 893 million four years later (Robins 1991: 101). The second oil shock of 1979 raised Turkey's oil import bill to over US$ 3.86 billion by 1980 (OECD 1982: 7, 43). From the 1970s onwards, Turkish governments tried to facilitate the formation of regional business networks, which required heavy reliance on government support of investments by Turkish contracting companies in oil-exporting countries.

In 1978 there were 22 Turkish contracting companies in the Middle East. By 1981 there were 113 (Robins 1991: 105). Their first major success was in Libya where in 1977 the Arab-Turkish Bank was established as a joint venture. Kuwait joined the venture sometime later (Ihsanoglu 1996: 83). Turkey also became an important transshipment route for Iraqi oil. In 1977, the first Turkish-Iraqi oil pipeline was completed to export oil from Kerkuk to Europe through the Turkish port of Yumurtalik. The Kerkuk–Yumurtalik oil pipeline had a capacity of approximately 800,000 barrels per day (Robins 1991: 59). With the start of the Iraq-Iran War in 1980, Iraq also exported large amounts of oil via Turkey in tanker trucks.

The Turkish rapprochement with Middle Eastern countries was aimed at reversing military dependence on the United States. In response to the arms embargo, the Turkish parliament passed the REMO defence appropriation bill in 1975. It required Turkish self-sufficiency in armaments and export weapons within and outside NATO (*Cumhuriyet Newspaper*, 30 June 1975). The bill also stipulated the terms of regional arms production. In 1975, Turkey signed a five-year economic agreement with Iran to establish a joint defence industry (*Hurriyet Newspaper*, 11 June 1975). The expansion of the Turkish tank industry in Kirikkale was also planned with Iranian financial assistance (*Hurriyet Newspaper*, 18 November 1975). In addition, Turkey undertook a series of joint industrial ventures with Libya. This included the establishment of an ammunition factory in Turkey, the construction of four submarines for Libya, and the sale of light and heavy machine guns, artillery pieces and shells to the Libyan army (*Gunaydin Newspaper*, 28 February 1978).

Transnational Islamic ties

In the period between the nationalization of the Suez Canal in 1956 and the Islamic Revolution in Iran in 1978-79, the Soviet Union achieved its greatest influence in the Middle East. During this time, Turkey, Iran, Egypt, Syria, Iraq, and Algeria received large amounts of Soviet economic and military aid. Egypt's debt to the Soviet Union, for example, was estimated to be US$ 11 billion by the early 1980s (Dawisha 1982: 11). After Nasser's death and Sadat's rise to power, Egypt and Saudi Arabia became closer, with the latter emerging as the strongest US ally in the region. Meanwhile, Soviet interests in Iraq and Libya increased.

Although Soviet-Iraqi relations were not based on an ideological alliance, the Soviet Union supported Iraq in its conflict with Iran over the Shatt al-Arab waterway in 1973 and 1974. Between 1972 and 1975 Iraq was able to double the size of its armed forces by doubling its procurement of Soviet arms supplies. This build-up of military strength was reflected in Iraq's dealings with the Iranian-supported Kurdish rebellion in the oil-producing areas around Kerkuk and Mosul, and in its conflict with Iran over the Iranian takeover of three islands in the Hormuz Strait. Iraq's suppression of Kurdish opposition also contributed to a convergence of interests between Iraq and Turkey.

In 1971, Iraq received a US$ 224 million Soviet loan for the construction of an oil refinery and two oil pipelines across Turkish territory. The loan was to be repaid in oil (Freedman 1978: 50). In 1972, with Soviet technical assistance and financial aid, Iraq was also able to nationalize the Iraq Petroleum Company (Golan 1990: 167).

Soviet influence over Libya was very slight. Qaddafi's coup d'état of 1969, considered one of the earliest manifestations of Islamic revolution (Anderson 1983), clashed with both Soviet and US interests. For Qaddafi, there was no difference between the Soviet Union, western Europe or the United States in terms of imperialist designs.

The Israeli-Egyptian peace agreement that followed the 1973 war brought Libya and Iraq closer to the Soviet Union, with Turkey providing a strategic link. The 1973 war created an environment conducive to Arab unity against the United States and Israel. Libya, Saudi Arabia, Kuwait, Qatar, Bahrain, and Dubai cut off all oil exports to the United States on 19 October 1973. The price of oil increased from US$ 2.59 per barrel in January 1973 to US$ 5.12 by October 1973 (Venn 1986: 199). However, the break with US foreign policy by Arab states did not improve their ability to exert greater economic and political influence in the region. Following an Egyptian-Israeli peace agreement on 19 March, major oil-producing Arab states led by Saudi Arabia lifted the oil embargo. Nevertheless, oil prices continued to rise to between US$ 16 and US$ 20 per barrel in December 1973. By 1980 the price reached US$ 40 per barrel. The Iranian Islamic Revolution and subsequent Iran-Iraq war had reduced the volume of oil available to world markets by between 4 million and 6 million barrels (Venn 1986: 202). Regardless, the Saudi-led termination of the oil embargo created disunity among Arab states and isolated Libya, Iraq, and Syria in the Middle East. This further circumscribed Soviet entanglements in the region.

While new political relations backed by the United States developed along the Saudi-Egyptian axis, the Soviet Union stepped up support for both Iraq and Syria. The Soviets also improved relations with Libya. The Soviet Union needed access to Middle East oil, even though it was a major oil-producing country. Warsaw Pact economic planning required the Soviet Union to provide 50 million tons of oil to its Pact partners between 1971 and 1975, and 70 million tons a year after that (*The Economist*, 22 July 1972: 82). Unless it raised the price of its oil or found additional sources of supply, the Soviet Union was not going to benefit from the increased oil prices of 1973-74. In 1974 the Soviet Union decided to raise the price of its oil to world market levels and demand that Warsaw Pact countries pay for it in hard currency (Sodaro 1990: 254). This was a pivotal turning point in Soviet-Warsaw Pact relations, pushing Warsaw Pact allies into a bilateral relationship with Western governments, private banks, and international lending agencies in order to secure economic aid (*The Economist*, 6 January 1973: 28). At the same time, it pushed the Soviet Union deeper into the shifting political and military alliances of the Middle East.

The Soviet Union centred its strategic thinking on the Islamic ties between Muslim states. Khrushchev (1953–64) had already employed this strategy when he cautiously mobilized Soviet Muslim intellectuals in the Middle East in an effort to promote the idea of Islamic unity against 'Western imperialism and Israeli aggression'. Soviet Muslims who were organized around the Afro-Asian Solidarity Committee and the Peace Partisans assembled several conferences in the Middle East. Kazakh writer Muhtar Auezov, a member of the Communist Party of Kazakhstan, was vice-chair of the Afro-Asian Solidarity Council. Saraf Rashidov, First Secretary of the Central Committee of the Communist Party of Uzbekistan, led the Cairo conference of the Afro-Asian Solidarity Committee in December 1957 and January 1958. And Soviet-Muslim Mirso Tursun Zade led the Baghdad conference of Peace Partisans in April 1959 (Bennigsen et al 1989: 29–34).

During the Brezhnev era (1964–80), the Soviet Union intensified its appeal to Islam in the face of Nasser's failure to unite Arabs. The Soviet Muslim religious establishment and Muslims from Central Asia and the Caucasus began to act as 'ambassadors' to the Muslim Middle East. The Soviet Muslim religious establishment, represented by four Muslim spiritual boards, was an effective instrument for advertising the 'freedom' offered to believers of Islam in the Soviet Union (Bennigsen et al 1989; Ro'i 1984). The boards promoted the idea that the Soviet Union, with a Muslim population of 50 million, was the best friend and partner of the Muslim world. At the Rawalpindi Islamic Conference in November 1968, the Soviet-Muslim delegation led by Babakhanov, head Mufti of the Muslim Spiritual Board of Tashkent, strongly protested US, Israeli, and British imperialism in the Middle East and presented the Soviet Union as a 'Muslim country' (Bennigsen et al 1989: 39).

In the 1970s, Islamic activity became increasingly connected on a global level through the informal exchange of intellectuals and preachers, and the hosting of international conferences. During this period, there was also an increase in the volume and intensity of exchanges linking the Soviet Union and Muslim Middle East. The Soviet-Muslim religious establishment focussed its activities on Islamic conferences in the Soviet Union, visits to the Middle East, and international journal publications. Between 1973 and 1979, official Soviet Muslim-religious delegations visited 20 Muslim countries. They visited Saudi Arabia seven times, North Yemen and Algeria twice, the Gulf states, Iraq,

Egypt, Syria, Jordan, Tunisia, Libya, Turkey, India, Pakistan, and Bangladesh once each, and several other Muslim countries in Africa. In the same period, 24 Muslim religious delegations from 20 Muslim countries visited the Muslim republics of the Soviet Union (Bennigsen et al 1989: 43–9). The most active Soviet Muslim journal at this time was *Muslims of the Soviet East.*

In October 1970, Babakhanov organized the first of many international conferences with the theme of 'Unity and Cooperation Among Muslim Peoples in the Struggle for Peace'. Official representatives from 24 Muslim countries and 100 Soviet Muslim functionaries attended the conference. In November 1973, the Tashkent conference was held with the theme of 'Soviet Muslims Support the Just Struggle of the Arab People against Israeli Imperialist Aggression'. Babakhanov chaired the meeting. In August 1974 a conference to commemorate the life and work of Imam Ismail al-Bukhari was held in the Soviet Union. This conference attracted high-level Muslim officials from 27 Muslim countries, including the Deputy Director of the Muslim World League. In 1979 a symposium was organized on 'The Contribution of Muslims From Central Asia, the Volga and Caucasus to the Development of Islamic Thought, the Cause of Peace and Social Progress'. It attracted delegates from 30 Muslim countries, as well as the Secretary General of the Muslim World League, Inanullah Khan (Bennigsen et al 1989: 50–2). Dr. Karacazmali from the Directorate of Religious Affairs represented Turkey at this conference. For his part, Foreign Minister Sa'ud al-Faisal expressed gratitude for 'the positive Soviet stance towards Arab causes' (Churba 1980: 355).

The Soviet invasion of Afghanistan in December 1979 was a significant setback for the Soviet anti-Western and anti-Israeli Islamic strategy. All Muslim states, with the exception of Libya, Syria, and South Yemen, condemned the Soviet invasion at the Organization of the Islamic Conference meetings convened in Islamabad in January and May of 1980. Khomeini publicly declared the Soviet Union 'the greatest Satan of all time'. The leaders of Saudi Arabia saw the invasion as part of a grand Soviet strategy to ultimately capture the oil-rich Persian Gulf (Goldberg 1984: 268).

With the occurrence of the Islamic Revolution in Iran and the Soviet invasion of Afghanistan, Islamic unity began to assume a different political and economic meaning than the 'anti-imperialism' of the Soviet Islamic strategy. The US government also switched its foreign policy from a pro-Israeli preoccupation to a positive engagement with Muslims. In addition to concerns that the growing power of political Islam in the Persian Gulf might deny US access to resources, the US government was motivated by a desire to render the Soviet Islamic strategy less effective. Moreover, the United States hoped to combat leftist political factions in pro-Western states of the Middle East, and to end the Soviet occupation of Afghanistan. In the process, Turkey was able at this time to restore its geo-strategic importance in the US-centred political and economic configuration of the Middle East.

The Organization of the Islamic Conference

The Organization of the Islamic Conference (OIC) was founded in 1972 as a transnational framework for an emerging Islamic bloc of Muslim states united on the basis of a common religion. The First Islamic Summit Conference of Kings and Presidents from 24 Muslim countries was held in Rabat, Morocco, in September 1969. Conference attendants agreed that Muslims should promote mutual assistance in the economic, scientific, cultural, and spiritual spheres. It was also decided that a permanent secretariat would be established to foster cooperation among member states. At the first Islamic Conference of Foreign Ministers held in Jeddah, Saudi Arabia, in 1970, decisions were made about the appointment of a secretary general. The Third Conference of Foreign Ministers held in 1972 approved its charter and declared the name of the organization to be the Organization of the Islamic Conference (Al-Ahsan 1988: 18–19). The OIC consists of 57 member states with a total combined population of approximately one billion people. Members are spread over an area of 26 million square kilometres extending from West Africa to Southeast Asia.

The organizational structure of the OIC consists of the Islamic Summit Conference of Kings and Heads of States and Governments, the Conference of Foreign Ministers, and the General Secretariat. The Islamic Summit determines general policies of the OIC, and the Conference of Foreign Ministers functions as the main decision-making body. The General Secretariat is the executive organ.

The General Secretariat works through various subsidiary organs. Its financial subsidiaries include the Islamic Solidarity Fund (ISF) (1974) and the Islamic Development Bank (IDB) (1975). Both are located in Jeddah and provide Muslim communities throughout the world with financial support for the social, cultural, and political empowerment of Muslims. Between 1976 and 1990, the IDB distributed funds totalling 2,013.64 million dinars (one dinar was equivalent to US$ 1.35 in July 1990) (Ihsanoglu 1996: 83–4). In the cultural field, the secretariat works through the Research Centre for Islamic History, Art and Culture, as well as the International Commission for Islamic Heritage. Both were founded in 1980 and are centred in Istanbul. The purpose of these research institutes is to reveal Islam as a complete way of life. The Rabitat al-Alam al-Islami, the ISF, and IDB provide their funding. In the commercial field, there are a number of subsidiary organizations. Among them are the Statistical, Economic and Social Research and Training Centre for Islamic Countries (1977), located in Ankara; the Islamic Foundation for Science, Technology and

Development (1975), located in Jeddah; the Islamic Centre for the Development of Trade (1981), located in Casablanca; and the Islamic Chamber of Commerce, Industry and Commodity Exchange (composed of national chambers situated in member countries of the OIC), located in Karachi. These organizations foster trade, investment, and labour migration among member states of the OIC.

There were earlier attempts to unite Muslims around an organization, prior to the founding of the OIC. From 1965, King Faisal of Saudi Arabia had wanted Muslims to unite as an *ummah* – one community 'believing in Allah, His Prophet and His laws' (Al-Ahsan 1988: 17). His calls aroused little excitement, however, as Arab states were divided between the pro-Western conservative monarchies of Saudi Arabia, Jordan, Kuwait, and Libya, and the nationalist and pro-Soviet revolutionary regimes of Egypt, Iraq, Syria, Algeria, and Yemen. Egyptians and Iraqi and Syrian nationalists had rejected Faisal's call for an *ummah*, believing that it represented an imperialist plot to take territorial control of Arab states out of the exclusive framework of nation-states (Moinuddin 1987: 70–1). With the Arab defeat in the 1967 Arab–Israeli War, the loss of Jerusalem, and the attempted arson at the al-Aqsa Mosque in 1969, King Faisal's Islamic unity idea gave way to the establishment of the OIC, supported financially by Saudi Arabia through the Rabitat al-Alam al-Islami.

The Rabitat al-Alam al-Islami (also known as the Muslim World League) is a Saudi-based transnational financial institution, founded in Mekkah in 1962. It was established to cover the cost of Islamic educational centres, places of worship, training courses, seminars, and Islamic conferences. It also provides funds to pay the salaries of imams and travelling preachers throughout the world. The Muslim Brotherhood and the Jamat-I Islami provide an ideological liaison that connects Rabitat al-Alam al-Islami funds to Islamic organizations worldwide. Particularly after the 1973 oil price hikes, when Saudi Arabia emerged as a financial giant, the Islamic Solidarity Fund, the Islamic Development Bank, and the Rabitat al-Alam al-Islami became very important to the expansion of Islamic organizational networks throughout the world.

The OIC declares that 'common belief constitutes a strong factor in rapprochement and solidarity among Muslim peoples, transcending ethnic/ racial and national differences' (Article 2 of the OIC Charter). Religion is the basis for membership. However, OIC members are nation-states, not individuals or non-governmental organizations. The OIC defines a Muslim state in terms of the number of Muslims living within the territorial boundaries of that state, but there is no consistent rule or policy. Not all of the citizens of member states are Muslims. Also, Muslim citizens of a non-member state are not included within the structure of the OIC. The Soviet Union, with a minority Muslim population of approximately 50 million, had presented itself as a Muslim society and participated in OIC meetings and conferences through the Soviet Muslim establishment. However, a number of countries with a Muslim majority, including Albania, the Ivory Coast, and Tanzania have not become part of the OIC. And, although the majority of its population is non-Muslim, Uganda has become a member. But Bulgaria, the former Yugoslavia, and other states with substantially larger Muslim populations have not become involved in OIC activities. The United States and Canada are not member states; neither Farakhan's Nation of Islam nor approximately 10 million Muslims living in the United States and Canada have been included in the OIC—but Turkish-Cypriots and the Moro Front of the Philippines have observer status. And, although a sizable number of its citizens are Muslims, the OIC has cancelled the membership of India (Al-Ahsan 1988: 45–55).

The First Islamic Summit Conference established that every 'Muslim state' is eligible to join the Organization of the Islamic Conference provided it is prepared to adopt the charter (Article 8). The OIC charter accepted the Islamic notion of *ummah* as the foundation for solidarity among Muslim countries (Al-Ahsan 1988). The Koran refers to *ummah* not only as a group of people bound tightly together by a common belief, but also to the belief itself (The Koran 6: 38; 10: 19; 16: 93; 43: 22-3; 16: 120; 7: 159; 11: 8; 28: 23; 7: 160; 2: 143; 5: 48). *Ummah* represents the religious unity found among all individuals who accept Islam as a way of life, regardless of the territorial division of Muslims by national states. This poses interesting questions for countries with secular constitutions or varied religious compositions. Turkey, a constitutionally secular state, has not ratified the charter, but continues to participate in OIC activities as a de facto member.

The charter does not require OIC member states to legislate Islamic principles or the *sharia* law in their constitutions. Rather, the OIC maintains a loose structure that relies on member states to apply its recommendations voluntarily. In order to furnish the OIC with legally binding power, Saudi Arabia has tried to establish the supremacy of *sharia* in OIC activities. Toward that end, the Rabitat al-Alam al-Islami organized an Islamic conference in Pakistan in 1976. At this meeting, also known as the International *Sharia* Congress, Turkey was represented by the Minister of State, Hasan Aksay, a member of the pro-Islamic NSP. The congress adopted the following principles to establish a legally binding framework for the OIC:

1) The constitutional frameworks of Muslim countries should be restructured according to Islamic principles and the Arabic language should be spread among Muslim people.
2) Civil laws should be replaced by the *sharia*.
3) Women should obey Islamic restrictions.
4) All necessary economic and political steps should be taken to establish modern Islamic states based on the *sharia*.
5) At every level of educational training, Islam should be taught as a mandatory subject.

6) The five principles of Islam should be memorized by all primary school students.

7) Secondary school students must learn the entire Koran.

8) In order to promote these goals, Islamic educational institutions must be established in each country.

9) In order to create Islamic unity, all Muslim states should first recognize and accept their Islamic attributes and then establish a confederation under the guidance of a commonly elected caliph (Mumcu 1994b: 174–5).

In a related development, the Third Islamic Summit of the OIC was convened in Mecca in 1981. It issued a document known as the 'Mecca Declaration', in which member states affirmed their willingness to promote solidarity on the basis of the Islamic principles of justice, equality, liberty, tolerance, and compassion. This document states that 'strict adherence to Islam and Islamic principles as a way of life constitutes the greatest protection for Muslims against the dangers which confront them' (Ihsanoglu 1996: 90). Member states also confirmed their commitment to the principles and aims of non-alignment. The Third Islamic Summit encouraged Muslim economic integration and created a 'Standing Committee for Commercial and Economic Cooperation' (COMCEC). COMCEC was based on a process of bilateral and multilateral trade liberalization among OIC member states. In essence, the OIC's emphasis on trade liberalization connected Muslim states to the neo-liberal structuring of the world economy as proclaimed by the UN during the Third Development Decade (1980–90).

As Moinuddin (1987: 108) suggests, the Mecca Declaration solidified the role of Islam as a strong moral influence on Muslim cooperation within the OIC framework. Turkish Prime Minister Ulusu saw the Mecca Declaration as reflecting the religious values and principles shared by Muslims throughout the world but reiterated that secularism was an unchangeable component of the Turkish constitution. He also stated that Turkey would remain within the Western security alliance. Nevertheless, Turkey has relied on Islam as a moral value in social and economic life. It continues to use the notion of Islamic solidarity, not as an alternative to its Western orientation but to strategically enlarge its foreign policy options and complement its relations with the EEC and the United States. As a result, Turkey has striven from the early 1980s to become a leading country in the economic and trade relationships of Muslim states through COMCEC.

The proliferation of transnational Islamic ties strengthened Erbakan's national vision of Turkish disengagement from a single Western orientation. At the same time, continued contact between Turkish migrant labour in Germany and homeland politics further reinforced Islamic activity beyond Turkey's national borders.

Turkish migrant labour and Islam

Although Germany banned labour recruitment in 1973, the overall number of Turkish workers in Germany continued to increase. Those who could obtain permission from the German authorities to stay brought their family members with them. In addition to family reunions, marriages with partners from Turkey and a high birth rate have contributed to an increase in the number of Turkish citizens in Germany. After the labour ban the Turkish population in Germany nearly doubled, reaching 30 per cent of the German foreign workforce by the early 1990s. With a population of more than 2 million, Turkish residents are now the largest minority group in Germany. Two out of three Turks in Germany are under the age of 30, the majority of whom are German-born (Kursat-Ahlers 1996: 119). Approximately 60 per cent of the new arrivals from Turkey who join their families are under 18 years old (Kolinsky 1996: 83, 89).

Germany does not accept immigration as a sufficient basis for granting German citizenship. It also refuses to link citizenship to place of birth. As a result, even those children born in Germany are given the nationality of their parents. Turkish migrants, then, live in Germany as 'foreign' citizens. About 38 per cent of these migrants live in poverty (Kursat-Ahlers 1996: 122), but most do not seek public assistance for fear of deportation. They live in ethnic enclaves, segregated from the larger society, uncertain of their status and residency rights, and subject to discrimination. Turks in Germany have experienced significant ethnic hostility and xenophobic violence, especially after the 1973 recruitment ban. The murder of Turks in Molln and Solinger in 1992 and 1993 is indicative of how extreme such hostility can be.

Many of Germany's Turkish residents prefer to live in either mixed neighbourhoods (53 per cent) or in predominantly German neighbourhoods (33 per cent) (Kursat-Ahlers 1996: 125). It appears that most do not wish to be isolated in ethnic enclaves. However, Germany provides migrants with no institutionalized channels of access to the political process, apart from the highly marginal foreigners' councils (Koopmans and Statham 1999: 665–6). The political context of discrimination and social exclusion in Germany, and the lack of citizenship rights have created and reinforced conditions for migrant identification with homeland politics. A significant aspect of this is the proliferation of Turkish Islamic associations in Europe.

As Levitt (2001) has demonstrated in the case of Dominican Republicans living in the United States, migrants maintain familial, religious, and political connections across national borders—between the country of origin and country of destination. These connections provide the means through which migrants form their cultural representation and exercise their group rights. Likewise, the Turkish residents of Germany configure claims to cultural community rights through their ties to Turkey.

Turkish-language newspapers and television channels closely connect migrants to homeland politics. In fact, some of the major Turkish newspapers have been printed and distributed in Europe since the 1970s. Among them are *Hurriyet*, with a nationalist liberal orientation; *Milliyet*, with a social democratic focus; *Milli Gazete*, with a pro-Islamic perspective; and *Tercuman*, with a strong nationalist focus. The state-owned Turkish Radio Television Network (TRT) has an international channel and is available on cable. Among the private channels based in Turkey are Euro Show, Euro Star, Euro D, Euro ATV, TGRT, Kanal 7, and HBB, all received on cable or via satellite in Europe. These channels broadcast news programmes from Turkey and produce programmes specifically for Turkish migrant communities in Europe. They also offer old Turkish movies, comedy shows, music, and sports for entertainment.

TRT-International plays a significant role in migrants' ability to establish claims of cultural belonging. The station holds 47 per cent of the Turkish audience (Kaya 2001: 97) and has become successful by broadcasting programmes that blend Kemalist principles of westernization and secularism with Islamic moral values. The TGRT and Kanal 7 channels have close connections to the pro-Islamic party in Turkey and attempt to depict daily social life through an interpretation of the Koran and Sunna.

The first transnational ties linking Turkish politics to Germany were established almost 30 years ago. There are now social democratic, conservative, and religiously oriented immigrant organizations in Germany. Social democratic and conservative organizations function as networks for state diplomacy, facilitating informal talks between Turkish and German politicians. These organizations also promote Turkey's membership in the EU and encourage the integration of Turks into German society as a culturally distinct group. There are about 2,000 Turkish Islamic organizations in Germany with an estimated membership of half a million people (Karakasoglu 1996: 168). The religious groups are diverse and divided between private and state-run organizations. Despite their differences, all aim to locate immigrant culture within the context of Islam.

The Federation of Social Democratic People's Associations was founded in Berlin in 1977 and currently represents approximately 40 organizations. It promotes Kemalist principles of secularism and is closely connected to the left-of-centre Republican People's Party (RPP). Indeed, one of its leaders, Ercan Karakas, has represented the RPP in the Turkish parliament. Germany's Ataturkist Thought Association, a close affiliate of the Federation of Social Democratic People's Association, has been organized to counter the spread of Islamic politics among Turkish migrants. And the Liberal Turkish German Friendship Association, founded in 1979 in Bonn, represents 55 Turkish associations in Germany (Ostergaard-Nielsen 2003: 52–5). It is closely connected to conservative political parties such as the Justice Party and its successors.

The *Suleymancilar* branch of the Naqshbandi order, the *Nurcu cemaati*, and the Association for a New World View in Europe (AMTG) are the most important privately run religious groups in Germany. They are among the first immigrant religious organizations founded in the country in the early 1970s. The AMTG has ties to the pro-Islamic National Salvation Party and its successors.

In the 1960s, when Turkish workers were recruited as guest workers, Islamic religious practice was considered a private matter. Pious Turkish migrants simply used available rooms in their hostels or factories as places of worship. Prayers were often led by someone in the community who took on the role of an *imam*. In the 1970s immigrants began to move out of temporary hostels to live with their wives and children as permanent residents in houses and flats. They also began to build mosques and open religious schools offering instruction on the Koran (Karakasoglu 1996). There are currently 1,350 mosques and prayer centres in Germany. The *Suleymancilar* and the *Nurcu cemaati* oversee the operation of 300 of them and the AMTG 275 (Ostergaard-Nielsen 2003: 56).

The *Suleymancilar* founded the Association of Islamic Cultural Centres in 1973 in Cologne. The organization, which has some 1,700 associations and 1,300 student dormitories throughout Germany, places great emphasis on religious education through private Koran courses (*Turkish Daily News*, 28 September 2002). Likewise, the *Nurcu cemaati*, founded in Cologne in 1979, has established approximately 200 schools in Germany where the *Risale-I Nur* of Said Nursi is studied and disseminated. The *Nurcu cemaati* has about 50,000 followers in Germany (Ostergaard-Nielsen 2003: 141).

In 1976, the Association for a New World View in Europe (AMTG) was founded in Berlin with the direct involvement of Necmettin Erbakan, pro-Islamic National Salvation Party leader. In 1997 its membership exceeded 160,000, with more than 57,000 mosque members. The AMTG's organization for women has a membership of 74,000. The ATMG publishes the monthly newsletter *National View and Perspectives*. The association has also founded the European Mosque Construction and Support Community to administer member organizations and property owned by the AMTG.

The AMTG does not have an organizational presence in Turkey. Many of its leaders are second generation, born and educated in Germany (Karakasoglu 1996: 169). Nevertheless, the leadership maintains strong ties to homeland politics. At present, the AMTG's secretary general is Erbakan's nephew, Mehmet Sabri Erbakan. Several members of the AMTG have been candidates in Turkish parliamentary elections; two of them were elected in 1995 and one in 1999.

The Turkish government has also established its own religious organization in Germany, the Diyanet Isleri Turk Islam Birligi (DITIB). An official religious organization founded by the Turkish state's Directorate of Religious

Affairs in 1982, the DITIB has 740 member associations compared with the AMTG's 262 (Karakasoglu 1996: 169). It oversees 775 mosques and prayer centres (Ostergaard-Nielsen 2003: 56). Leaders of the DITIB are employees of the Turkish state, appointed on a five-year basis and paid by the Turkish government. Many do not know German and provide religious instruction in Turkish using course materials devised by the Minister of Education in Turkey. While the Turkish state supports religious expression by Turks in Germany through the DITIB, it does so with the express purpose of blending Islamic sentiments with Turkish secular nationalism.

Privately run Islamic organizations promote Muslim integration into German society and work to improve the social and legal position of Muslims in Germany. They take an active stand on issues relevant to migrants' daily life experience, such as racism and discrimination in housing and employment. The programmes of private Islamic organizations cover a wide variety of leisure and social support activities including holiday camps, sports clubs, amateur radio courses, computer training, handicrafts, homework assistance for students, legal aid, school and work-place support programmes, translation services, and sex education.

The private Islamic organizations in Germany make cultural claims on the basis of principles of equality and individual rights and freedoms (Soysal 1997). When these organizations establish claims using universal referents to human rights discourse, they are not suggesting a belonging to a unitary nation-state of country of origin and residence. Rather, they are identifying with a transnational Islamic community of *ummah*. This is consistent with the content of the Mecca Declaration of the OIC, which states that loyalty to Islamic principles is the greatest protection for Muslims living in 'non-Islamic' environments.

Suleymancilar, Nurcu cemaati, and the AMTG provide funds for the construction of mosques, religious schools, student residences, boarding schools, and Koran courses throughout Europe and North America. Membership fees are their primary source of income. These organizations also receive financial support from Saudi-based financial institutions such as the Rabitat al Alam al-Islami and the Islamic Development Bank of the OIC through special funds allocated for Muslim communities abroad. The principal goal of these organizations and funding agencies is the refashioning of homeland politics and the worldwide promotion of Islam as a way of life. The ties established through workers' remittances and organizational leaders play a key role in linking homeland politics to global Islamic formations. The importance of transnational economic forces and their interaction with Islamic beliefs is the subject of the following chapter.

6

Cosmopolitan Islamists and Globalization

In earlier chapters, I described how the Turkish modernization project subordinated small- and medium-sized fractions of private capital to large industrial interests. I also examined the transformation of wheat-producing peasants into an urban wage-earning class and marginal workers. These groups were often the source of political conflict in Turkey, which various governments were able to contain within the favourable conditions of the Cold War. During détente, and under the impact of a debt crisis and subsequent economic recession, political conflict among the groups seeking to influence government allocation of scarce resources became commonplace. The military coup in 1980 suppressed political dissent, and subsequent civilian governments subordinated smaller fractions of private capital, rural populations, and labour within an export-oriented economic policy. This chapter examines the restructuring of the economy from the time of the military coup. It explores the emergence of a new group of Islamist capitalists within the economy and their relative position with one another, different capital groups, and the pro-Islamic political party.

The following analysis highlights the connection between participation in the global economy and Islamic beliefs. Max Weber (1971), who was interested in the effects of the Protestant ethic on the advent of capitalism in Europe, has shown the importance of cultural practices in mediating economic activity. However, the study of Islamic politics in functional terms does not allow us to uncover a much stronger link that exists between changes in the power configurations of the state, political regimes, and religion. Islamists interact with the deployment of state power, affecting the shape of that power and economic strategy. This interaction is based on the relationship between national political strategies and shifting patterns in the global economy of capitalism. In this light, the present chapter focusses on the shaping of an Islamic ideology. It does so by considering the political choices made by state ruling elites—including civil and military bureaucrats, and political parties—within the context created after the Islamic Revolution in Iran and the Soviet invasion of Afghanistan.

The reorganization of the global economy

Beginning in the 1970s the global economy experienced a major restructuring of the economic and political arrangements that had long been identified with the overwhelming dominance of the United States. The rising strength of western Europe and Japan, the impact of the Vietnam War, and the unwillingness of certain countries in the Third World to accept subordination—among them Vietnam, China, and Cuba—all contributed to the weakening of US hegemony (Wallerstein 2000). In 1971, the international monetary system became much more unstable when the Nixon administration unilaterally abandoned the gold standard by devaluing the dollar (Block 1977). This coincided with the collapse of the Bretton Woods system and the worldwide economic recession. Increasing protectionism between western Europe and the United States undermined Atlantic integration (van der Pijl 1989a). The Atlantic capitalists responded to declining profits by relocating industrial production from western Europe and North America to the newly industrializing countries of southern Europe, Latin America, and Southeast Asia (Hoogvelt 1997: 46–7).

Industrial relocation became a critical feature in the reconstruction of patterns of global capital accumulation. It represented a reversal in the development projects of Third World countries, away from import-substitution industrialization towards export-oriented industrialization (EOI) (Froebel et al 1980). EOI laid the foundation for the reorganization of the global economy around a 'global manufacturing system' (Gereffi 1994). In this system, transnational corporations integrate countries at diverse levels of development into commodity chains to produce part of an overall product for market sale. The financial resources required to organize the system were obtained from transnational banks eager to recycle Euro and Arab petrodollar surpluses generated from oil price hikes in the 1970s (Hoogvelt 1997: 49–50; 163).

The recycling of funds resulted in the accumulation of massive debt loads for Third World countries. By the end of the 1980s that debt reached US$ 1 trillion (Hoogvelt 1997: 50). As the number of countries unable to repay increased, multilateral agencies—notably the IMF and World Bank—instituted a global debt management regime to reschedule Third World debts (McMichael 2000: 113–46). These agencies tied debt rescheduling to the restructuring of production priorities and government programmes in debtor states—all within the intensively integrated global manufacturing system.

The process of global debt management institutionalized the authority of the IMF and World Bank within the organization and behaviour of states. As a consequence, state policy orientations have shifted away from the social goals of full employment, welfare provision, and public investment to debt-payment obligations. Although there is no agreement on the role of states (Arrighi 1999; McMichael and Mhyre 1991; Sassen 1996), national states and cultures have become subordinated to world capitalist production and its structure of class domination (Atasoy 2003c: 4). These changes have also introduced the 'nightwatchman' state of classical liberalism, with a new emphasis on the state's police powers and other control structures (van der Pijl 1989b).

The remaking of the global economy has been as much a cultural and political operation as an economic one. The assertion that market integration is inevitable reflects an ideological 'consensus' formation that simply 'accepts' growing extremes in wealth and poverty as inevitable (Carroll 2003). However, this consensus must continually be renewed, defended, and modified (Williams 1977: 112). Market consensus exists only by virtue of the political decisions of state managers in response to domestic and international political, economic, and cultural pressures.

In Turkey, the total foreign debt rose from US$ 13.5 billion in 1980 to US$ 104.5 billion in 1999, more than 50 per cent of the gross domestic product (Kazgan 1999: 224, 270). Beginning in 1978, the IMF imposed a debt repayment programme, transferring short-term private loans, which then constituted more than 60 per cent of the total debt, into long-term public loans. Considering that more than 75 per cent of the short-term loans were private loans, the state's ability to repay its debt was further diminished.

With the IMF rescheduling debts and the World Bank promising foreign loans, Turkey adopted the 24 January measures in 1980 to shift its development model to one emphasizing export-oriented industrialization. Turkey's debt rescheduling accounted for nearly 70 per cent of the total volume of debt renegotiated by all Third World countries between 1978 and 1980 (Celasun and Rodrik 1991: 193). Between 1980 and 1984 Turkey negotiated a three-year standby agreement of 1.2 billion SDR (Special Drawing Rights) with the IMF and five structural adjustment loans totalling US$ 1.6 billion with the World Bank. During this time, Turkey became a Baker Plan country. The plan was named after then Secretary of the US Treasury James Baker, who tied debt rescheduling to IMF- and World Bank-imposed structural adjustment programmes. Through the Baker Plan, Turkey received aid worth between US$ 10 billion and US$ 15 billion over a five-year period beginning in 1979 (US Congress 1979: 5633–4). These funds were intended to accelerate Turkey's process of structural adjustment to a market-oriented economic model.

The military regime (1980–83) and subsequent civilian government of Ozal's Motherland Party (1983–87) implemented the 24 January measures. The military leadership consolidated the market-orientation of the economy, and, as Evans (1985) has argued in relation to other Third World states, this involved strengthening the bureaucratic capacity of the state. Towards that end, the military coup successfully eliminated opposition to the 24 January measures. Almost immediately, coup leaders banned all political parties, and, with the exception of Turk-Is, shut down all three trade union confederations

(DISK, Hak-Is, and MISK) (Sakallioglu 1991: 57–69). The 1982 Constitution concentrated political power in the executive and limited the rights and freedoms of individuals. It also restricted the activity of trade unions and other associations. As a result, the government was able to change Turkey's development trajectory with virtually no scrutiny from its citizens.

Under Ozal's government, the Turkish economy shifted from a state-dominated and heavily protectionist economic model to a neoliberal market orientation. The neoliberal restructuring of the Turkish economy substantially changed the structure of relative pricing and income distribution in society. Between 1979 and 1985 there was a 40 per cent reduction in real wages and a 17 per cent reduction in agricultural incomes (Boratav 1990). Combined with the unemployment rate, which rose to 16.1 per cent in 1983, sharp reductions in wages and income pushed many into poverty. With the restructuring of society, the majority of citizens found their social welfare policies taken away, while only a small minority of large exporters benefited from the changes.

The 1980 Act on Foreign Trade Companies redefined large exporting companies that surpass a pre-specified export target as foreign trade companies. It also offered extensive tax and credit incentives, export-tax rebates, and exclusive trading rights. In 1985, there were between 24 and 30 large exporting companies, many of whom were subsidiaries of Turkey's largest industrial-holding companies (Ilkin 1991). This resulted in a spectacular growth in exports between 1980 and 1987 (World Bank 1987), averaging 25 per cent annually (Kiray 1990: 261). Exports rose in value from US$ 2.3 billion in 1979 to US$ 10.2 billion in 1987, accounting for 14.9 per cent of the GNP in 1985. By the end of the decade, the large foreign trade companies accounted for approximately 50 per cent of Turkish exports. Still, the subsidy effect of government incentives equalled roughly 55 per cent of the value of exports (*Milliyet Newspaper*, 20 June 1985).

In allowing the recycling of funds and debt rescheduling programmes of the IMF and World Bank to restructure Turkish society, the state consolidated the political power of the prime minister's office and high-level bureaucrats, particularly in relation to the government and the legislature. For example, the Undersecretary of the Treasury and Foreign Trade, created by the prime minister's office, significantly weakened the powers of both the ministry of finance and the ministry of commerce (Oncu and Gokce 1991). Without control over the treasury, the ministry of finance's role was reduced to a general directorate of customs and taxation, akin to a department of internal revenue. Similarly, the decision-making power of the ministry of commerce declined with the severing of foreign trade responsibilities. Other newly created departments included the Department of Foreign Investment, and the Department of Investment and Export Promotion and Implementation, all created by the prime minister's office. These departments held the powers of a ministry, but remained non-cabinet posts headed by an appointed technocrat answering directly to the prime minister. Managerial bureaucrats were largely independent of political and intra-bureaucratic pressures. As a result of these organizational changes in the state structure, funds were spent at the discretion of the prime minister without the prior approval of the government and parliament. Extra budgetary funds spent in this way by the prime minister's office reached 11.2 per cent of public investment in 1988 (Onis 1991: 33).

Changing geopolitical relations and Islam

The escalation of the war in Vietnam precipitated crises in relation to US military power and the legitimacy of Cold War ideology. The war in Vietnam and détente both weakened anti-communist sentiments and marked a rise in Third World nationalist movements. However, the Islamic Revolution in Iran and the Soviet invasion of Afghanistan represented a turning point for the US government's military power. During what Halliday (1984) has called the second Cold War, between 1978 and 1982, the United States intensified its military capacity to contain latent and growing challenges to US hegemony.

With the implementation of the Carter Doctrine in January 1980, the United States moved to reassert its military might. In the Persian Gulf region, the doctrine required the protection of Western oil and security interests, by military force if necessary (Kuniholm 1986). The United States also endeavoured to create a moderate Sunni Islamic bloc in the Middle East under the leadership of Saudi Arabia, with ties to NATO through Turkey (Churba 1980). The Organization of the Islamic Conference (OIC) prepared the political and technical ground for an Islamic economic union among member states (Moinuddin 1987: 120–7). The circulation of huge amounts of Saudi money among Muslim states in the Middle East helped to strengthen economic ties within the OIC. Saudi Arabia accounted for 42 per cent of the US\$ 450.5 billion petrodollar surplus held by OPEC members (Atasoy 2003b: 64). The Rabitat al-Alam al-Islami, the Dar al-Maal al Islami, and the Al Baraka Group circulated Saudi petrodollars among OIC states, along with the Islamic Development Bank, a subsidiary of the OIC.

With the second Cold War, Turkey regained the geopolitical advantage that was undermined during détente and the Cyprus War. The reward for Turkey's renewed status as an important Middle East player was the provision of aid. There is no doubt that Ozal's Motherland Party government used official aid funds to link Turkey's structural adjustment measures to the OIC.

The Ozal government allowed Saudi-based Faisal Finance and the Al-Baraka Group to establish themselves in Turkey. Together with the Islamic Development Bank, they were given special exemptions from Turkish bankruptcy laws (Mumcu 1994b: 183). The politically important and Naqshbandi-affiliated capital groups mediated the founding of these Saudi-based finance institutions in Turkey. Faisal Finance of Turkey was established with the active involvement of parliamentarians such as Salih Ozcan and Ahmet Tevfik Paksu (Mumcu 1994b: 180–3). The Al-Baraka Turk was founded as a joint venture with Korkut Ozal and Eymen Topbas. Korkut Ozal is a prominent Naqshbandi, a former NSP parliamentarian and minister of agriculture. He also worked as a consultant for the Islamic Development Bank. Eymen Topbas is a former chairperson of the Motherland Party's Istanbul provincial branch. By the early 1990s the Al-Baraka Turk and Faisal Finance of Turkey held an estimated one-tenth of all domestic bank deposits (Moore 1990).

Faisal Finance of Turkey, the Al-Baraka Turk, and the Islamic Development Bank (IDB) contributed to the expansion of Naqshbandi-affiliated companies. Well over 90 per cent of their funds were used to finance trade on the basis of non-interest-charging Islamic banking methods. These methods include a profit/loss sharing partnership with a client, and *murabaha* (Baldwin 1990: 32). The commonly used *murabaha* method involves a bank purchasing goods that a trader wants and then selling them at an agreed mark-up price (Khouri 1987: 18). In the early 1980s, the Islamic Development Bank held only 0.67 per cent of total foreign investments in Turkey. Between 1979 and 1983, Turkey received an average of US$ 75 million per year from the IDB. It received US$ 3 billion from the World Bank during the same period (Kazgan 1988: 331). Despite its relatively small contribution, Saudi capital and investment in the banking sector helped to strengthen newly emerging pro-Islamic business groups in Turkey.

By taking advantage of the overabundance of petrodollar funds in international markets, Turkey was able to connect with global circuits of capital. Set against the political backdrop of the US government's crisis management philosophy, Turkey found its niche within the framework of Islamic solidarity. The large exporting capital groups organized around TUSIAD and newly emerging Islamist capitalists came to appreciate the increasing possibilities for prosperity in the Middle East. Turkey intensified its economic ties with Iran, Iraq, Libya, and Saudi Arabia—countries that were responsible for 45.5 per cent of the total growth in Turkey's manufactured exports between 1980 and 1985 (Senses 1990: 64–5). Fuelled also by the outbreak of the Iran–Iraq war in 1980, Turkey's exports to the Middle East rose higher than its exports to EEC countries.

The inflow of foreign currency from Turkish contracting companies operating in the Middle East, and the workers' remittances from Turkish labour employed by these companies, represented Turkey's largest gains in revenue. By the mid-1980s, there were more than 300 Turkish contracting companies in the Middle East, with some of the largest revenues generated in Libya, Saudi Arabia, and Iraq. In 1986, the cumulative value of their contracts was approximately US$ 17 billion (Orhon 1989: 89–91). Between 1980 and 1986, the total number of Turkish migrant workers in Arab countries increased over 210 per cent, reaching 207,696. Saudi Arabia and Libya alone absorbed 72.7 per cent of these workers. By 1985, Saudi Arabia had the second largest number of Turkish migrant workers in the world; only West Germany had more. As a result, Turkey experienced a sharp increase in the inflow of workers' remittances, from US$ 983 million in 1978 to US$ 2,187 million in 1982 (State Planning Organization 1985: 351). This made up 35.8 per cent of Turkey's total export income in 1982 (World Bank 1984).

However, the collapse of oil prices in 1986 adversely affected Turkey's exports and its contracting companies in the Middle East, as Turkey's oil-exporting trade partners became debtor states. Although Turkey benefited from an oil bill that fell by over US$ 1.5 billion in 1986, its exports declined some 30 per cent, and the value of its contracts dropped considerably, reaching only US$ 18.5 billion by 1990. In 1987, the slowdown caused a 27 per cent reduction in the number of workers employed by these companies (Robins 1991: 109-10). Workers' remittances as a share of total export income also fell to 21.2 per cent by 1991 (Ongun 2002: 79).

With the weakening economies of oil exporting countries after 1986, Turkey participated in the creation of Muslim sub-regional arrangements. These included the Regional Cooperation for Development (Turkey, Iran, and Pakistan), the Association of South East Asian Nations (Malaysia and Indonesia), the Bangkok Agreement (Bangladesh), the Asian Clearing Union (Bangladesh, Iran, Pakistan), and the Economic Cooperation Organization (Turkey, Kazakhstan, Azerbaijan, Kyrgyzstan, Turkmenistan, Uzbekistan, and Afghanistan). These regional arrangements put together countries comprising more than 25 per cent of the world's Muslim population. By cultivating ties with Muslim countries, Turkey has demonstrated its continuing interest in the idea of 'Islamic unity' and has recognized Islam as an essential ingredient in its struggle for competitive advantage in the capitalist world economy. This has been the case for a number of successive governments including the military regime (1980–83), and subsequent civilian governments of the Motherland Party (1983–91), the True Path Party—in coalition with the Social Democrat Populist Party (1991–95), and the pro-Islamic Welfare Party—in coalition with the True Path (1995-97).

The collapse of the Soviet Union in 1989–91 transferred the global dynamics of political economy. Development strategies, class interests, the role of the state, and geopolitics have all been changed. The implications of these changes for the political structuring of capitalism are by no means clear (Hobsbawm 1994). As the US government persists in its desire to create a new world order, Turkey will continue its struggle to find a niche within this order in terms of its strategic relevance to the changing economy of capitalist accumulation. Turkey has long been in pursuit of the status of a truly Western state, but this has been conditional on its playing a subordinate role. However, there are now groups within the Islamic movement in Turkey that yearn to find strength through Islam in the global political economy. These groups include Islamist engineers, business groups, and industrialists. They maintain historically rooted ambiguities towards Western dominance in the global system, but their ideas are shaped as much by Western ideology as by Islamic references. These Islamic groups call for the union of Muslim states around a common market in the Middle East, the Caucasus, Central Asia, and Southeast Asia. Nonetheless, they support Turkey's proposed membership in the EU.

Turkish-Islamic synthesis ideology

The principal goal of the military regime was to depoliticize urban marginal groups and youth who came to play an important role in the growth of political tension during the 1970s. This required the suppression of every manifestation of ideological politics, especially leftist activity. The military promoted Islam while restructuring state organs and institutionalizing neoliberal policies in Turkey. The military also believed the Islamic concept of *ummah* was a panacea for containing the Left. Since the military was suspicious of more radical manifestations of Islamic politics, *ummah* was placed under state control. Thus, the military regime sought to combine Turkish nationalism with Islam by using the ideology of a Turkish-Islamic synthesis. Civilian governments also later adopted this approach. After coming to power in 1983, the Motherland Party (MP) gave the Turkish-Islamic synthesis ideology its particular form.

Although not an Islamist party, the MP's ideology, under the unique leadership of Turgut Ozal, represented a mixture of economic liberalism and nationalism, with some Islamic elements. According to Onis (1997: 757), it was Ozal's personality and his ability to combine a liberal Western orientation with a strong attachment to Islam that held the liberal and Islamic factions of the party together around the cause of economic liberalization. Under Ozal's leadership the MP managed to establish a broad-based coalition and promote the view that Turkey's economic development projects should rest on the moral/cultural legitimacy of Islam (Cakir 1993: 33, 38). After Ozal's withdrawal from active party politics, the ideological outlook of the party shifted to the centre-right.

The presence of a strong pro-Islamic faction within the party was a crucial dimension of the strategy that forged a link between Muslim cultural values and economic development. A holy alliance (*kutsal ittifak*) was formed between liberal and pro-Islamic groups within the Motherland Party, pressing for the institutionalization of a Turkish-Islamic synthesis in the state structure (*Turkish Daily News*, 20–25 June 1988). Great emphasis was placed on the role of religion within the state educational system in cementing conflicting societal demands. A more tolerant approach to the Sufi orders was also part of the national consensus project.

This new formulation of official state ideology settled one persistent question in the political debate over the role of Islam in defining the nation. The debate dates back to the second half of the nineteenth century when Ottoman reformers initiated a wholesale westernization programme to restructure the Ottoman state along secular principles. Islamists opposed the secularization project, and, as previously noted, advocated the adoption of Western technology but not its culture. However, founding leaders of the Turkish nation-state believed that technology and culture were constituent elements of a unified whole. Industrialization, then, would require the wholesale adoption of Western cultural values. With the establishment of the multi-party regime in 1945 and the rise to power of the DP in 1950, the intellectual debate on Islam re-emerged. By incorporating rural producers into the national economy the DP also integrated their Muslim beliefs and practices. During the 1970s, the debate over culture versus technology was revived within the pro-Islamic NSP. The national view ideology of the NSP popularized the theme of Western imperialism and questioned the presumed universality of a Western model. Under Ozal's leadership during the 1980s, the Turkish-Islamic synthesis ideology of the MP integrated Islam as a moral cultural value into the strategy of a competitive export-oriented economic model. MP ideology also connected Islam to a liberal Western orientation. The combined effect of these ideological shifts was that the West was no longer perceived as a coherent cultural unit of modernity but an economic power within the larger space of global competition.

It is indisputable that Islam has been a permanent partner in the ideological configuration of cultural politics since 1945. The strategy of the state has been to contain real or potential leftist and radical Islamist opposition within a modernist assertion of Islam in the state structure. However, this has not prevented the rise of an Islamic movement in national politics in which older Islamic Sufi orders and other religious communities are main players. What is especially interesting is their engagement with the process of globalization and their search for a way to participate in new markets using innovative technologies without becoming Western.

The political decision to develop a religious educational system played a significant role in the creation of a new genre of Muslim professionals employed mainly as engineers in the state bureaucracy and private sector. These professionals were the children of religiously minded rural small producers and urban lower classes. The intention was never to subvert existing hierarchies but to more effectively articulate a cultural link between the state and Muslims from rural and urban lower classes. The cultural articulation of these groups within the state structure was an urgent matter for leaders of the military coup. After the

1970s' economic crisis, Turkey could no longer export 'excess' labour to Europe. These workers entered into urban class politics as marginals making a living in the informal urban economy (Kilic 2002). For them, radical ideologies, leftist in particular, became strategic resources for political and economic empowerment. And for leaders of the military coup, state-run religious education became a strategic means for containing the radicalization of these groups.

Islamic education

In 1983, the State Planning Organization prepared a *Report on National Culture*. The report stated that the crisis of the 1970s was due to the corruption of Turkish moral and cultural values by 'divisive foreign' ideologies (State Planning Organization 1983). According to the report, these foreign ideologies prompted Turkish youth and intellectuals to imitate Western cultural values—a process destructive to national culture. Preservation of the nation's culture was a duty of the state, and national culture, according to the report, was the sum of tradition and belief culminating in religion.

Religious courses have been mandatory in the school curriculum in Turkey since the 1982 Constitution. This includes primary schools, middle-level high schools, and lycées. Religious instruction in the educational system reflects both the military's commitment to creating a new national culture and the determination of the state to regulate the practice of Islam. General Evren, leader of the 1980 military coup, explains the importance of state control over religion:

> Families should not give religious education to children. This would be improper since it may be taught incorrectly, incompletely, or through the family's own point of view ... I ask you ... not to send your children to illegal Koran schools ... religion will be taught to our children by the state in state schools (Evren 1991: 301).

The increasing importance of *imam-hatip* schools (for prayer leaders and preachers) and Koran schools underscores the role of Islamic education in Turkey. In 1951–52, there were only seven middle-level and lycée-level *imam-hatip* schools; by 1980 there were 588. From 1980 to 1986 the number of *imam-hatip* schools increased by 22 per cent to 717. The number of students enrolled in these schools also increased by 34 per cent, from 178,000 to approximately 240,000. In the 1985/6 academic year there were 5,600 official general high schools (including middle-level schools and lycées) in Turkey with 2.4 million students. The ratio of *imam-hatip* students to general high school students increased from one in 37 in the 1965/6 academic year to one in ten by 1985/6 (State Institute of Statistics). There are now 446,429 students, most from urban lower-class and rural families, attending middle-level and lycée-level *imam-hatip* schools. These schools provide them with alternative channels of upward mobility (Gokce et al 1984: 123).

The original purpose of these schools was to meet the demand for educated religious personnel, but this appears to be of secondary importance today. Although founded as vocational-religious institutions, *imam-hatip* schools were integrated into the secondary educational system in 1973 by the coalition government of the centre-left RPP and pro-Islamic NSP. This has transformed them into an alternative educational system that trains students to perform religious services and also prepares them for higher education. Most graduates continue their education in various university departments for careers in engineering, law, and medicine. They enter the job market as professionals and civil servants. In 1987, nearly 40 per cent of students in the Public Administration Department of Ankara University's prestigious Faculty of Political Science were graduates of *imam-hatip* lycées (*Cumhuriyet Newspaper*, various issues, 1987). The only institution not affected by this trend is the military. Military schools reject *imam-hatip* graduates. Nevertheless, the Sufi orders and *Nurcu cemaati* try to recruit young students who enter the military lycées by providing them with Islamic instruction in their homes on weekends.

The government strictly regulates the content of religious education in *imam-hatip* schools. The curriculum offers a blend of religious and secular courses so that students are able to gain employment in areas outside the religious profession. The schools are similar to private Catholic schools in North America. A study conducted by Aksit (1986) found that *imam-hatip* students expressed preferences for courses in mathematics, physics, literature, English, and Arabic, as well as courses in the Koran. Most of these students express a desire to continue their university education in engineering, medicine, law, and public administration; only a few plan to become prayer leaders and clerics. In fact, only 10 per cent of *imam-hatip* graduates are employed as prayer leaders and preachers (Directorate of Religious Affairs 1990). One-sixth of them are female. Female clergy are not yet accepted in Islam, so most of these women are unemployable in their professions. Table 6 presents data on the number of graduates from *imam-hatip* lycées who have obtained jobs in religious professions from 1980 to 1989.

Table 6: *Imam-Hatip* Lycée Graduates Who Have Taken Jobs in the Clerical Professions

Years	Number of graduates	Number of graduates employed by the Directorate of Religious Affairs
1980-1981	4393	0
1981-1982	9865	0
1982-1983	11222	2238
1093-1984	14347	3876
1984-1985	18467	3444
1985-1986	15257	4039
1986-1987	15971	7432
1987-1988	17758	7281
1988-1989	16640	5917

Source: Directorate of Religious Affairs Statistics (1990)

There is no data to suggest a link between the graduates of these schools and Islamists. We do not know how many Muslim professionals have *imam-hatip* school diplomas. However, it is well known that these schools create an attachment between young, upwardly mobile, and religiously educated Muslims, and the secular values and ideology of the state.

Koran schools are also part of the state-led Islamic educational system in Turkey. There are 4,925 Koran schools with 176,892 regular and 52,028 evening students. In 1996, 1,326,443 children attended summer courses in these state-controlled schools (Ayata 1996: 47). The Sufi orders and religious communities have also established unofficial private Koran schools and youth hostels, largely outside the official sphere of state control. Their mission is to provide private instruction in Islam to youth who have come from smaller urban and rural areas for an education in state schools. Fethullah Gulen's *nur evleri* (light houses) and the *Suleymanci* schools are the best-known examples of private Koran schools and hostels.

There is no publicly available data on the exact number of these private schools or their student enrolment and management. There is also no indication from the literature on whether there is interaction between the two types of Islamic education in shaping an Islamic mode of thinking in Turkey. In order to gain insight into the possible influence of private religious schools on the Islamic education of students in state-run schools, I conducted 18 interviews in Ankara during 2003. I also interviewed the principal of a *Suleymanci* youth hostel in a small Turkish town in 2002. To maintain the anonymity of my interviewees,

I refer to them only as 'respondents'. My interviews offer insight into how students in private Islamic schools become attuned to the norms and values of devout Muslims while pursuing higher education in the state-controlled secular environment of universities.

Nur evleri

The *nur evleri* are student houses affiliated with *Nurcu cemaati* that operates under the leadership of Fethullah Gulen. The *cemaat* has a rigidly structured hierarchical order and Gulen is its sole leader. The *mutevellis* (community organizers), *Abiler* (elder brothers), and *ablalar* (elder sisters) run *cemaat* activities at the neighbourhood level. Their exact number is not known, but as the *cemaat* has expanded throughout Turkey, the number of those who supervise and oversee *cemaat* activities has also increased. *Mutevellis* are those given a high rank in the *cemaat* hierarchy. They are selected from the most educated and dedicated *Risale-I Nur* students and receive advanced education from an even higher rank known as the *Nur talebesi*. Their education is based on studies of the Koran and the Prophet's Sunna, as well as the *Risale-I Nur* collection of Said Nursi, and Fethullah Gulen's books. The *mutevellis* periodically hold written and oral examinations. *Abiler* and *ablalar* are positioned in the lower ranks of the *cemaat* hierarchy and have limited knowledge of the activities of higher ranks.

The *nur evleri* are single-sex rented apartment flats, each housing seven students, and situated close to students' schools. *Abiler* operate the flats for male students while *ablalar* are responsible for the flats of female students. *Abiler/ablalar* are also students who live in the *nur evleri*, and are highly self-disciplined in the practice of Islam. There are no clearly stated rules which determine one's status as an *abi* or *abla*. The higher ranked *mutevellis* assign appointments in terms of one's level of knowledge and degree of maturity within the *cemaat*. My information here is limited mostly to the activities of women *mutevelli*. I am aware that men operate in a different manner but have very limited data regarding their activities. For security reasons, *mutavellis* reveal their identity only within trust-based networks. I was able to meet a female *mutavelli* through the personal connections of one of my respondents. My limited data on male *mutavellis* is due to my lack of connections to such networks.

The *mutevellis* connect students with Muslim business groups through monies collected for student scholarships. In general, male *mutevellis* collect funds from business groups, while female *mutevellis* organize fairs and other fundraising activities. The fairs, in which women sell homemade food and handcrafts, are highly successful. My respondent informed me that approximately US$ 25,000 was raised during one month's fundraising alone. *Mutevellis* also collect the required material for the goods they sell free of charge from Muslim commercial groups.

The *mutevellis* forward the monies raised to the *abiler/ablalar* to be distributed as scholarships and for household expenses. One *Fethullahci* woman told me that her husband gives about US$ 600 a year to their local *mutevelli* in equal monthly instalments. The sum is determined by the *mutevellis* on the basis of one student's monthly spending needs. The *mutevelli* I interviewed said that they decide on students' eligibility for scholarships after carefully examining their parents' socio-economic background. In particular, they try to assist lower-class students from smaller towns who have moved to the city for their schooling.

Students become aware of these houses and generally ask for financial support through their informal connections with other students in the schools. They also seek support through their parents' neighbourhood *cemaat* activities and while they are attending *dersanes* before university. *Dersanes* are privately run schools that offer students preparation courses for university entrance examinations. The *Fethullahci cemaati* often offers courses in their *dersanes* free of charge or for a small fee. The courses are taught by upper-level university student *abiler* and *ablalar*. The *abiler/ablalar* sometimes take these students who are preparing for university entrance exams to their *nur evleri*. One of my respondents told me that she spent two months in a *nur evi* preparing for her exams. Another respondent indicated that her parents could not afford the *dersane* fee when she was preparing for the exams, but through the help of one of her high school teachers she was able to enrol in a *Fethullahci dersane* in Ankara for free. She has since graduated from the Department of Chemistry at Ankara University and is now working voluntarily for the *dersane*.

According to one of my respondents, the *nur evleri* also often function as dormitories or hostels for out-of-town university students from modest lower and middle class families in small Anatolian cities or towns. They prefer these flats because they know that their daily activities will have a moral-religious focus. They organize daily religious *sohbets* under the supervision of the household *abi/abla*, and read and discuss the *Risale-I Nur* collection of Said Nursi, as well as the books of Fethullah Gulen. These students are also mindful of their daily prayers and endeavour to live their lives in accordance with the norms expected of a believing Muslim. The respondents whom I interviewed are pursuing their university education in the natural sciences and various technical subjects. They firmly believe that Islam will provide a spiritual foundation for them, which, when combined with the values of Turkish national culture, will allow them to become successful as they venture into the competitive relations of the economy.

A Suleymanci youth hostel near Ankara

In 2002, in a small town near Ankara, I interviewed the principal of a youth hostel run by *Suleymancilar*. I also interviewed a prominent and well-informed town resident. These sources provided me with valuable information on the importance of religious education in Turkey.

The youth hostel is in Gudul, a town of 3,000 Sunni Muslim inhabitants. Many are small family farmers involved in wheat, fruit, and vegetable production. Gudul is well known for the high quality of its cherries and grapes. The town has lost many of its younger people to Ankara, where they have found employment in small businesses established by former Gudul residents. Those who stay behind are generally older. Gudul also receives some new migrants from smaller villages nearby, but there is no migration from Gudul to Europe.

The former residents of Gudul who have migrated to Ankara maintain close ties with each other. Many are co-founders of the Association for the Development of Gudul, a group that organizes various fundraising activities. The association is small but ties between its members are strong, especially for self-employed members of the community. Members of the association are among the small- and medium-sized segments of private capital groups in Ankara. They are self-employed, mostly in the production and sale of fresh fruits and vegetables, as well as the animal hide trade and leather-processing industries. These migrants, some of whom are quite wealthy, maintain close attachments to their hometown and are considered their communities' most prominent, successful residents. Many provide the town with financial assistance through communal fundraising activities and private donations when necessary. In short, they have gained great respect as trusted, highly valued members of the Gudul community.

What is particularly interesting about this town is its school system. The number of school-aged inhabitants in Gudul is very small, but the town acts as a central administrative unit for surrounding villages, thereby attracting numerous students. Gudul has two primary schools and one public lycée run by the state, as well as a private youth hostel run by *Suleymancilar*. It also once had a middle-level *imam-hatip* school, which was closed down in 1998 after the so-called 28 February process, a repressive military campaign against Islamists.

The 28 February process led to the resignation in 1997 of the coalition government of the pro-Islamic Welfare Party. The military charged that the Welfare Party was behind the growth of reactionary religious forces directed against the secular regime. The party was consequently closed down and its leader Erbakan banned from politics for life. The military's manoeuvre is generally regarded as a 'soft military coup' because it did not actually result in the overthrow of the government by force. Nevertheless, it was decisive in firmly establishing tutelage over civilian governments. The 28 February process also banned all middle-level *imam-hatip* schools. Lycée-level *imam-hatip* schools were allowed, but could only operate as 'vocational and technical' schools for the training of religious personnel. The number of recruits was to be kept low and not exceed the number of expected job vacancies in various religious professions. The intention here was to prevent the growth of *imam-hatip* schools as an alternative educational system for students wishing to continue their university education in fields unrelated to religion. This is ironic, however, because military generals had initially supported the spread of *imam-hatip* schools and Koran courses in Turkey after the 1980 military coup.

The *Suleymanci* youth hostel was opened in Gudul in 1994 as a private residential school to serve students travelling back and forth every day from their villages to town to attend the state-run lycée and primary schools. The 28 February process prohibited primary school students from staying in private residential schools and hostels. Consequently, the hostel only accepts lycée students. It operates in accordance with the rules and regulations set out by the Ministry of National Education.

The *Suleymanci* hostel has a capacity of 86 students. At the time of my interview there were 31 students between 14 and 18 years of age residing there and three full-time certified teachers working voluntarily. Children who stay at the hostel are from lower-class peasant families and are not charged a residency fee while attending the lycée.

The public educational system in Turkey has suffered from cuts in state spending since the adoption of neoliberal economic policies in the 1980s. State-run schools now have double time instruction, the number of students per classroom has increased, and extra-curricular activities have been cut (Acar and Ayata 2002: 102–3). Nonetheless, students still receive instruction in 14 different subjects ranging from mathematics, literature, history, the natural sciences, and foreign languages, to physical education, music, and fine arts. My respondent from the *Suleymanci* hostel reports that the education received in the hostel complements and upgrades the quality of education provided by the public lycée. He points to the low level of university enrollment among public-lycée graduates compared to graduates of private foreign-language schools and the reputable Anadolu and science lycées. According to my respondent, graduates of the public lycées cannot compete with the graduates from these prestigious schools in the competitive, nationally administered university entrance examinations. As a result, he argues, the complementary education offered by the hostels is essential if these students are expected to move on to higher education. He states:

> There are 1,430,000 students who will write their university entrance exams but only 18 per cent of them will be accepted into the universities. The successful ones are most likely graduates of these elite schools. These children complement their education with private lessons to prepare for the university entrance exams. They are the children of rich families who can afford to pay for private lessons. Low-income families cannot afford such lessons and their children will remain high school graduates, with no chance of

going to university. They will be left without the necessary skills for employment in well-paying jobs. In my hostel we educate these students to be ready for the university entrance examinations. We are helping them to improve their chances in life. They deserve it.

The hostel provides a disciplined environment for religious and secular education. Students are expected to review the lessons they have learned during the day in the lycée. The hostel's principal and three teachers regularly attend these review sessions, which take approximately two hours in the afternoon and two hours after dinner. In addition, students are required to live in accordance with Islamic principles. They recite the Koran, learn about the life and practices of Prophet Mohammed, and fulfil the daily requirements of their religion. My respondent indicated that the hostel offers a mixed curriculum emphasizing the importance of both scientific technical knowledge and Islamic religious and moral values. This is reminiscent of the educational programme adopted in the Ottoman Empire during the Abdulhamit era. According to my respondent, this holistic type of education empowers students. In his words:

> State-run schools generate a feeling of powerlessness among the children of poor families. They have no chance of going to university. Our goal is to create a feeling of empowerment among them that will continue throughout their lives. They will learn how to become devout practicing Muslims, and develop a generalized orientation to Islam in their lives. They will also learn to connect their actions to moral judgements and principles. This will be their source of success.

My respondent adds: 'The hostel aims to counteract the degeneration of Turkish youth's moral and cultural values under the influence of a television culture that transmits loose and dissolute ways of un-Islamic, non-Turkish living.' To achieve this goal, the hostel supervises students' daily activities inside and outside the hostel. It also encourages students to be disciplined in their behaviour and act in ways consistent with Islamic moral teachings. It appears that the inhabitants of Gudul are keenly aware of this kind of moral instruction, although the pro-Islamic party does not receive any support from Gudul. One of the residents of Gudul whom I interviewed, a 65-year-old man, explained on the basis of his own personal experience how the hostel teaches students to act in a morally disciplined manner:

> I have cherry trees in my garden. One day last summer, I realized that some of the nearly ripe cherries from one tree suddenly disappeared. Judging from the pits scattered about, I realized that someone had

helped themselves. Not a big deal, I thought—only a few cherries. But I was waiting so patiently for them to ripen. So I was curious and wanted to find out who did it. I asked around a bit, mentioned this incident in the local coffee house, and then simply forgot about it. Not exactly a serious matter. It turns out that the principal of the hostel happened to be in the coffee house that day. A few days later two schoolchildren came to my home and apologized. They told me they saw the cherries on their way to school and decided to indulge. They also told me that their teacher had sent them to my house to ask what kind of punishment I believed appropriate for their behaviour [At this point my respondent was so touched he was crying.] Of course, I had no intention of punishing them. I told the students at once that they were forgiven. You know what ... they were from the *Suleymanci* school. Their principal had obviously made inquiries and the 'guilty' students immediately admitted that they had eaten the cherries. After the children left, I was again moved to tears. I thought to myself, that hostel is teaching them good moral values. And what is wrong with that? Do you think that the children of the state lycée would do the same thing? I don't think so. Quite the contrary, they most likely would have 'talked back' to me, and called me a stingy old man.

This respondent is a devout Muslim, but not a supporter of the pro-Islamic party. To his way of thinking, the *Suleymanci* hostel offers a solid religious education and teaches values that are desirable within the general culture.

The *Suleymanci* hostel receives monies raised by the Association for the Development of Gudul, as well as charitable donations from successful members of the Gudul community now living in Ankara. These donations are particularly generous during the Muslim month of Ramadan and the Festival of Sacrifices. However, the exact amount and source of monies raised for the *Suleymanci* hostel and other private religious schools is not known. There is no publicly available data to clearly establish external financial connections. There is evidence, however, to suggest that remittances from Turkish migrant workers, especially those in Germany, have funded an ever-growing number of private Koran schools and youth hostels organized by religious orders. During the 1980s, Saudi capital was also a source of funding for these schools and hostels.

Saudi capital and Islamic education

Through Faisal Finance of Turkey and the Al-Baraka Turk, Saudi capital has played a significant role in the founding of several *vakifs* (religious charity and educational foundations) and private Koran schools. Naqshbandi-affiliated members of the new and growing Muslim business sector provided the liaison (Atasoy 1998). Among these *vakifs* are the Bereket Vakfi and the Ozbag Vakfi.

The Bereket Vakfi provides students with scholarships for religious education, organizes conferences, and offers financial support for religious publications. For example, Al-Baraka Finance supplied the pro-Islamic newspaper *Turkiye* with 833 tonnes of paper between 1984 and 1985 (Mumcu 1994b: 194). The Ozbag Vakfi was established to build new mosques, open Koran schools, provide financial assistance to students receiving a religious education, and support research.

There is no firmly established link between the *imam-hatip* schools and transnational Islamic institutions. However, it has been documented that from 1982 to 1984, the Saudi-based financial institution Rabitat al-Alam al-Islami paid monthly salaries of US$ 1100 to Turkish *imams* working in western Europe. These religious leaders were state employees appointed by the Directorate of Religious Affairs (Mumcu 1994b: 171–3). Between 1984 and 1987, Saudi finance was also used to pay the salaries of many Turkish university instructors teaching Arabic in Turkey. The Imam Mohammed Ibn-Saud Islamic University of Saudi Arabia supplied the funding. In addition, the Saudis have contributed to the construction of many new mosques on university campuses.

I should note that these schools constitute half of the antinomy in the emergence of Islamist alternative schooling. The schools have also become an effective means for the state to gain moral control over the rural and urban lower classes through a formal curriculum that articulates Islamic and secular education. This is a compelling finding. It demonstrates that religious education allows students to combine a secular line of thought, as advocated by the state, with Islam—thus supporting my earlier contention that Islam and modern/ global cultural values cannot accurately be seen in opposition to one another.

A conceptualization of the role of Islamic education in creating congruence between Islam and the modern/global would be incomplete if it failed to take into account the position of newly emerging Muslim professionals in the post-1980 neoliberal globalization era.

Islamist engineers and Western modernity

An examination of the biographies of a group of professional Islamist engineers illustrates how their education bridges the presumed divide between Islamic and modern ways. This group is actively involved in the assertion of cultural meanings in an effort to reposition itself in the global circuits of the world economy.

Interestingly, most of the new engineering managers come from modest lower-middle class families in small Anatolian cities and towns (Gole 1993).

During the 1980s, they came to hold highly strategic positions of power within the state bureaucracy. Much of their upward social mobility was due to significant achievement in technical education. We do not know how many engineers have *imam-hatip* diplomas, but some do have such a background. What is well known, however, is that their Islamist orientation is largely related to their family background and education in private Koran schools.

Their biographies clearly illustrate the presence of a very strict Muslim morality in their work ethic—an important factor in the struggle of these Islamists to reposition themselves as a distinct capital fraction, competing in both national and global circuits of capital. I offer two illustrative quotations from Gole's biographical study of these engineers. The first pertains to a manager from an Islamic banking institution.

> I am 42 years old. I was born in Eskisehir, and completed my secondary education there ... I was brought up in a Muslim family, in a Muslim environment. At the university, I studied mechanical engineering. Then I attended a one-year postgraduate programme in business administration. I spent a year and a half in England and, for three years, taught at a university in Saudi Arabia. Then, for four years, I worked as an expert at the SPO. Now I am working in a private company (Gole 1993: 207-8).

The second quotation relates to an engineer who also has a combined religious and secular education.

> I was born in Maras. I am the first engineer in my family. Since the time of my grandfather, every member of my family has been well educated. But they all studied religion [through private lessons]. It was only I who studied the 'profane sciences'. I graduated from the Engineering Faculty of Istanbul Technical University, and ran an engineering project company. Then I taught at a university. I resigned from my post at the university on 17 September 1983, and became a founding member of the MP (Gole 1993: 208).

These engineers played a prominent role in formulating Turkey's new export-oriented industrialization model. They claim that their logical-scientific approach, mathematical reasoning, and access to technical language enable them to provide better solutions to Turkey's problems.

The Muslim engineers do not have a preconceived, stereotypical image of the West. Rather, their view reflects a give-and-take relationship within a strategy of economic competition. The West, accordingly, does not pose a threat to the moral-cultural integrity of Muslims, and Islam ceases to be an ideological force in opposition to Western ways. These engineers see no contradiction or conflict between Islamic values and competitive participation in the market economy. One engineer clarifies this point:

> There are several dynamics which shaped the West. First of all, there is the idea expressed by Dostoyevsky in his book *The Brothers Karamazov*, namely: 'If God does not exist everything is permissible'. Since the period of the Enlightenment, there is an approach which only accepts the reality of the five senses of human beings. Another dynamic is the one that deifies the will of the individual, which comes from liberalism and is identified with the formula, laissez-faire, laissez-passer. And finally, the aspiration to engage in consumption—that is the ultimate goal of these societies; to consume means to be happy. One of the alternatives to this material civilization is Islam (Gole 1993: 214).

For Muslim engineers, Islam does not require a complete rejection of the West. Rather, Islam is seen as a cultural component of the economic activity that these engineers promote. It is part of an effort to strengthen their entrance into the competitive relations of the economy. As another Muslim engineer states:

> We have to be an open society. We have to leave behind the dogmas of the Left and Right, and keep an atmosphere of debate. Turkey is, in fact, beginning to display vitality. There is a new generation, between 30 and 35 years old, in blossom. They are the ambitious young professionals who speak two foreign languages and are impatient to expand towards the world market (Gole 1993: 216).

Muslim engineers articulate an Islamist position that combines Muslim cultural values, pragmatism, and the competitive logic of the globalized economy. In concert with other Islamist groups, they argue that the Turkish economy could be among the most dynamic in the world economy if the younger generation was given a knowledge of national culture based on their Muslim heritage. This position explicitly incorporates Islamic references in the integration of the Turkish economy with Muslim countries of the former Soviet Union, the Balkans, and the Middle East.

The fusion of Islam and the modern gives a distinctive character to Turkish society. It highlights the growing importance of Islamist capitalists in the economy. But the blending of Islam and the modern is not only a general consequence of a particular Islamic education. It depends on a political-economic context that stimulates such a fusion. That context has shaped a strategy now being used in the competitive class politics of various capital groups. The blending of Islam with secular thinking implies increased opportunities for Islamists to advance new demands within the state structure. It also suggests that they are using this opportunity to produce well-articulated economic strategies and to search for a way to participate in new markets without becoming subordinate to the West or Western lifestyles.

Islamic political economy in Turkey

Islamists, like other devout Muslims in Turkey, root their individual and collective social lives in religious beliefs and values. Islamist groups who are among the small, medium, and large capital fractions also refer to their Islamic faith and cultural community. Members of large capital fractions in particular strive to increase their competitiveness in the global economy. They are highly educated professionals adept at using new technology. However, they are not fully incorporated into the political structure of the state. Nevertheless, their reference to Islamic moral principles of justice and equality equips them with a sense of entitlement. Similarly, Islamists of small- and medium-sized capital fractions hope to increase their economic opportunities and their access to state resources and incentives.

Islam appears to help construct cross-class alliances. It brings small- and medium-sized Islamist capital fractions together with globally competitive Islamist professionals under the unifying rubric of social justice and equality. Moreover, the Islamic education of Muslim children who attend state-run religious or secular schools helps build bridges between Islamic values and the competitive relations of market capitalism.

It is important to underscore the fact that there is no unified community of Islamists, nor is there one coherent Islamic ideology. Political Islam in Turkey can more accurately be characterized as consisting of internal cleavages between the pro-Islamic political party, Sufi orders, professionals, and intellectuals. The following section offers an analysis of the pro-Islamic party in Turkey.

Pro-Islamic parties

The changes in the organization of the economy and the state structure in the 1980s and 1990s transformed Turkey into a country of disillusioned citizens, repressed workers, neglected rural communities, and disempowered small producers. Excluded from government incentives, smaller companies either went bankrupt or were swallowed up by mergers. The political suppression of small capital interests and labour resurfaced as the pro-Islamic party articulated an agenda of social justice based on Islamic morality. The coalition politics of the Motherland Party fragmented as some members of the Islamic faction joined the

Welfare Party, while other members of the liberal faction moved to the centre-right True Path. Even though the Islamic movement cannot be reduced to a single ideological orientation, overall it gained considerable momentum during the late 1980s and 1990s. The Welfare Party (WP) emerged as an oppositional movement in response to a particular strategy designed to integrate Turkey within the global economy. It shared the national view ideology of former pro-Islamic parties.

The WP, which arose in the 1980s, and then the Virtue Party of the late 1990s, articulated a strategy that elevates the protection of small- and medium-sized capital interests to a position of central importance in Turkish politics. The Islamic political movement has favoured the protection of smaller capital interests and labour against a globalization project based on the free trade economy. This is evident in the public statements delivered by Erbakan (1990), leader of the party. There is no hard evidence that the pro-Islamic party supports reinstatement of a theologically-centred politics, but there is a basis for arguing that the pro-Islamic party cultivates an ideology based on moral responsiveness to smaller capital interests.

The pro-Islamic party blamed the development managers of the state, whom they defined as corrupt, for appropriating the nation's wealth and wasting it on a small number of large-private industrialists from the Istanbul region. In addition to having concerns over Western imperialism, the just economic order rhetoric of the WP focussed great attention on moral and cultural issues related to improving the material position of the poor (Onis 1997: 753). This was the WP's response to the negative impact of neoliberal economic restructuring for the masses in Turkey.

According to State Planning Organization statistics (1996), the wealthiest 20 per cent of the population in Turkey increased their share of income distribution from 49.9 per cent in 1987 to 54.9 per cent in 1994. The income of the poorest 20 per cent of the population decreased from a very low 5.2 per cent of total incomes in 1987 to 4.9 per cent in 1994. While 80 per cent of the population (excluding the wealthiest segment) experienced income decline between 1987 and 1994, the incomes of the wealthiest 20 per cent increased. Middle class incomes declined from a share of 35 per cent in 1987 to 31 per cent in 1991. There were also regional differences in the distribution of incomes; cities in central and eastern Turkey fared much worse than Istanbul and the surrounding area. While the just economic order rhetoric of the WP was built on these consequences of neoliberal restructuring in the Turkish economy, the party did not see any contradiction between a social justice-oriented distributional programme and private wealth accumulation. Such wealth accumulation was seen as perfectly consistent with basic Islamic principles (Atasoy 2003b: 67).

Despite a commonly held principle of social justice in redistributive policies, the NSP and WP diverged in their approach to the role of the state in the economy. During the 1970s, the NSP's emphasis was on active state involvement in heavy industrialization projects (Erbakan 1975). The WP advocated the adoption of an export-oriented economic model similar to that of Southeast Asian countries (Erbakan 1990). This difference is related to the fact that the WP tried to accommodate the interests of newly emerging Islamist capitalists in its party programme. Both parties, however, shared the belief that economic growth is facilitated by education in modern sciences and advanced technology. They also shared a Third Worldist perspective on economic 'imperialism' and the global spread of Western cultural values. The NSP and WP promoted an Islamic world-view and rejected the appropriation of Euro-American values, customs, and fashions (Atasoy 2003b: 67–8). The two parties further agreed that national principles are enhanced by the Islamic moral and spiritual values of daily life experience. This reflects the Islamist desire to be moored to an Islamic moral-spiritual universe in the social realm. I have examined the significance of this earlier in my coverage of the ideas of Necip Fazil Kisakurek, Said Nursi, and the Naqshbandi order.

The following analysis of Islamist business covers the economic activity and ideological position of the Sufi orders, Muslim business associations, and Islamic financial institutions. I pay special attention to the differences among these Islamists relative to a particular Islamic ideology advocated by the pro-Islamic party—one based on the protection of small capital interests.

It is very difficult to differentiate Islamist capital groups from secularists. Islamists are an integral part of the larger Turkish economy, and are subject to the rules established by the secular state. There are no specifically Islamic rules of conduct to distinguish Islamist activities from other secular business groups. Even the Islamic prohibition on paying or receiving interest is not strictly observed by all Islamists (Bugra 1998). Therefore, I have restricted my analysis to those business groups with ties to religious communities and the business associations in which Islam is used as an organizational strategy.

Islamist business

The Naqshbandi order and the *Nurcu cemaati* direct Islamic ethical thought strategically towards the establishment of entitled groups that recognize Muslims as members of a previously marginalized cultural category. This is consistent with the ideological position of the pro-Islamic party vis-à-vis small capital groups. As civil society–based movements (Ozdalga and Persson 1997), religious communities prepare these entitled groups to participate in the global economy.

Religious communities emphasize the moral self-renewal of individuals, but this has not influenced Islamists to rethink the global economy or to find ways of reversing it. While interest in re-establishing a connection with community-based living is evident in the general critical scholarship on globalization (Mander and Goldsmith 1996), a critical approach to globalization is largely absent within Islamist thinking, with the exception of a few Muslim intellectuals. Ali Bulac (1978, 1983) and Ismet Ozel (1976) are two of the exceptions who are highly critical of capitalism. For the most part, however, religious orders and communities play an active role in preparing Islamists to venture into transnational power relations in business. The invisible universities of the religious orders increase the power of Islamists to respond to the highly competitive relations within the global economy (Gurdogan 1991). Individual self-renewal is directed towards developing an Islamic work ethic and enhancing the cultural capacity to think above and beyond community-based economic activity. This vision does not include alternative principles and practices to the present market economy, industry, and technology. Rather, it actively promotes Islamists' involvement within the global economy. As a result, the number of large companies with direct connections to religious orders and communities has increased.

By the mid-1980s, the Naqshbandi and *Nurcu* movements began to constitute the core of Islamist-led large capital groups. Holding companies and financial institutions with direct links to these movements are now expanding into global markets and have invested in Bulgaria, Romania, Albania, Bosnia, Russia, the Muslim republics of the former Soviet Union, the Middle East, Germany, and the United States. The Naqshbandi order has played a significant role in the wealth accumulation of Islamist families with trade and investment ventures in the Middle East—most notably, the Ozal and Topbas families (Mumcu 1994b). The Server Holding Company, which comprises 38 firms operating in various sectors of the economy, is directly affiliated with the Naqshbandi order (Bulut 1999: 75-6). Another business group affiliated with a particular branch of the Naqshbandi order is the Ihlas Holding Company, part of the *Isikcilar* community of Enver Oren. It has economic investments in the media, the automotive industry, marketing and finance, insurance, electrical appliances, machinery, food, construction, and foreign trade.

Another religious community affiliated with the *Nurcu cemaati* operates under the leadership of Fethullah Gulen. Gulen is a retired *imam* who previously worked as a state employee for the Directorate of Religious Affairs. He has a large group of followers known as the *Fethullahcilar*, which began to increase in size after the 1980 military coup. Gulen's approach to Islam is moderate and combines Turkish nationalism with Islamic values to form a liberal brand of Turkish Islam (Aras and Caha 2000). Gulen views Islam as a private matter and wants to create a Muslim community that opposes politicized Islam. He has frequently criticized the policies of the WP for creating a political crisis situation that threatens the secular system in Turkey. In 1996, Gulen rejected comments made by Prime Minister Recep Tayyip Erdogan, who was then mayor of

Istanbul. Erdogan, had stated that: 'The minarets are our bayonets, the domes our helmets, and the mosques our barracks'. For Gulen, these words represented an attempt to bring down a democratically elected government and undermine a constitutionally grounded political system.

Gulen, who received both a secular and religious education in his training as an *imam*, shows a remarkable ability to fuse Islam with Western modernity. In a manner reminiscent of Weber's *Protestant Ethic and the Spirit of Capitalism*, Gulen's (1997) ideas can be aptly described as an examination of the Islamic ethic and the spirit of global capitalism. However, in contrast to Weber's (1947) belief that Islam leads to mystical contemplation or otherworldly asceticism, Gulen's Islamism is not built on the Weberian idea of tension between mysticism and asceticism. In fact, Gulen sees no contradiction between Islam and a market economy. Rather, he envisions an economic model based on continued capital accumulation through scientific and technological innovation. For Gulen, the worldly affairs of the economy should not be conflated with the spiritual rules of religion; they are separate, although economic activity should not go against the spirit of religion. The Fethullah Gulen *cemaati* mobilizes small- and medium-sized business groups based largely in smaller Anatolian cities. This expanding group of export-oriented capitalists exerts pressure on the state to increase their access to resources, thus allowing them to compete with large industrialists and commercial groups. Gulen argues that ways must be found to mobilize the hidden wealth of devout Muslims in support of these business groups and to establish large-scale firms capable of entering foreign markets. He further emphasizes the importance of 'self-discipline' and hard work to the success of these firms. In *Altin Nesil* (Golden Generation) published in 1978, Gulen stresses the need for young Turks to learn about modern science and technology, and to combine this secular knowledge with Islamic morality for the purpose of contributing to the financial power of the state. This is known as *hizmet* (service) to one's country, which Gulen (1996) believes is the most important way to gain God's favour and a place in paradise. However, *hizmet* can only be met through discipline and perseverance in the highly competitive relations of the capitalist global economy.

The Gulen group appears to be among the richest of Islamist groups and the fastest growing of all capital fractions in Turkey, with about 500 affiliated firms. In 1996, it also founded Asya Finance and Isik Insurance. Asya Finance raises funds for investment in the Turkic republics of the former Soviet Union. Gulen is particularly interested in founding schools abroad, as well as in Turkey. The Gulen group has established more than 250 middle- and lycée-level schools in the Central Asian republics of the former Soviet Union and the Balkans. Asya Finance acts as an intermediary between the Gulen schools and the funds collected from Muslim business groups by the *mutevellis*. These schools provide high-quality education in English and therefore attract children of the elite and high-level government officials in Central Asia. I was told by a *mutevelli* that the teachers in these schools are from Turkey and working abroad on a voluntary basis. The Gulen schools promote cultural identity formation among Turkic-Muslim populations on the basis of a Turkish-Islamic synthesis model. According to Ozdalga (1999), students who graduate from these schools are suitably prepared to hold important positions in their countries. Gulen wants his schools to contribute to the development of political elites in the Muslim countries of Central Asia and the Balkans, countries that view Turkey as their state model. There are now more than 20,000 schools founded by the Gulen group in Turkey. In addition to teaching moral-religious values, these schools use the same curriculum as state schools and operate under state regulation. The Gulen group operates seven universities, five abroad and two in Turkey (Bulut 1999: 57, 83–6, 300). It publishes a monthly journal, *Sizinti* (Disclosures), and two academic journals, *Yeni Umit* (New Hope) and the *Fountain*. It also organizes national and international conferences in which participants discuss issues related to Islam and science, democracy, modernity, and religious tolerance. The Fethullah Gulen *cemaati* publishes a daily newspaper and operates a TV and radio station as well.

Both the Fethullah Gulen group and the Naqshbandi-associated-holding companies, along with their affiliated agencies, combine an Islamic sensibility with a strong nationalist ideology. This strategy is directed towards the protection of newly emerging capital groups and expansion into the markets of the former Soviet Union and the Balkans. It makes effective use of Islam as an ethical instrument for mobilizing Islamist economic activity in the competitive relations of the market economy.

The Association of Independent Industrialists and Businessmen (MUSIAD)

MUSIAD, which presents an alternative class strategy to that formulated by the Association of Turkish Industrialists and Businessmen (TUSIAD), is a non-governmental umbrella organization, founded in 1990 by a group of young businessmen. In 1996, there were close to 4,000 member firms. TUSIAD, with a membership of approximately 400, represents the largest industrialists and advocates an open-trade regime, as well as integration with EU markets (Ilkin 1993). MUSIAD, on the other hand, has a different membership base with wider regional representation from smaller Anatolian cities. It aims to sustain and improve its members' competitive capacity in national and international markets. It also promotes closer economic ties between Muslim countries. Most MUSIAD member firms were established during the 1980s and vary greatly in size.

MUSIAD generally represents smaller firms employing fewer than 50 workers. In terms of geographical distribution, Istanbul has the highest number of MUSIAD members (523 in total), but most of the firms are located in smaller cities. The largest sectors of concentration for these companies are construction and construction materials, textile and leather, and food and beverages (Bulut 1999: 102).

MUSIAD has in general articulated a class strategy favouring the small-business interests of less advantaged cities. Its mission statement indicates that MUSIAD 'activates and spreads entrepreneurial spirit based on the free initiative' of its members. Nonetheless, MUSIAD's position in relation to a free trade economy is not clearly established compared to the secularist TUSIAD. Looking at the relative position of large Islamist companies within MUSIAD, the degree to which small capital interests are incorporated into MUSIAD's strategy also seems less clear. The number of large companies within MUSIAD employing over 100 workers is significant. The very largest companies include Kombassan Holding, Yimpas Holding, the Ulker Group, Saray Biscuits, and Al-Baraka Turk.

Kombassan, for example, was established in 1988 by a school teacher in Konya, a small Anatolian city. The biography of its founder, Hasim Bayram, resembles that of other Anatolian Islamic capitalists who came from similarly modest family backgrounds. Bayram was born into a very poor family in a village near Konya. His family owned a small plot of land that was used to grow grain for household consumption. His father was often unemployed. Bayram received his religious education in the private Koran school of his village and from his family. His upward social mobility was largely due to his education in state schools and the support of his father, who worked for some time as a janitor. Bayram graduated from university as a chemistry teacher, and then continued his studies in chemical engineering. In the immediate aftermath of the 1980 military coup he resigned from teaching after being demoted to the position of janitor because of his pro-Islamic political orientation. After being unemployed for a few years, he worked as a teacher in a private *dersane*—a school designed to prepare students for their university entrance examinations. Bayram then opened his own private *dersane* where he improved his financial and business skills. In 1988, he founded Kombassan with the encouragement of a friend working in the State Planning Organization (Dincel 1999: 151–65).

Kombassan began by producing paper products and then expanded into tourism, transportation, finance, a retail sales chain, and various manufacturing interests. With 60 factories and 100 firms, Kombassan now employs almost 30,000 people in Turkey. It has investments in the Balkans, the Central Asian republics of the former Soviet Union, Germany, and the United States (Bulut 1999: 302–4). Kombassan has more than 40,000 shareholders, none of whom is allowed to hold more than a 1 per cent stake in the company (Morris 1999). The source of the investment funds is the 'hidden' wealth that pious Muslims keep 'under their pillows', frequently in the form of gold jewellery, and particularly the bracelets worn by Muslim women. For many devout Muslims, depositing money in conventional banks is sacrilegious, since they believe that earning interest is against the teachings of the Koran. Bayram estimates that Turkey has as much as US$ 400 billion in such 'idle' wealth (Dincel 1999: 163). By opening up its companies to public investment, Kombassan mobilizes this hidden wealth. According to unofficial estimates, several billion dollars have been invested in Muslim companies in this manner. The other major source of capital is the remittances from Turkish workers in Germany, although there is no hard data on the transfer of workers' remittances from Europe to Islamist corporations in Turkey. This kind of capital movement is mostly funnelled through the informal channels of religious communities. Enormous investment funds have been mobilized from abroad in this way. Bayram, for example, visited Turkish migrant communities in Europe and received monies from them. Although he does not reveal his connections to religious communities in Europe, Bayram has stated that Turkish workers in Europe constitute the largest group of Kombassan shareholders. It is also well known that the Association for a New World View in Europe—AMTG—(the national view organization in Europe) collects cash donations from migrants in the mosques and sends them to Islamic corporations by private courier (Bolugiray 2000: 127–48).

MUSIAD has ideological ties to the pro-Islamic party and other Islamist groups in Turkey. It would be wrong, however, to assume that all small- and medium-sized companies that have an Islamic orientation are represented under the umbrella of MUSIAD. Large firms affiliated with MUSIAD do have an Islamic outlook, but according to Onis (1997: 759), only a fraction of highly successful small- and medium-sized firms with an Islamic orientation are affiliated with MUSIAD. The representation of smaller firms that have an Islamic orientation is not unique to MUSIAD. There are other organizations in Turkey, such as TOB, that have such firms within their membership. According to Bugra (1998: 528–30), what is unique to MUSIAD is its use of Islam as a basis for co-operation and solidarity among business groups. For MUSIAD, Islam has become a means to create secure market niches and sources of investment finance, as well as a way of containing potential social unrest and labour militancy.

MUSIAD organizes conferences on political and economic issues, establishes special commissions and professional committees, and arranges international fairs in Turkey and abroad. In all of these efforts MUSIAD aims to enhance the solidarity of its members. It is also committed to providing its members with access to information on recent technological innovations, marketing, and global production and trade patterns. In general, Islam is used as an important resource in MUSIAD's class strategy to create a sense of unity among smaller capital groups. This strategy is intended to promote the establishment of larger companies capable of competing in external markets.

These companies represent newly emerging Anatolian small-town capital in competition with the traditional business establishment in Istanbul.

MUSIAD has constructed a cultural-political category of Muslimness to describe those who are marginalized in the Turkish economy. It does not demand that their members be active practitioners of Islam, but they must be believers. One common theme discussed in MUSIAD's publication *Homo-Islamicus* (1993–97) is how to reassert Islam as a source of morality within the competitive relations of the economy, and how to link it to modern technology. MUSIAD urges Islamist businessmen to do everything necessary to be successful in the markets without sacrificing Islamic morality. This is seen as a form of worship, as it is carried out in the service of God. Writing against a certain association of Islam with the mystical realm, Erol Yarar (n.d: 3), the first president of MUSIAD, states: 'One mouthful food, one short coat was misconceived and opened the way to sluggishness. As a result, motivation toward the world was lost completely.'

The Islamist encouragement of wealth accumulation, as I have illustrated through the examples of MUSIAD, the Sufi orders, and other religious communities, leads to the following question. To what extent is the Islamist desire for wealth accumulation framed with reference to the distinction between the West and non-West in the competitive relations of the global economy? Islamic projects in Turkey promote the idea that Islam is compatible with the competitive logic of the global economy and the major features of global culture. This is also evident in the cosmopolitan approach Islamist engineers have adopted to underline their ideological orientation. Here the relevance of the non-West is played out with respect to the promotion of Islamic solidarity among Muslim nations, both to secure markets and to strengthen Turkey's ties with Muslim countries such as Malaysia and Indonesia (MUSIAD 1996). Yarar opposed any kind of trade relations with European Union countries, as well as the customs union agreement into which Turkey entered in 1996. Alternatively, he advocated an economic union with Islamic and Central Asian countries. In 1996, MUSIAD proposed that a cotton union be established among Turkey, Pakistan, Uzbekistan, and Turkmenistan (Atasoy 2003b: 74).

In this chapter, I have shown that various fractions within newly emerging Islamist capital groups use Islam as a strategic resource for capital accumulation. There is also an increasing number of economically mobile and morally motivated Islamist capital groups. To be sure, some Islamists, especially those organized within the pro-Islamic political party, focus on protecting small capital groups and labour from the negative effects of market competition. However, the strategies of the newly rich Islamist groups are directed at participation in the global economy. These Islamists formulate a cultural disposition of openness to the world rooted in an Islamic morality through which Islamic culture embraces international economic competitiveness.

The Islamist focus on competitive engagement with the global economy breaks the ideological connection between the cultural arrangements of the West, as described by Weber, and the economy. Islamists view Muslim values as a distinct element in the competitive strategy. This reflects a political desire to emerge as a competitive force in both the national and global circuits of the economy. The West now represents a competitive partner, and not a model for emulation in the cultural realm. This dimension of the Islamist project expresses an ultramodern instrumentality that is caught between westernizing social practices and global economic competition. Herein lies the ambivalence involved in Islamic politics—buying into Western ways while challenging the West's claim to general cultural superiority.

The issue may prove to be more complex and contentious than merely identifying the relevance of Islam to the global economy. This is related to the subordination of cultural values and practices to the requirements of the market economy. Polanyi describes the emergence of political movements for self-protection as being embedded in the cycles between the market economy and the local space of territorial states. Drawing from Polanyi, one can argue that Islamic politics shapes a strategy for protecting and strengthening those who are adversely affected by global market forces. This reflects an Islamist desire to gain better access to resources while making a competitive principle in class politics spiritually acceptable. Such a Polanyian interpretation of Islamic politics in Turkey adds a twist, in terms of political culture, to an understanding of the state and economy. However, the potential conflicts between locally and globally oriented Islamist groups might involve more than a process of reshaping relations between the national state and a market economy. Whether or not Islamists will solidify into a unified position is uncertain, but for the time being they are engaged in promoting Islam as a strategic resource in the class politics of Turkey. This may very well signal the beginning of a new kind of political economic formation emerging out of regional cultural-political attachments. There is no clear indication as to what exact form it will take in the near future. But it is quite clear that Islamists are repositioning themselves. This requires rethinking the political economy of Islamic politics and its relationship to the market and the state. And it certainly compels us to reconceptualize Islam beyond a binary opposition between the global and culturally local.

7

Turkish Islamists in the Post-Cold War State System

In the previous chapter I demonstrated that even if the Islamist critique aims to graft Muslim moral and cultural practices onto economic activity, it does not represent an alternative to a neoliberal way of organizing the economy. Rather, Islamists are formulating a cultural disposition for competitive engagement with the global economy. In fact, Islamists appear to be adopting elements of nineteenth-century evolutionary thought based on scientific knowledge. That knowledge engenders the modern myth of a universal modernity built around what Polanyi has called the 'self-regulating market'.

Moreover, Islamist groups have emerged as contending forces struggling to shape the political agenda. However, it is not clear what it means to connect Islamic politics to the state, culture, and economic organization. It definitely leads us away from a conventional theoretical emphasis on the resurgence of traditional local culture that rejects market competition and capital accumulation, but it also involves more than merely identifying the relevance of Islam to the global economy. The Islamic political standpoint may very well signal Islamic cultural entanglement in the intensification of global capitalist rivalries. This is a complicated issue. In earlier chapters I illustrated that Islamist groups in Turkey are not offering qualitatively different ways of organizing economic and social life. They continue to anchor their politics in the realization of modernity through European progress ideology. As Islamists act to reposition themselves in society and the economy, they also move away from univocal cultural interpretations.

It is surprising that some scholars continue to position Islamic politics within a binary view of 'Islamic' and 'Western', thereby claiming an ideological and political opposition between the two. Although we have seen a proliferation of publications on Islam in recent years, little sustained attention has been given to the meaning and character of Islamic politics in the global reshaping of the post–Cold War economy. Interestingly, scholarly analysis occasioned by recent events such as the attacks of 11 September 2001, and the US war on al-Qaeda, Iraq, and the Taliban regime in Afghanistan, continues to conceptualize Islamic politics in a confrontational manner. If an understanding of Islam in the current context of global political and military uncertainties is important, we must provide a clear historical account of Islam, as well as an assessment of its mass appeal in the world today.

Islam and the global economy

According to Hobsbawm (1994), the end of the Cold War produced tremendous uncertainty in the geopolitical ordering of the world economy. Wallerstein (1995) has expressed a similar view. He believes present insecurity in world politics is rooted in the ideological confusion created by the end of the Cold War and the collapse of liberalism. The liberal ideal that emerged in the aftermath of the French Revolution triumphed under US dominance in the post-1945 state system as a global ideology of the world capitalist system. In Wallerstein's view, the Cold War had contained international inequalities with the promise of modernization and a means to 'catch up' with Western states. But modernization failed to achieve a democratic and egalitarian social-economic system in non-Western societies. Islam has now become a political project for those who wish to build solidarity in the struggle to '"catch up" and move to the head of the line' (Wallerstein 1995: 7).

According to Huntington (1996), the main purpose of the West's universal pretensions to cultural superiority was to win over the political and military loyalty of non-Western nations to the capitalist camp of the NATO alliance. With the end of the Cold War, Islam emerged as an antithesis to the universality of Western cultural practices and political dominance in the state system. In contrast to Wallerstein, who believes Islamic politics is rooted in the failure of modernization, Huntington argues that the Islamic revival is based on the growing power of non-Western societies, which is being fostered by the success of modernization itself. Either way, Wallerstein and Huntington both conceptualize Islamic politics as constituting the ideological battleground in the capitalist world economy after the Cold War. The confrontation is rooted in the political response of the non-Western Islamic world to the dominance of the United States. The United States has reacted to the challenge by employing military force when required to protect the global status quo.

Thus far, the United States has shown no sign that it will refrain from taking military action to assert its military supremacy and protect its geopolitical position in the non-Western world. Since WWII, the United States has been at war many times and in many places, including: China (1945–46, 1950–53); Korea (1950–53); Guatemala (1954, 1967–69); Indonesia (1958); Cuba (1959–60); the Belgian Congo (1964); Peru (1965); Laos (1964–73); Vietnam (1961–75); Cambodia (1969–70); Grenada (1983); Libya (1986); El Salvador (1980s); Nicaragua (1980s); Panama (1989); Bosnia (1995); Sudan (1998); Yugoslavia (1999); Afghanistan (2001–present); and Iraq (1991–present). Although defeat in

Vietnam weakened its hegemonic position, the Islamic Revolution of 1978-79 in Iran posed a greater challenge to US dominance. Both these events underscored the inability of the United States to enforce its vision of the geopolitical ordering of the world.

It was at this juncture that the US government began to focus on what Halliday (1984) has called the second Cold War. It started with President Carter's undermining of the Nixon-Brezhnev détente in the late 1970s, and then deepened with Reagan's Star Wars initiative in the 1980s. The second Cold War was also fought in Africa and Asia through US support of moderate Sunni Islamist groups (Gaddis 1982; Rashid 2000). Initially, the Carter administration was concerned about the possible unsettling effects of the Iranian Islamic Revolution on Turkey, Iraq, and the Arabian Peninsula. One of Carter's senior advisors, Zbigniew Brzezinski, even lobbied for military intervention in Iran. After coming to power in 1980, Reagan frequently referred to Islamists as radical anti-Western extremists and became increasingly confrontational with them. Nevertheless, both the Carter and Reagan administrations saw the Soviet Union, and not Islam, as the real threat to the United States and its allies in the Third World. The US administration sought to solve a range of regional problems through its support of monarchical and conservative 'Islamic' regimes in Saudi Arabia, Pakistan, and Afghanistan. CIA support of Islamist groups in Afghanistan was an extension of the US Cold War policy of containing socialist and nationalist movements in the Third World. The 11 September 2001 attack appears to be a 'blowback' from the US Cold War policy of fostering Islam as a strategic alternative to the growth of Soviet influence and indigenous national independence movements.

With US assistance, Islamist groups eventually drove the Soviets out of Afghanistan. By 1991 the Soviet Union had collapsed and the Cold War was over. With the election of George Bush in 1989, Islamic politics was redefined in relation to the upsurge of radical Islam against Western domination of the global system. A number of key events figures in this redefinition. At the regional level, these include the 1989 military coup in the Sudan, which installed an administration allied with the Islamic National Front, and the 1991 electoral victory of the Islamic Salvation Front in Algeria. In the latter case, a subsequent civil war claimed 80,000 lives after the Algerian military's annulment of the elections in 1992 (Gerges 1999: 73–85).

The Gulf crisis of 1990–91, triggered by Iraq's invasion of Kuwait, represents a significant attempt by the United States to re-establish dominance over its allies in the post–Cold War period. The concept of a new international order coined by President Bush demonstrates the United States' willingness to use military force to solve conflicts in and between non-Western states. And yet, the US-led military intervention by coalition forces in Iraq, similar to Anglo-French actions at Suez in 1956, spurred the growth of nationalist opposition against Western interference in the Arab Middle East. This rise in nationalism rapidly became entangled with Islamic sentiments and a new Third World assertiveness.

Khomeini in Iran, Turabi in the Sudan, and the Muslim Brotherhood in Egypt shaped their politics by perpetuating the idea of a perennial conflict with the West. The new international order rhetoric of US policy-makers suggests that they expected this conflict to be revived at the end of the Cold War. In reality, as previous chapters in this book show, the invocation of Islam in Turkish politics is not an outcome of anti-Western attitudes embedded in a transhistorical understanding of what is 'Islamic' and what is 'Western'. Rather, it coincides with the emergence of national groups engaged in a struggle to reposition themselves in society and the economy. In their identification with an Islamic political perspective, these groups espouse a rights and freedoms discourse directed against state oppression, economic inequality, and external domination. Interestingly, when the US administration backed Islamist groups in Afghanistan and supported conservative regimes in the region, it inadvertently helped Islamic political factions to mobilize opposition movements. The appearance of Islamist groups on the front stage of Turkish politics also took place in the context of the second US Cold War, particularly during the Gulf War when George Bush and Turgut Ozal established closer relations. From the Turkish pro-Islamic parties to the Egyptian Muslim Brotherhood, these groups demand greater representation in national politics. All are committed to changing social and economic structures that generate oppression and inequality.

The Clinton administration agreed with the former Bush administration that Islam poses a challenge to the centrality of the US role in rerouting world capitalism. The United States did not have a coherent foreign policy to deal with the geopolitical and ideological uncertainties of the post-Cold War era. Nevertheless, the fear of what was interpreted as reactionary anti-modernism by Islamist terrorists led the Clinton administration to closely follow Islamic political activities in the Persian Gulf, Egypt, Algeria, Saudi Arabia, and Turkey. At the same time, the United States isolated Iran, the Sudan, and Libya for assisting international Islamic terrorism.

The 1995 election victory of the pro-Islamic Welfare Party in Turkey and the formation of the Welfare-led coalition government in 1996 were matters of great concern to the United States. Prime Minister Erbakan visited Iran and Libya in 1996 and signed a US$ 20 billion agreement with Iran to buy natural gas. The gas deal came just one week after the US congress passed an anti-terrorism law (on 5 August 1997) barring other countries from trading with Iran and Libya, since they were seen as sponsoring international terrorism (Celik 1999: 84). Erbakan's desire to form an Islamic commonwealth called the Developing Eight (D-8)—including Turkey, Iran, Pakistan, Indonesia, Bangladesh, Egypt, Malaysia, and Nigeria—was interpreted as a sign that he was slowly moving Turkey towards an anti-US alliance with radical Islamic states, particularly Iran. But Turkey has remained firmly within the US-led Western security alliance. The Welfare government also retained military and security cooperation agreements with Israel (Aybak 2002: 224). Nevertheless, the Clinton administration was uncomfortable with the pro-Islamic Welfare government establishing ties with Iran and Libya.

It is not credible to think that Turkish rapprochement with Iran and Libya challenged US security interests in the region. Erbakan did not change the foreign policy orientation of Turkey; he was a nationalist who hoped to make Turkey the regional leader by balancing Turkey's relations between Western and Muslim states. The US administration doubted that the pro-Islamic Welfare government could contribute to the continuation of US military and financial power in the region. Interestingly, when the Welfare government resigned under pressure from the Turkish military following the 28 February process, the Clinton administration had already shown a willingness to maintain ties with a pro-Islamic government that did not threaten US interests in the region. The US strategy was to pacify nationalist challenges to its position in the global system, rather than changing internal political regimes, Islamic or otherwise.

The United States does not require an Islamic 'enemy' to assert its post–Cold War hegemony. In fact, the global economy of capitalism requires no enemy at all, whether it be communism, Islam or anything else (Halliday 1999: 107–32). The weakness experienced in the US economy since the 1970s has made the United States unable to use its leadership to deflect world economic crises. Nevertheless, a faction within the US political elite continues to use coercion—military, economic, and political—as the only viable means for maintaining the global status quo (McCormick 1989: 186–90). The end of the Cold War environment has extended the US military and political capacity to realign its international power by responding to challenges to its global leadership. From this perspective, the ability of the United States to tie Islamic regimes to the West is central to its international position. To this end, the United States recruits subordinate allies and enlists their support in times of need.

The Clinton administration refashioned the global pre-eminence of the US state through neoliberal globalization (Panitch and Gindin 2003), which is essentially a political experiment in corporate regulation. It sweeps away the ability of national powers to regulate capital and subordinates their cultures to a presumed universal Western model of modernity (Atasoy 2003c). Islam does not tell us whether or not devout Muslims should embrace neoliberal globalization or modernize according to a European model. In reality, Islam is best understood as an attempt to realize European modernity through the application of scientific knowledge and progress ideology (Gray 2003). In order to enforce its international power, suppress oppositional movements, and reconcile with disputants, the United States supports monarchical and conservative regimes. This is certainly the response of the United States to its fears of an Islamic assault on the West. McCormick (1989: 186) argues that America's capacity to act as a world police force works through the formation of sub-imperialism—the use of substitute secondary powers to act on behalf of the dominant power in a given region.

Turkey is an important ally in the regional configuration of US hegemony. The Clinton administration did not see the pro-Islamic Welfare government as aggressively anti-Western and it was not against its removal from power as long as it did not involve a military coup. In light of the tragic outcome of the Bush administration's sanctioning of the military coup in Algeria (Gerges 1999: 78), US policy-makers were worried about a possible military coup in Turkey. Secretary of State Madeleine Albright's message was clear when she stated: 'Whatever changes people are thinking about they [should pursue them] in a democratic context' (Gerges 1999: 216). The Turkish military saw this as a sign that the US government was supportive of the military's concerted efforts to pressure the nationalist Erbakan and the Welfare Party to resign. With the founding of the AKP in 2001 the pro-Islamic party's references to capitalism assumed a more neoliberal perspective, while maintaining a sensitivity to the power of Islamic cultural practices.

The divergence of the AKP from the Islamic national view ideology of Erbakan represents a change in the class relations of Islamist capital groups in Turkey. Newly rich Islamist capitalists want to integrate into the processes of capital accumulation as a culturally distinct group within a global capitalist economy. They believe that the basic economic interests of Islamic enterprises will thrive within the global economy. In contrast to the rhetoric of the national view ideology, Turkish Islamists now raise the possibility that Turkey may very well become an industrial and economic powerhouse in the region, and play a dominant role in connecting the Islamic world to the West as partners in a global economy. The AKP's push for Turkey's full membership in the EU reinforces this as a political possibility—that Islamist capitalists be incorporated into a broadening of the political alliances of corporate regulation.

The state system after the Cold War

The complement to neoliberal globalization is a reworking of the international state system. However, its political structure is unknown. The Clinton administration tried multilateralism as a means to reconstitute US dominance in the world capitalist economy. It redefined the international role of the United States in managing the global economy through the help of the World Trade Organization (WTO), by promoting a policy of strategic cooperation and partnership with Russia, China, and North Korea. This policy alternative has shifted towards an aggressive unilateralism with the current administration of

George W. Bush. Bush's unilateralism does not obliterate the trend towards an open market economy in favour of a policy favouring only US national interests (Atasoy 2003d: 200). Despite growing economic difficulties, the capitalist market economy is broadening and deepening in most parts of the world, including the Muslim world. The new rhetoric of George W. Bush has redirected US foreign policy towards international competition. For example, as China becomes more powerful, the United States, under the Bush administration, is moving away from a policy option of promoting partnership and, instead, embracing strategic competition. This move was centred on the probability of a conflict with China over the Taiwan Strait. The Bush administration has initiated a new arms race with China, coinciding with the prospect of arms sales, including the Aegis missile radar system, to Taiwan. The emergency landing of a US surveillance aircraft on Chinese soil after a mid-air collision with a Chinese F8 fighter plane in 2001 has only served to intensify this combative stance. The Bush administration has also distanced itself from Europe and Europe's Balkan problems in Macedonia, Kosovo, and Bosnia. Bringing the Arab-Israeli conflict to an end was not on the agenda either.

Of course, the Bush administration's position on national interest is not confined to strategic-military relations. In addition to flexing its muscle with Canada and Europe over new missile defence proposals, and keeping North Korea and Iraq in focus as active enemies, the decision to pull out of the Kyoto Protocol and hostility towards the UN conference on racism are among the policy initiatives designed to push the US national interest agenda forward. All these examples are indicators of US unilateralism under the Bush administration. This does not terminate the multilateralism of the Clinton era. However, by aggressively projecting US world supremacy, the Bush administration twists multilateralism to suit US interests. The 11 September 2001 attacks on the World Trade Center and Pentagon have privileged the US administration with the 'right' to deploy military power and assert military supremacy in the global system.

When the air-strikes began on Afghanistan, Osama bin Laden was personified as evil incarnate, and the Taliban were targeted for harbouring that evil. The Taliban collapsed almost immediately during the US military campaign, but the war on terrorism did not end there. The US administration developed what appeared to be an open-ended list of 'terrorist' targets, including groups such as Hezbollah and Hamas, and states such as Iraq. But it was a highly arbitrary list. Syria and Iran were listed as terrorist states before the September 2001 attacks, but accepted into the loop of coalition building against terrorism. On 9 October 2001 Syria was even elected a new member of the UN Security Council. Iraq was defined as a terrorist state before its war with Iran, but taken off the list of terrorist states during the conflict. Then, after it invaded Kuwait, Iraq was returned to the list (Atasoy 2003d: 196).

While war against Iraq was justified by claims that it possessed weapons of mass destruction, the war did not receive UN approval. Although the Bush administration clearly sought to internationalize the war, the fact remains that this conflict was waged by the United States and Britain primarily to impose a 'friendly' regime and gain greater control over the region. Turkey's newly elected pro-Islamic AKP government supports Turkey's military alliance with the United States but it does not support the US war on Iraq.

At the international level, the question facing the Bush administration is not how to punish Islamist terrorists and undermine their political strength. What is at stake here is the reputation of the United States as a bulwark of stability and its ability to govern the world capitalist economy in the face of challenges to its power (Atasoy 2003d: 197). The US administration has put its military vision of international dominance in play by waging war, and the terrorist attacks have created opportunities for the United States to exploit. The key issue for the US government is how to rearrange the political-military framework of the global economic system to suit US interests.

In *The Grand Chessboard*, Zbigniew Brzezinski (1997) explains that US governments were never interested in eradicating the political power of Islamists in Muslim countries. The real issue is the form that political Islam, or any other nationalist movement, will take and whether it will be cooperative or competitive with US interests. This concern is closely linked to the reconstruction of international political alliances with moderate Muslim countries—alliances that favour the enhancement of economic relations within the global economy of capitalism. However, there is a danger that the war on terror will foster anti-American feelings and create long-term instability in the region. This prospect, and the extent of US power in the region, depends on US alliances with countries bordering Iraq—Kuwait, Saudi Arabia, Jordan, Syria, Iran, and Turkey.

With the exception of Kuwait, Turkey is by far the most co-operative of these countries towards US interests, although the AKP government continues to be uneasy with the war. The AKP has policy differences and differences in style and image with the former pro-Islamic parties led by Erbakan. It works to strengthen linkages between the United States and Turkey far more than Erbakan's national view-oriented parties. The AKP emphasizes Turkey's full integration with the European Union, and promotes greater involvement in the world capitalist economy. It also embraces neoliberal ideology and wants to solidify Western 'individual rights and freedoms' discourse within an Islamic political framework.

There is no consensus on the political shaping of a globalized future. The events of 11 September 2001 have heightened the perception that the United States no longer projects an untarnished image of stability and strength. There is no credible evidence to suggest that the terrorists were motivated by their hatred of the freedoms enjoyed by Americans. What the attack actually shows is that US global power is not invincible. As the only superpower in the world today, the United States has decided to rely on its military power as the principal strategy for integrating the world economy, supported by a highly fragile coalition of states in Europe and the Middle East.

The Bush administration was well aware that the Iraq war would trigger widespread hostilities against US forces in Iraq and US allies abroad, including civilians. Attacks on a synagogue and HSBC bank in Istanbul, and the bombing of a Bali nightclub in Indonesia and commuter train in Spain are notable examples. With the assistance of its 'coalition' partners, the current Bush administration is using terrorism as a vehicle for asserting US dominance in the world. This was clearly reflected in a statement made shortly after 11 September 2001 by Tony Blair, prime minister of Britain and staunch ally of the United States. In a televised public statement Blair said 'We must re-order the world around us'. The US administration appears prepared to wage a permanent war to reorient the world around its power. President Bush initially called this war a crusade, with no forethought given to what the term implies. He then called it 'operation infinite justice', which was not well thought out either, as he appeared to conflate US military might with God's own divine justice. The Pentagon soon adopted another name to describe the war against al-Qaeda: 'operation enduring freedom'. Significantly, the war in Iraq was also called 'operation Iraqi Freedom'. Tony Blair directed the world's attention to the 'necessity' of this war by stating that 'we will either defeat it or be defeated by it'. George W. Bush has tried to consolidate world order by coercing other states into making a choice between 'the forces of evil and the forces of freedom'. He has also used the phrase you are either with us or against us to bring states into line with US interests (Atasoy 2003d: 201).

Apparently, the realignment of the world is to take place along an ideological divide between the enemies of freedom, as Bush has called them, and the free world of the United States and its allies. His attempt to forge a worldwide political and military alliance is built on the assumption that non-alignment is immoral. This is reminiscent of the Cold War re-ordering of the world after the Second World War. During the Cold War it was also deemed immoral not to be an ally of the free world in the battle against communism. Today it is immoral not to be allied against terrorists and the enemies of freedom (Atasoy 2003d: 202). This sounds like a new global war (Kaldor 2002: 176) organized on the premise of Huntington's 'clash of civilizations' rhetoric and waged to redefine regional geopolitics based on coercive US power.

Turkey and US global supremacy

The new US militarism is refashioning the politics of Central Asia and redrawing the map of oil flowing into Europe (Atasoy 2003d: 203–3). Will the

United States be able to impose control in the region? What role will Turkey play as an emerging regional power? These are significant questions, the answers to which, while complex, require our attention.

The Caspian region consists of the states of the former Soviet Union in the Caucasus and Central Asia. It consists of the world's largest and most undeveloped sources of oil and gas. Geo-strategic control of this region, stretching from Azerbaijan through the Central Asian states of Turkmenistan, Uzbekistan, Kazakhstan, Tajikistan, and Kyrgyzstan, represents a counterweight to the Persian Gulf oil fields (Croissant and Aras 1999: 250). The energy fields of the Caspian region are landlocked, which means that gaining access to gas and oil requires building thousands of kilometres of pipeline across mountains and deserts.

There has been intense competition in determining the exact location of the pipelines and deciding who will build them. In the early 1990s the United States supported the Taliban, hoping that they would end the civil war and ensure the safety of pipelines linking Caspian oil to the Pakistan port of Karachi via Afghanistan. During the Afghan civil war the Taliban received arms and funding in their struggle against the Northern Alliance, a close ally of both Russia and Iran (Rashid 2000). But the Taliban never succeeded in building a stable, pro-American Afghanistan. Moreover, Russia and Iran had a vested interest in maintaining instability in Afghanistan. Both countries wanted to prevent Pakistan from building its Termez-Karachi pipeline, which would have brought Caspian oil across Uzbekistan and Afghanistan to Pakistan's Arabian Sea (*Los Angeles Times*, 28 November 2001). Since the Taliban were not able to stabilize Afghanistan, the US government began in 1996 to isolate Taliban in Central Asia. The Taliban responded by taking an increasingly anti-American stand and welcoming Osama bin Laden and al-Qaeda into Afghanistan. The US administration believed that the Taliban and al-Qaeda were sponsoring Islamic movements in Central Asia, especially in Uzbekistan, and stirring up anti-Western sentiments.

In the struggle to control Caspian oil, various powers have disrupted rival pipeline projects and coalitions have shifted. The US administration is now trying to establish dominance by cultivating pro-American alliances in the region. Turkey occupies a position of central importance in this strategic alignment. The inhabitants of oil rich Azerbaijan and much of Central Asia are Turkic people who share a language and culture with Turkey. Given that Turkey is the only Muslim NATO member and long-term ally of the United States, it could bring Azerbaijan, Turkmenistan, and Uzbekistan into a close co-operative relationship with the United States and western Europe. Turkey wants oil to be piped under the Caspian Sea to Baku in Azerbaijan where it can then flow to Turkey's Mediterranean port of Ceyhan. The Baku-Ceyhan pipeline would bypass Russia and Iran, carrying Central Asian oil and natural gas directly to Europe.

Russia has supported the Northern Alliance against the Pakistani-supported Taliban since the early 1990s, and rearmed them after 11 September 2001. However, the rebellion in Chechnya has prevented Russia from building a pipeline from Central Asia into Russian territory. While Russia tried to brutally suppress Chechen rebels, both Pakistan and Saudi Arabia supported the insurgents in order to disrupt Russian oil pipelines. Meanwhile, Iran is worried that US military ties to the Central Asian republics, and wars in Afghanistan and Iraq, are part of a US strategy to encircle and isolate Iran. Given this situation, Turkish governments hope to raise Turkey's international standing to that of a regional power capable of countering radical Islamic movements.

Turkey, then, wants to become a regional power by extending the ideological authority of Western modernity to the Muslim states of the Caucasus and Central Asia. Against the spread of radical Islam in the region, Turkey is promoting the coexistence of moderate Islam and modernization according to a European model. It wants to cultivate a political culture that is democratic, pro-Western, and secular yet Muslim. This does not represent a departure from Turkey's long-standing desire to be part of the European Union. Rather, it complements its relations with Western allies.

In 1992, the Black Sea Economic Cooperation Project (BSEC) was founded to promote economic, political, and cultural ties between states in the Caucasus, the Balkans, and the Middle East. Members include Turkey, Albania, Armenia, Azerbaijan, Bulgaria, Georgia, Greece, Moldova, Romania, Russia, and Ukraine. Countries given observer status in the BSEC include Poland, Slovakia, Italy, Austria, Tunisia, Egypt, and Israel. The project was created to foster democratic political systems and encourage market-based economies in the region. The Economic Cooperation Organization (ECO) was also founded in 1992 to encourage greater cooperation between Turkey, Iran, and Pakistan. Turkey was instrumental in enabling Azerbaijan, Kyrgyzstan, Turkmenistan, Uzbekistan, and Tajikistan to join the ECO. Kazakhstan presently has observer status. Turkey believes these organizations are vital if Turkey is to assert itself as a regional superpower capable of connecting Central Asia and Caucasus to the Middle East and Europe.

In addition to encouraging regional economic cooperation, Turkey has intensified its effort to bring about cultural unity in the Turkic world. Toward that end it has organized pan-Turkic summits in 1992 and 1994. It has also installed telephone systems in Central Asia and begun regularly scheduled flights between Ankara and the Central Asian capitals (Celik 1999: 125–7).

Moreover, the Turkish government has allocated many scholarships for students from Central Asia and accommodated 2,000 students from each Turkic state. In 1997 there were 6,439 Central Asian students studying in Turkey, compared to just 1,634 students in 1993 (Bal 2000: 90). The Turkish Ministry of Education has also prepared history textbooks to be adopted in Central Asia, where the adopted Turkish Latin alphabet now predominates rather than Arabic script (Celik 1999: 127–34). It is believed that the use of the Latin alphabet will make it easier for Turkic states to be connected to the Western world. Strong cultural links are maintained through state-run and private TV channels. The state-run Turkish Radio Television Company transmits programmes through its *Avrasya* (Eurasia) station, which has been broadcasting via satellite since 1992. The company promotes Turkey as a model secular democratic state and upholds Turkish cultural values and Muslim moral principles.

Since 1990, the Turkish government has sent tens of thousands of copies of the Koran to Central Asia through the Directorate of Religious Affairs. The directorate also supports mosque construction and religious education. Within a year of the Soviet Union's collapse Turkey sent 68 *imams* into the Turkic world. In addition, Turkish schools have accepted more than 600 students from Central Asia and the Balkans to study religion. In 1992 the Turkish government began to open Turkish schools in the Caucasus and Central Asia; by 1996, there were eight in Uzbekistan, three in Turkmenistan, two in Kyrgyzstan, and one in Azerbaijan (Bal 2000: 87–9).

There are also private Turkish schools in Central Asia. The Fethullah Gulen *cemaati* plays an active role in opening these schools but do not receive financial support from the state. Turkish Muslim business groups finance the schools through private donations channelled to Central Asia by Asya Finance. The Turkish state welcomes the school-building activities of the Fethullah Gulen *cemaati* because they support the Turkish state policy of combining secularism with a moderate Islam. The group also stresses the importance of achieving excellence in modern science and technology.

Despite Turkey's promotion of itself as a regional powerhouse and a bulwark of stability against radical Islamic movements, it has not resulted in the acceptance of Turkey as a Western state. Western European states want to assert their Europeanness and not be dominated by the United States. This has manifested itself not only in French and German opposition to the US war on Iraq but also in the EU's rejection to date of Turkey as a full member. The United States, however, supports Turkey's full membership in the EU.

The EU rejected Turkey's full membership in 1987. Nevertheless, Turkey intensified its efforts, concluding a customs union with the EU in 1995. The customs union began in 1996 when the pro-Islamic Welfare Party came to power. The expectation was that this would expedite the process of Turkey becoming a full EU member (Balkir 2001: 200–6). However, in 1997, a sense of crisis in Turkey's relations with the EU arose when the EU Summit in Luxembourg excluded Turkey from the enlargement process. At the summit the EU concluded agreements with central and eastern European states, as well as Cyprus, and ceded the possibility of their eventual full membership, but no place was given to Turkey in the accession queue. Remarks were made at the summit that the EU was a 'civilizational project', and European unity came to be seen as a political/cultural entity. The Luxembourg Summit questioned Turkey's Europeanness on the basis of cultural difference. This created immense uncertainty in Turkish foreign policy (Aybak 2002: 232). Interestingly, following rejection by the EU, Turkey forged closer ties with the United States, Israel, and Central Asian states, though it did not abandon the long-term objective of full EU membership. In 1999 the EU officially recognized Turkey's candidacy at the Helsinki Summit and placed it within the enlargement process. At the Copenhagen Summit of 2002 the EU decided to review Turkey's candidacy in December 2004. The EU's decision on whether to open formal negotiations on Turkey's membership was contingent upon Turkey achieving progress in fulfilling EU expectations on human rights, democracy, and the rule of law—as listed in the so-called 'Copenhagen Criteria'.

In its push towards full membership, Turkey adopted a series of constitutional and legislative reforms between 2001 and 2004. These changes were aimed at bringing Turkey into line with the EU. They included the improvement of human rights standards and democratic reforms, the imposition of stiffer penalties for torture, asserting greater government control over the military, and providing additional religious freedoms and minority rights. Most notable is the host of major reforms introduced to replace the 78-year-old Turkish penal code, originally adopted in 1926 from the Italian penal code and the code of criminal procedure. On 17 December 2004 leaders of the 25-member EU responded positively to these efforts by finally deciding to begin accession negotiations with Turkey in October 2005. Turkey's goal of achieving full membership may take ten to 15 years to realize, during which time the EU will monitor the implementation of these reforms in Turkey. Negotiations can be suspended if EU member states decide that there has been a Turkish breach of democratic or human rights principles, in which case Turkey would not succeed in joining the EU.

The EU is directly concerned with the future political, cultural, and military composition of Europe, as it seeks greater autonomy within the Atlantic Alliance. With the changes taking place in the post–Cold War state system, crucial questions arise over future relations between Europe and the United States, as well as significant changes to strategic alliances. In the face of a growing number of alliances in Asia and the Middle East, consideration of Turkey's attempt to join the EU should not be confined to the question of whether Turkey can become a Western society. The relationship between the EU and the United States is asymmetrical and contains the seeds of multiple tensions created by the pre-eminent military position of the United States in NATO. Turkey's EU membership has the potential to contribute to the unity of

NATO vis-à-vis Europe. In relation to EU attempts to achieve greater European autonomy from NATO, Turkey's EU membership would counter its potential marginalization in Europe and enable it to actively participate in the future reshaping of European politics. This possibility appears to be more attractive to Turkish policy-makers, given the rise in tension between Turkey and the United States following the Turkish parliament's 2003 decision to deny the US military the right to station troops in Turkey for deployment in the war on Iraq. At the same time, Turkey wants to demonstrate that a Muslim country can be both democratic and comfortable with the Western world. Turkey's membership in the EU has the potential to redefine the meaning and values associated with what is Western and what is Islamic.

Since the end of the Second World War, western Europe has been a subordinate member of the Atlantic Alliance dominated by the United States. While the invasion of Iraq and the use of overwhelming military power have established US military supremacy, a failure in Iraq might weaken the capacity of the United States to enforce its global dominance. But it is not at all clear what it means if US power declines and the EU acquires control over the definition of the 'West' in shaping a global strategy.

Turkey has long been a subordinate state within the Western sphere, yet it has forged important ties to the United States and the EU, as well as Muslim countries in the Middle East, the Caucasus, and Asia. This presents a compelling and complex case against the dichotomous positioning of the West and Islam in the current ideological configuration of world power. There are many Islamist groups in Turkey, each with their own dynamic and history, but all are engaged in a process of modernization based on a European model. Moreover, all are interacting with state power and reshaping their politics within the geo-historical context of Turkey's position in the global economy. This is the complicated story of an embodiment of Western modernity that manifests historically situated social relations. The Islamic engagement with the material and discursive conditions of the capitalist economy enters into the current processes constituting the global system. This underscores the reality of globalization as a highly contradictory process. It compels us to raise questions as to whether or not the West can claim unity in asserting a cultural authority over a globalized economy without turning itself into an armed fortress.

These issues should cause us to rethink the form and content of domestic politics as well as broader geopolitical relations. The fashioning of meanings associated with Islam and the West points to the need to find new ways to consider the organization of social life, particularly in light of structural shifts in the world economy and the global elite enforcement of a confrontational view. This in turn depends on the ability to capture the historical relations through which our social existence is re-constituted and incorporated into an economic reality that imposes a singular logic over a vastly diverse world.

References

Abu-Lughod, Lila (ed.) (1997). <u>Remaking Women: Feminism and Modernity in the Middle East</u> (Princeton, Princeton University Press).

Acar, Feride and Ayse Ayata (2002). 'Discipline, Success, and Stability: The Reproduction of Gender and Class in Turkish Secondary Education', in Deniz Kandiyoti and Ayse Saktanber (eds), <u>Fragments of Culture: The Everyday of Modern Turkey</u> (London and New York, I.B. Tauris).

Adams, T.W and A.J. Conttrell (1968). <u>Cyprus Between East and West</u> (Baltimore, The John Hopkins University Press).

Afshar, Halef (1998). <u>Islam and Feminisms: An Iranian Case</u> (London, Macmillan).

Aglietta, Michel (1979). <u>A Theory of Capitalist Regulation: The US Experience</u> (London, Verso).

Ahmed, Leila (1992). <u>Women and Gender in Islam</u> (New Haven, Yale University Press).

Akgul, N (1976). 'Turkiye'de Montaj Sanayi', in <u>Turkiye Sanayiinin Yapisal Sorunlari</u> (Ankara, Chamber of Mechanical Engineers Publication, Vol. 106, No. 4).

Aksit, Bahattin (1986). 'Imam-Hatip and Other Secondary Schools in the Context of Political and Cultural Modernization of Turkey', <u>Journal of Human Sciences</u>, Vol. 5, No. 1.

Aktar, Ayhan (1998). 'Varlik Vergisi Sirasinda Gayrimenkul Satislari, Istanbul Tapu Kayitlarinin Analizi: 26 Aralik 1942 – 30 Haziran 1943' (Unpublished Paper Presented at the VIIIth International Congress on the Economic and Social History of Turkey, Bursa, 18-21 June 1998).

Al-Ahsan, Abdullah (1988). <u>The Organization of the Islamic Conference: An Introduction to Islamic Political Institution</u> (Herndon, The International Institute of Islamic Thought).

Al-Azmeh, Aziz (1993). <u>Islams and Modernities</u> (London, Verso).

Albayrak, Sadik (1991). <u>Turkiye'de Din Kavgasi</u> (Istanbul, Arastirma Yayinlari).

Algar, Hamit (1983). 'The Naqshbandi Order in Republican Turkey' (Unpublished Paper).

---------- (1979). 'The Said Nursi and the Risale-i Nur, An Aspect of Islam in Contemporary Turkey', in Khurshid Ahmad and Zafer Ishaq Ansari (eds), Islamic Perspectives: Studies in Honour of Sayyid Abul Ala Mavdudi (Leicester, Islamic Foundation).

Ambrose, E. Stephen (1983). Rise to Globalism (Harmondsworth, Penguin).

Amin, Samir (1976). Unequal Development (New York, Monthly Review Press).

Anderson, Benedict (1991). Imagined Communities (London, Verso).

Anderson, Lisa (1983). 'Qaddafi's Islam', in John L. Esposito (ed.), Voices of Resurgent Islam (New York, Oxford University Press).

Aras, Bulent and Omer Caha (2000). 'Fethullah Gulen and His Liberal "Turkish Islam" Movement', Middle East Review of International Affairs, Vol. 4, No. 4.

Arcayurek, Cuneyt (1984). Yeni Demokrasi Yeni Arayislar, 1960-1965 (Ankara, Bilgi Yayinevi).

Armstrong, Philip, Andrew Glyn, and John Harrison (1991). Capitalism Since 1945 (Oxford: Basil Blackwell).

Arrighi, Giovanni (1999). 'Globalization and Historical Macrosociology', in Janet Abu-Lughod (ed.), Sociology for the Twenty-First Century (Chicago, University of Chicago Press).

Arrighi, Giovanni and Beverley J. Silver (eds) (1999). Chaos and Governance in the Modern World System (Minneapolis, University of Minnesota Press).

Arrighi, Giovanni, et al (1999). 'Geopolitics and High Finance', in Giovanni Arrighi and Beverley Silver (eds), Chaos and Governance in the Modern World System (Minneapolis, University of Minnesota Press).

Atasoy, Yildiz (2003a). 'Cosmopolitan Islamists in Turkey: Rethinking the Local in a Global Era', Studies in Political Economy, Vol. 71/72.

---------- (2003b). 'Explaining Local-Global Nexus: Muslim Politics in Turkey', in Yildiz Atasoy and William K. Carroll (eds), Global Shaping and Its Alternatives (Aurora and Bloomfield, Garamond Press and Kumarian Press).

---------- (2003c). 'Explaining Globalization', in Yildiz Atasoy and William K. Carroll (eds), Global Shaping and Its Alternatives (Aurora and Bloomfield, Garamond Press and Kumarian Press).

---------- (2003d). 'Afterword: September 11 and the Reorganization of the World Economy', in Yildiz Atasoy and William K. Carroll (eds), Global Shaping and Its Alternatives (Aurora and Bloomfield, Garamond Press and Kumarian Press).

---------- (2003e). 'Muslim Organizations in Canada: Gender Ideology and Women's Veiling', Sociological Focus, Vol. 36, No. 2.

---------- (1998). Beyond Tradition and Resistance: Islamic Politics and Global Relations of Power: The Case of Turkey, 1839-1999 (Unpublished PhD Thesis, University of Toronto).

---------- (1986). State, Order, and Change: Ismet Inonu and Transition to Democracy in Turkey (Unpublished MSc Thesis, Middle East Technical University).

Avcioglu, Dogan (1979). Turkiye'nin Duzeni, Vol. 2 (Istanbul, Tekin Yayinevi).

---------- (1978). Turkiye'nin Duzeni, Vol. 1 (Istanbul, Tekin Yayinevi).

Ayata, Sencer (1996). 'Patronage, Party, and the State: The Politicization of Islam in Turkey', Middle East Report, Vol. 50, No. 1.

Aybak, Tunc (2002). 'Foregin Policy in the New Century', in Brian Beeley (ed.), Turkish Transformation: New Century—New Challenges (Cambridgeshire, The Eothen Press).

Aydemir, S. Sureyya (1983). Ikinci Adam, Vol. 1 (Istanbul, Remzi Yayinevi).

---------- (1979). Ikinci Adam, Vol. 2 (Istanbul, Remzi Kitabevi).

---------- (1969). Menderes'in Drami (Istanbul, Remzi Kitabevi).

Bademli, R. (1978). 'Turkiye'de Kucuk Uretim' in Sanayide Kucuk Uretim, Toplumsal ve Mekansal Boyutlar (Ankara, Chamber of Architects).

Bal, Idris (2000). Turkey's Relations with the West and the Turkic Republics: The Rise and Fall of the 'Turkish Model' (Aldershot, Ashgate).

Baldwin, David (1990). 'Islamic Banking in a Secularist Context' (Unpublished Paper Presented at the Center for Middle Eastern and Islamic Studies, University of Durham).

Balkir, Canan (2001). 'International Relations: From Europe to Central Asia', in Debbie Lovatt (ed.), Turkey Since 1970: Politics, Economics, and Society (New York, Palgrave).

---------- (1993). 'Turkey and the European Community', in Canan Balkir and A.M. Williams (eds), Turkey and Europe (London, Pinter Publishers).

Barber, Benjamin (1995). Jihad vs. McWorld (New York, Balantine Books).

Barkan, O. Lutfi (1975). 'The Price Revolution of the Sixteenth Century', International Journal of Middle East Studies, Vol. VI, No. 1.

---------- (1945). 'Ciftciyi Topraklandirma Kanunu ve Turkiye'de Zirai Bir Reformun Temel Meseleleri', Istanbul Universitesi Iktisat Fakultesi Mecmuasi, Vol. 6, No. 1-2.

Barkey, J. H. (1990). The State and Industrialization Crisis in Turkey (Boulder, Westview Press).

Barutcu, A. Faruk (1977). Siyasi Anilar, 1939-1954 (Istanbul, Milliyet Yayinlari).

Basgil, A. Fuat (1962). Din ve Laiklik (Istanbul, Yagmur Yayinevi).

Baxter, R.D. (1871). National Debts (London, Robert John Bush, 32, Charing Cross, S.W.).

Bayar, Celal (1951). Celal Bayar Diyorki: 1920-1950 Nutuk, Hitabe, Beyanat, Hasbihal (Istanbul, Tan Matbaasi).

Behar, E. Busra (1992). Iktidar ve Tarih, Turkiye'de 'Resmi Tarih' Tezinin Olusumu: 1929-1937 (Istanbul, AFA Yayincilik).

Bennigsen, Alexandre, et al (1989). Soviet Strategy and Islam (London, Macmillan).

Berkes, Niyazi (1959). Turkish Nationalism and Turkish Civilization, Selected Essays of Ziya Gokalp (New York, Columbia University Press).

Besikci, Ismail (1991). Turk Tarih Tezi, Gunes-Dil Teorisi, ve Kurt Sorunu (Ankara, Yurt Kitap Yayinevi).

Betin, S.U. (1951). Ataturk Inkilabi ve Ziya Gokalp, Yahya Kemal, Halide Adivar (Istanbul, Guven Yayinevi).

Bianchi, R. (1984). Interest Groups and Political Development in Turkey (Princeton, Princeton University Press).

Birand, Mehmet Ali (2000). Turkiye'nin Avrupa Macerasi: 1959-1999 (Istanbul, Dogan Kitap).

Blaisdell, D.C. (1929). European Financial Control in the Ottoman Empire: A Study of the Establishment, Activities, and Significance of the Administration of the Ottoman Public Debt (New York, Columbia University Press).

Block, Fred (1990). Postindustrial Possibilities: A Critique of Economic Discourse (Berkeley, University of California Press).

---------- (1986). 'Political Choice and the Multiple "Logics' of Capital"', Theory and Society, Vol. 15.

---------- (1977). The Origins of International Economic Disorder (Berkeley, University of California Press).

Boll, M.M. (1979). 'Turkey's New National Security Concept: What It Means For NATO', Orbis, Fall.

Bolugiray, Nevzat (2000). 28 Subat Sureci Vol. 2 (Istanbul, Tekin Yayinevi).

Bolukbasi, Suha (1988). The Superpowers and the Third World: Turkish-American Relations and Cyprus (New York, University of Virginia Press).

Boratav, Korkut (1990). 'Inter-Class and Intra-Class Relations of Distribution Under "Structural Adjustment": Turkey During the 1980s', in Tosun Aricanli and D. Rodrik (eds), The Political Economy of Turkey: Debt, Adjustment, and Sustainability (London, Macmillan).

---------- (1982). Turkiye'de Devletcilik (Ankara, Savas Yayinlari).

---------- (1981). 'Kemalist Economic Policies and Etatism', in Ali Kazancigil and Ergun Ozbudun (eds), Ataturk Founder of a Modern State (Hamden, Archon Books).

Bozdogan, Sibel and Resat Kasaba (eds) (1997). Rethinking Modernity and National Identity in Turkey (Seattle and London, University of Washington Press).

Bromley, Simon (1994). Rethinking Middle East Politics (Austin, University of Texas Press).

---------- (1991). American Hegemony and World Oil (Pennsylvania, Pennsylvania State University Press).

Brown, L.C. (2000). Religion and State: The Muslim Approach to Politics (New York, Columbia University Press).

Brzezinski, Zbigniew (1997). The Grand Chessboard: American Primacy and Its Geostrategic Imperatives (New York, Basic Books).

Bugra, Ayse (2002). 'Political Islam in Turkey in Historical Context: Strengths and Weaknesses', in Nesecan Balkan and Sungur Savran (eds), The Politics of Permanent Crisis: Class, Ideology and State in Turkey (New York, Nova Science Publishers, Inc.).

---------- (1999). 'Turk Isadamlari ve Turk Devleti', in Oya Baydar and Gulay Dincel (eds), 75 Yilda Carklari Dondurenler (Istanbul, Turkiye IS Bankasi Tarih Vakfi Yayinlari).

---------- (1998). 'Class, Culture, and State: An Analysis of Interest Representation by Two Turkish Business Associations', International Journal of Middle East Studies, Vol. 30.

Bulac, Ali (1983). Islam Dunyasinda Dusunce Sorunlari (Istanbul, Isaret Yayinlari).

---------- 1978). Cagdas Kavramlar ve Duzenler (Istanbul, Dusunce Yayinlari.)

Bulut, Faik (1999). Yesil Sermaye Nereye? (Istanbul, Su Yayinlari).

Bulutoglu, Kenan (1974). Yuz Soruda Turkiye de Yabanci Sermaye (Istanbul, Gercek)

Burcak, R.Saim (1979). Turkiye'de Demokrasiye Gecis (Ankara, Olgac Matbaasi).

Cakir, Rusen (1993). 'Devlet Islami Istiyor', Birikim, Vol. 55.

---------- (1990). Ayet ve Slogan: Turkiye'de Islami Olusumlar (Istanbul, Metis Yayinlari).

Cakir, Rusen and F. Calmuk (2001). Recep Tayyip Erdogan: Bir Donusum Oykusu (Istanbul, Metis).

Cakir, Rusen and L. Cinemre (1991). Sol Kemalizme Bakiyor (Istanbul, Metis).

Calleo, David (1970). The Atlantic Fantasy: The US, NATO, and Europe (Baltimore, The Johns Hopkins University).

Carroll, K. William (2003). 'Undoing the End of History: Canada-Centred Reflections on the Challenge of Globalization', in Yildiz Atasoy and William K. Carroll (eds), Global Shaping and Its Alternatives (Aurora and Bloomfield, Garamond Press and Kumarian Press).

Celasun, M. and D. Rodrik (1991). 'Turkish Experience with Debt: Macroeconomic Policy and Performence', in Jeffrey D. Sachs (ed.), Developing Country Debt and the World Economy (Chicago, University of Chicago Press).

Celik, Yasemin (1999). Contemporary Turkish Foreign Policy (Westport and London, Praeger).

Chatterjee, Partha (1993). The Nation and Its Fragments: Colonial and Postcolonial Histories (Princeton, Princeton University Press).

Churba, J. (1980). 'The Eroding Security Structure Balance in the Middle East', Orbis, Summer.

Colasan, Emin (1983). 24 Ocak: Bir Donemin Perde Arkasi (Istanbul, Milliyet Yayinlari).

Cooper, John, Ronald Nettler, and Mohamed Mahmoud (eds) (2000). Islam and Modernity: Muslim Intellectuals Respond (London and New York, I.B. Tauris).

Coronil, Fernando (1997). The Magical State: Nature, Money, and Modernity in Venezuela (Chicago, University of Chicago Press).

Couloumbis, T.A. (1983). The United States, Greece, and Turkey: The Troubled Triangle (New York, Praeger).

Council on Foreign Relations (1962). Documents on American Foreign Relations (New York, Harper and Brothers).

Cowen, M.P and R.W. Shenton (1996). Doctrines of Development (London, Routledge).

Croissant, P.M. and B. Aras (eds) (1999). Oil and Geopolitics in the Caspian Sea Region (London, Praeger).

Culhaoglu, Metin (2002). 'The History of the Socialist-Communist Movement in Turkey by Four Major Indicators', in Nesecan Balkan and Sungur Savran (eds), The Politics of Permanent Crisis: Class, Ideology, and State in Turkey (New York, Nova Science Publishers, Inc.).

Davison, R.H. (1993). 'Turkish Attitudes Concerning Christian-Muslim Equality in the Nineteenth Century', in Albert Hourani, Philip S. Khoury, and Mary C. Wilson (eds), The Modern Middle East: A Reader (Berkeley, University of California Press).

Dawisha, Adeed (1982). 'The Soviet Union in the Arab World: The Limits to Superpower Influence', in Adeed Dawisha and Karen Dawisha (eds), The Soviet Union in the Middle East: Policies and Perspectives (New York, Holmes & Meier).

Demirel, H., U. Simsek, and B. Ates (1977). Islami Hareket ve MSP (Istanbul, Yeni Asya).

Dincel, Gulay (1999). 'Konya'nin Kombassani ve Hasim Bayram'in Yukselisi', in Oya Baydar and Gulay Dincel (eds), 75 Yilda Carklari Dondurenler (Istanbul, Turkiye IS Bankasi Tarih Vakfi Yayinlari).

Directorate of Religious Affairs (1990). Istatistiklerle Diyanet Isleri Baskanligi (Ankara, T.C. Basbakanlik Diyanet Isleri Baskanligi APK Dairesi Baskanligi)

Dodd, C.H. (1979). Democracy and Development in Turkey (Hull, The Eothen Press).

Dogan, Muzaffer (1983). 'Mursid ve Murid', Turk Edebiyati, Vol. 117.

Dumont, Paul (1987). 'Islam as a Factor of Change and Revival in Modern Turkey', in S.M. Akural (ed.), <u>Turkic Culture: Continuity and Change</u> (Bloomington, Indiana University Press).

Duru, O. (1978). <u>American Gizli Belgeleriyle Turkiye'nin Kurtulus Yillari</u> (Istanbul, Milliyet Yayinlari).

Ecevit, Bulent (1976). <u>Dis Politika</u> (Ankara, Ajans Turk).

---------- (1965). 'Donum Noktasi', <u>Milliyet Newspaper</u>, 26 April 1965.

Ehrlich, T. (1974). <u>International Crisis and the Role of Law: Cyprus 1858-1967</u> (London, Oxford University Press).

Eichengreen, Barry (1996). <u>Globalizing Capital: A History of the International Monetary System</u> (Princeton, Princeton University Press).

Elwell-Sutton, E.P. (1955). <u>Persian Oil: A Study in Power Politics</u> (London, Lawrence and Wishart).

Eralp, Atilla (1993). 'Turkey and the EC in the Changing Post-War International System', in Canan Balkir and A.M. Williams (eds), <u>Turkey and Europe</u> (London, Pinter Publishers).

---------- (1990). 'The Politics of Turkish Development Strategies', in A. Finkel and Nukhet Sirman (eds), <u>Turkish State, Turkish Society</u> (London, Routledge).

Erbakan, Necmettin (1990). 'Refah Partisi 3. Olagan Buyuk Kongresi: Genel Baskan Professor Necmettin Erbakan'in Acis Konusmasi' (Pamphlet Published by the Welfare Party).

---------- (1975). <u>Milli Gorus</u> (Istanbul, Dergah Yayinlari).

---------- (1972). <u>Mecliste Ortak Pazar</u> (Izmir, Istiklal Matbaasi).

Erdemir, Sebahat (ed.) (1962). <u>Muhalefette Ismet Inonu, 1959-1960</u> (Istanbul, Ekicigil Matbaasi).

Ergil, Dogu (1975). 'Class Conflict and Turkish Transformation', <u>Studia Islamica Fasicule</u>, Vol. XLI.

Escobar, Arturo (1995). <u>Encountering Development</u> (Princeton, Princeton University Press).

Esposito, L. John. (1992). <u>The Islamic Threat: Myth or Reality</u> (New York and Oxford, Oxford University Press).

---------- (1987). <u>Islam and Politics</u> (New York, Syracuse Press).

Esteva, Gustavo (1992). 'Development', in Wolfgang Sachs (ed.), <u>The Development Dictionary</u> (London, Zed Books).

Esteva, Gustavo and Madhu S. Prakash (1998). <u>Grassroots Postmodernism: Remaking the Soil of Cultures</u> (London, Zed Books).

Evans, Peter (1985). 'Transnational Linkages and the Economic Role of the State: An Analysis of Developing and Industrialized Nations in the Post-World War II Period', in Peter Evans, Dietrich Rueschemeyer, and Theda Skocpol (eds), <u>Bringing the State Back In</u> (New York, Cambridge University Press).

Evren, Kenan (1991). Kenan Evren'in Anilari 4 (Istanbul, Milliyet Yayinlari).

Faroqhi, Suraiya (2000). Culture and Daily Life in the Ottoman Empire (London and New York, I.B. Tauris).

Featherstone, Kevin (1989). 'The Mediterranean Challenge: Cohesion and External Preferences', in Juliet Lodge (ed.), The European Community and the Challenge of the Future (New York, St. Martin's Press).

Findley, C. (1980). Bureaucratic Reform in the Ottoman Empire: The Sublime Porte, 1789-1922 (Princeton, Princeton University Press).

Fleming, D.F. (1961). The Cold War and Its Origins, 1917-1960 (London, George Allen and Unwin Ltd).

Fortna, C. Benjamin (2002). Imperial Classroom: Islam, the State, and Education in the Late Ottoman Empire (New York, Oxford University Press).

Freedman, R.O. (1978). Soviet Policy Toward the Middle East Since 1970 (New York, Praeger).

Frey, Frederick (1964). 'Education', in R.W. Ward and D.A. Rustow (eds), Political Modernization in Japan and Turkey (Princeton, Princeton University Press).

Friedmann, Harriet (1993). 'The Political Economy of Food: A Global Crisis', New Left Review, No. 197.

---------- (1992). 'Distance and Durability: Shaky Foundations of the World Food Economy', Third World Quarterly, Vol. 13, No. 2.

---------- (1982). 'The Political Economy of Food: The Rise and Fall of the Postwar International Food Order', in Michael Buraway and T. Skocpol (eds), Marxist Inquiries: Studies of Labour, Class, and Capital (Chicago, University of Chicago Press).

Froebel, Folker, Jurgen Heinrichs, and Otto Kreye (1980). The New International Division of Labour (Cambridge, Cambridge University Press).

Gaddis, L. John (1982). Strategies of Containment (New York, Oxford University Press).

Gellner, Ernest (1983). Nations and Nationalism (London, Basil Blackwell).

Genc, S. (1971). 12 Mart'a Nasil Gelindi: Bir Devrin Perde Arkasi, 1960-1971 (Ankara).

Gendzier, Irene (1985). Managing Political Change: Social Scientists and the Third World (Boulder, Westview).

Gereffi, Gary (1994). 'The International Economy and Economic Development', in Neil Smelser and Richard Swedberg (eds), The Handbook of Economic Sociology (Princeton and New York, Princeton University Press and Russell Sage Foundation).

Gerges, A. Fawaz (1999). America and Political Islam: Clash of Cultures or Clash of Interests? (Cambridge, Cambridge University Press).

Gevgili, Ali (1973). Turkiye'de 1971 Regimi (Istanbul, Milliyet Yayinlari).

Gill, Stephen (1992). 'Economic Globalization and Internationalization of Authority: Limits and Contradictions', Geoforum, Vol. 23.

Giritlioglu, Fahir (1965). Turk Siyasi Tarihinde CHP'nin Mevkii Vol. 1 (Ankara, Ayyildiz Matbaasi).

Gocek, F. Muge (1996). Rise of Bourgeoisie, Demise of Empire: Ottoman Westernization and Social Change (New York, Oxford University Press).

Goffman, Erving (1959). The Presentation of the Self in Everyday Life (Garden City, Anchor Doubleday).

Gokce, Birsen, et al (1984). Orta Ogretim Gencliginin Beklenti ve Sorunlari (Ankara, Milli Egitim Genclik ve Spor Bakanligi Yayinlari).

Golan, Galia (1990). Soviet Policies in the Middle East from World War II to Gorbachev (Cambridge, Cambridge University Press).

Goldberg, J. (1984). 'Saudi Arabia's Attitude Toward the USSR, 1977-80', in Yaacov Ro'i (ed.), The USSR and the Muslim World: Issues in Domestic and Foreign Policy (London, George Allen & Unwin).

Gole, Nilufer (1996). The Forbidden Modern (Ann Arbor, University of Michigan Press).

---------- (1993). 'Engineers: Technocratic Democracy', in Metin Heper, Ayse Oncu, and H. Kramer (eds), Turkey and the West: Changing Political and Cultural Identities (London and New York, I.B. Tauris).

Gologlu, Mahmut (1974). Milli Sef Donemi, 1939-1945 (Ankara, Turhan Kitabevi).

Gonlubol, Mehmet (1971). 'NATO and Turkey, An Overall Appraisal', Milletlerarasi Munasebetler Turk Yilligi, Vol. XI.

Gonlubol, Mehmet, et al (1987). Olaylarla Turk Dis Politikasi (Ankara, Ankara University Press).

Goodwin, Jeff (2001). No Other Way Out: States and Revolutionary Movements, 1945-1991 (Cambridge, Cambridge University Press).

Gorst, Anthony and Lewis Johnman (1997). The Suez Crisis (London, Routledge).

Graebner, A.N. (1970). 'The United States and the Soviet Union: The Elusive Peace', Current History, Vol. 59, No. 350.

Gray, John (2003). Al Qaeda and What It Means to Be Modern (New York and London, The New Press).

Griswold, Wendy (2004). Cultures and Societies in a Changing World (Thousand Oaks, Pine Forge Press).

Gulalp, Haldun (1997). 'Globalizing Postmodernism: Islamists and Western Social Theory' Economy and Society, Vol. 26, No. 3.

Gulen, Fethullah (1997). Prizma: 2 (Izmir, Nil).

---------- (1996). Prizma: 1 (Izmir, Nil).

---------- (1978). Altin Nesil (Erzurum, Gulen Matbaasi).

Gunaltay, Semsi and H.R. Tankut (1938). Dil ve Tarih Tezlerimiz Uzerine Gerekli Bazi Izahlar (Istanbul, Devlet Basimevi).

Gunduz, Irfan (1983). Osmanlilarda Devlet-Tekke Munasebetleri (Ankara, Seha Yayinlari).

Gurdogan, Ersin (1991). Gorunmeyen Universite (Istanbul, Iz Yayinlari).

Haddad, Y. Yvonne (1994). 'Muhammad Abduh: Pioneer of Islamic reform', in Ali Rahnema (ed.), Pioneers of Islamic Revival (London and New Jersey, Zed Books).

Hale, William (2000). Turkish Foreign Policy: 1774-2000 (London and Portland, Frank Cass).

---------- (1981). The Political and Economic Development of Modern Turkey (London, Croom Helm).

Halliday, Fred (1999). Islam and the Myth of Confrontation: Religion and Politics in the Middle East (London and New York, I.B. Tauris).

---------- (1994). 'The Politics of Islamic Fundamentalism: Iran, Tunisia, and the Challenge of the Secular State', in A.S. Ahmed and H. Donnan (eds), Islam, Globalization and Postmodernity (London and New York, Routledge).

---------- (1984). The New Cold War (London, Verso).

---------- (1979). Arabia Without Sultans (Harmondsworth, Penguin).

Harris, S. George (1972). The Troubled Alliance: Turkish-American Problems in Historical Perspective, 1945-1971 (Washington, American Enterprise Institute for Public Policy Research, Hoover Policy Studies, No. 2).

Hart, T. Parker (1990). The Two Allies at the Threshold of War: Cyprus, a Firsthand Account of Crisis Management, 1965-1968 (Durham, Duke University Press).

Hassan, Riaz (2002). Faithlines: Muslim Conceptions of Islam and Society (London, Oxford University Press).

Hatipoglu, S.R. (1936). Turkiye'de Zirai Buhran (Ankara).

Hatipoglu, Z. (1978). An Unconventional Analysis of Turkish Economy (Istanbul, Aktif Buro Basim Organizasyon).

Hershlag, Z.Y. (1968). Turkey: The Challenge of Growth (Leiden, E.J. Brill).

Hitchens, C. (1984). Cyprus (London, Quartet Books).

Hobsbawm, Eric (1994). The Age of Extremes (New York, Vintage).

Hoodfar, Homa (1997). 'Return to the Veil: Personal Strategy and Public Participation in Egypt', in Nalini Visvanathan, Lynn Duggan, Laurie Nisonoff, and Nan Wiegersma (eds), The Women, Gender & Development Reader (London and New Jersey, Zed Books).

Hoogvelt, Ankie (1997). Globalization and the Postcolonial World: The New Political Economy of Development (Baltimore, The Johns Hopkins University Press).

Hourani, Albert (1991). A History of the Arab Peoples (London, Faber and Faber).

Huntington, Samuel (1996). The Clash of Civilizations (New York, Touchstone).

Ihsanoglu, Ekmeleddin (1996). 'Turkey in the Organization of the Islamic Conference: An Overview', in Kemal Karpat (ed.) , Turkish Foreign Policy: Recent Developments (Madison, University of Wisconsin Press).

Ilkin, Selim (1993). 'Businessmen: Democratic Stability', in Metin Heper, Ayse Oncu, and H. Kramer (eds), Turkey and the West: Changing Political and Cultural Identities (London and New York, I.B. Tauris).

---------- (1991). 'Exporters: Favoured Dependency', in Metin Heper (ed.), Strong State and Economic Interest Groups: The Post-1980 Turkish Experience (Berlin and New York, Walter de Gruyter).

Inalcik, Halik (1994). The Ottoman Empire: The Classical Age, 1300-1600 (London, Phoenix).

---------- (1987). 'When and How British Cotton Goods Invaded the Levant Markets', in Huri Islamoglu-Inan (ed.), The Ottoman Empire and the World Economy (Cambridge, Cambridge University Press).

---------- (1969). 'Capital Formation in the Ottoman Empire', Journal of Economic History, Vol. XXIX, No. 1.

Inonu, Ismet (1946). Inonu'nun Soylev ve Demecleri (Istanbul, Milli Egitim Basimevi).

Issawi, Charles (1980). The Economic History of Turkey: 1800-1914 (Chicago, University of Chicago Press).

Istanbul Chamber of Industry (1981). Istanbul Sanayi Odasi Dergisi, 15 October 1981, No.188.

Jaschke, G. (1972). Yeni Turkiye'de Islamlik (Ankara, Bilgi Yayinevi).

Kabakli, Ahmet (1983). 'Son Sohbet', Turk Edebiyati, Vol. 117.

Kaldor, Mary (2002). 'Beyond Militarism, Arms Races, and Arms Control', in Craig Calhoun, Paul Price, and Ashley Timmer (ed.), Understanding September 11 (New York, The New Press).

Kandemir, Feridun (1955). Ataturk-Ismet Inonu, Inonu-Maresal Darginligi, Vol. 6. (Istanbul, Ekicigil Matbaasi).

Kandiyoti, Deniz (1996). Gendering the Middle East: Emerging Perspectives (London and New York, I.B. Tauris).

Kandiyoti, Deniz and Ayse Saktanber (eds) (2002). Fragments of Culture: The Everyday of Modern Turkey (London and New York, I.B. Tauris).

Kara, Mustafa (1979). 'Cumhuriyet Oncesi Tasavvufi Yayin Organlari ve Cemiyetler', Hareket, Vol. VIII.

Karabekir, Kazim (1951). Istiklal Harbimizin Esaslari (Ankara, Sinan Matbaasi).

Karahasanoglu, M. (1975). Masona-Komuniste-Renksize Karsi Tek Adam Erbakan (Istanbul).

Karakasoglu, Yasemin (1996). 'Turkish Cultural Orientations in Germany and the Role of Islam', in David Horrocks and Eva Kolinsky (eds), Turkish Culture in German Society Today (Providence and Oxford, Berghahn Books).

Karluk, S. Ridvan (1990). Avrupa Topluluklari ve Turkiye (Istanbul, Bilim Teknik Yayinevi).

Karpat, Kemal (1976). Gecekondu: Rural Migration and Urbanization (Cambridge, Cambridge University Press).

---------- (1959). Turkey's Politics: The Transition to a Multi-Party System (Princeton, Princeton University Press).

---------- (1957). Transition of Turkey's Political Regime to a Multi-Party Political System (New York, New York University Press).

Kasaba, Resat (1993). 'Treaties and Friendships: British Imperialism, the Ottoman Empire, and China in the Nineteenth Century', Journal of World History, Vol. 2, No. 2.

Kaya, Ayhan (2001). Sicher in Kreuzberg: Constructing Diasporas: Turkish Hip-Hop Youth in Berlin (Bielefeld, Transcript).

Kazgan, Gulten (1999). Tanzimat'tan XXI. Yuzyila Turkiye Eonomisi (Istanbul, Altin Kitaplar Yayinevi).

---------- (1988). Ekonomide Disa Acik Buyume (Istanbul, Altin Kitaplar Yayinevi).

---------- (1976). 'Agricultural Exports to the EC', in Osman Okyar and Okan Aktan (eds), Economic Relations between Turkey and the EEC: Proceedings of a Seminar, Antalya, 11-14 October 1976 (Ankara, Hacettepe University Press).

Keddie, Nikki (1994). 'Sayyid Jamal al-Din 'al-Afghani'', in Ali Rahnema (ed.), Pioneers of Islamic Revival (London and New Jersey, Zed Books).

Kent, Mariam (1976). Oil and Empire: British Policy and Mesopotamian Oil: 1900-1920 (London, Macmillan).

Keohane, O. Robert (1984). After Hegemony: Cooperation and Discord in the World Political Economy (Princeton, Princeton University Press).

Kepenek, Yakup (1984). Turkiye Ekonomisi (Ankara, Savas Yayinlari).

---------- (1983). Gelisimi, Uretim Yapisi, ve Sorunlariyla Turkiye Ekonomisi (Ankara, Middle East Technical University Press).

Keyder, Caglar (1997). 'Whither the Project of Modernity? Turkey in the 1990s', in Sibel Bozdogan and Resat Kasaba (eds), Rethinking Modernity and National Identity in Turkey (Seattle and London, University of Washington Press).

---------- (1987). State and Class in Turkey (London, Verso).

---------- (1981). The Definition of a Peripheral Economy, Turkey: 1923-1929 (Cambridge, Cambridge University Press).

Khouri, R.G. (1987). 'Knotting a New Network', <u>ARAMCO World Magazine</u>, Vol. 38, No.2.

Kilic Ali (1955). <u>Kilic Ali Hatiralarini Anlatiyor</u> (Istanbul, Sel Yayinlari).

Kilic, Cem (2002). 'Turkiye'de Isgucu Piyasasi ve Kriz', in Omer Faruk Colak (ed.), <u>Kriz ve IMF Politikalari</u> (Istanbul, Alkim).

Kiray, Emine (1990). 'Turkish Debt and Conditionality in Historical Perspective: A Comparison of the 1980s with the 1860s', in Tosun Aricanli and Dani Rodrik (eds), <u>The Political Economy of Turkey: Debt, Adjustment, and Sustainability</u> (London, Macmillan).

Kisakurek, N. Fazil (1990). <u>Son Devrin Din Mazlumlari</u> (Istanbul, Buyuk Dogu).

---------- (1979/1962). <u>Cile</u> (Istanbul, Buyuk Dogu).

---------- (1978). <u>O ve Ben</u> (Istanbul, Buyuk Dogu).

---------- (1976). <u>Ideolocya Orgusu</u> (Istanbul, Buyuk Dogu).

Kocak, Cemil (1986). <u>Turkiye'de Milli Sef Donemi, 1938-1945</u> (Ankara, Yurt Yayinlari).

Koksal, E. (1971). 'Agricultural Credit in Turkey', <u>Studies in Development</u>, No. 3.

Kolinsky, Eva (1996). 'Non-German Minorities in Contemporary German Society', in David Horrocks and Eva Kolinsky (eds), <u>Turkish Culture in German Society Today</u> (Providence and Oxford, Berghahn Books).

Kolko, Gabriel (1990). <u>The Politics of War: The World and United States Foreign Policy, 1943-1945</u> (New York, Pantheon Books).

Kolko, Joyce and Gabriel Kolko (1972). <u>The Limits of Power: The World and United States Foreign Policy, 1945-1954</u> (New York, Harper and Row).

Koopmans, Ruud and Paul Statham (1999). 'Challenging the Liberal Nation-State? Postnationalism, Multiculturalism, and the Collective Claims Making of Migrants and Ethnic Minorities in Britain and Germany', <u>American Journal of Sociology</u>, Vol. 105, No. 3.

Kop, K.K. (1945). <u>Milli Sefin Soylev, Demec, ve Mesajlari</u> (Ankara, Akay Kitabevi).

Koprulu, Fuat (1964). <u>Demokrasi Yolunda</u> (The Hague, Mouton, Columbia University Publications in Near and Middle East Studies Series A, No. 3).

<u>The Koran</u> (1999). Bi-lingual Edition: 2 (English Trans. Marmaduke Pickthall) (Istanbul, Cagri Yayinlari).

Korum, U. (1976). 'Import Substitution in Turkey in Relation to Integration with the EEC', in Osman Okyar and Okan Aktan (eds), <u>Economic Relations between Turkey and the EEC</u> (Ankara, Hacettepe University Press).

Kotku, M. Zahit (1995). <u>Tenbihler</u> (Istanbul, Seha).

---------- (1994). <u>Cennet Yollari</u> (Istanbul, Seha).

---------- (1984a). <u>Cihad</u> (Ankara, Seha).

---------- (1984b). <u>Mu'minin Vasiflari</u> (Ankara, Seha).

Krane, E. Ronald (1979). International Labour Migration in Europe (New York, Praeger).

Krueger, Ann (1974). Foreign Trade Regimes and Economic Development, Turkey (New York, Columbia University Press).

Kucuk, Yalcin (1984). Turkiye Uzerine Tezler, Vol. 2, 1908-1978 (Istanbul, Tekin Yayinevi).

Kuniholm, B.R. (1986). 'The Carter Doctrine, the Reagan Corollary, and Prospects for United States Policy in Soutwest Asia', International Journal, Vol. 41.

---------- (1980). The Origins of the Cold War in the Near East: Great Power Conflict and Diplomacy in Iran, Turkey, and Greece (Princeton, Princeton University Press).

Kursat-Ahlers, Elcin (1996). 'The Turkish Minority in German Society', in David Horrocks and Eva Kolinsky (eds), Turkish Culture in German Society Today (Providence and Oxford, Berghahn Books).

Kuruc, Bilsay (1970). Iktisat Politikasinin Resmi Belgeleri (Istanbul).

Landau, Jacob (1976). 'National Salvation Party in Turkey', Asian and African Studies, Vol. 11, No. 1.

Leithauser, Gerhard (1988). 'Crisis Despite Flexibility: The Case of West Germany', in Robert Boyer (ed.), The Search for Labour Market Flexibility (Oxford, Clarendon Press).

Lerner, Daniel (1958). The Passing of Traditional Society (New York, Free Press).

Levitt, Peggy (2001). The Transnational Villagers (Berkeley, Los Angeles, and London, University of California Press).

Lewis, Bernard (1988). The Political Language of Islam (Chicago, University of Chicago Press).

---------- (1968). The Emergence of Modern Turkey (London, Oxford University Press).

Leys, Colin (1996). The Rise and Fall of Development Theory (Nairobi, Bloomington, and London, EAEP, Indiana University Press, and James Currey).

Lipietz, Alain (1987). Mirages and Miracles (London, Verso).

Mackie, J.B. (1939). 'Turkish Industrialization', Journal of Royal Central Asian Society, July.

Majid, Anouar (2000). Unveiling Traditions: Postcolonial Islam in a Polycentric World (Durham and London, Duke University Press).

Mango, Andrew (1994). Turkey: The Challenge of a New Role (Westport and London, Praeger).

Mander, Jerry and Edward Goldsmith (1996). The Case Against the Global Economy and For a Turn Toward the Local (San Francisco, Sierra Club Books).

Mann, C. (1980). 'The Effects of Government Policy on Income Distribution: A Case Study of Wheat Production in Turkey Since World War II', in Ergun Ozbudun and Ahmet Ulusan (eds), The Political Economy of Income Distribution in Turkey (New York, Holmes & Meier).

Mardin, Serif (1997). 'Projects as Methodology: Some Thoughts on Modern Turkish Science', in Sibel Bozdogan and Resat Kasaba (eds), Rethinking Modernity and National Identity in Turkey (Seattle and London, University of Washington Press).

---------- (1991). 'The Naqshbandi Order in Turkish History', in Richard Tapper (ed.), Islam in Modern Turkey: Religion, Politics, and Literature in a Secular State (London and New York, I.B. Tauris).

---------- (1989). Religion and Social Change in Modern Turkey: The Case of Bediuzzaman Said Nursi (Albany, State University of New York Press).

---------- (1986). 'Religion and Politics in Modern Turkey', in James Piscatori (ed.), Islam in Political Process (Cambridge, Cambridge University Press).

---------- (1980). 'Turkey: The Transformation of an Economic Code', in Ergun Ozbudun and Ahmet Ulusan (eds), The Political Economy of Income Distribution in Turkey (New York, Holmes and Meier).

---------- (1973). 'Center-Periphery Relations: A Key to Turkish Politics', Daedalus, Vol. 102, No. 1.

------------ (1962). The Genesis of Young Ottoman Thought: A Study in the Modernization of Turkey's Political Ideals (Princeton, Princeton University Press).

---------- (1957). 'DP'nin Dayandigi Kuvvetler', Vatan Newspaper, 29 November 1957.

Margulies, Ronnie and Ergin Yildizoglu (1987). 'Agrarian Change: 1923-1970', Irvin Cemil Schick and Ahmet Tonak (eds), Turkey in Transition (Oxford, Oxford University Press).

Marriot, J.A.R. (1924). The Eastern Question: A Historical Study in European Diplomacy (Oxford, Clarendon Press).

McCormick, J. Thomas (1989). America's Half Century: United States Foreign Policy in the Cold War (Baltimore, The Johns Hopkins University Press).

McMichael, Philip (2000). Development and Social Change (Thousand Oaks, Pine Forge Press).

McMichael, Philip and David Myhre (1991). 'Global Regulation vs. the Nation-State: Agro-Food Systems and the New Politics of Capital', Capital and Class, No. 5.

Mead, G. Herbert (1934). Mind, Self, & Society (Chicago, University of Chicago Press).

Meeker, E. Michael (2002). A Nation of Empire: The Ottoman Legacy of Turkish Modernity (Berkeley, University of California Press).

Mejcher, H. (1976). Imperial Quest for Oil: Iraq 1910-1928 (London, Ithaca Press, St Antony's Middle East Monographs, No. 6).

Melzig, H. (1944). Inonu Diyor ki (Istanbul, Ulku Basimevi).

Menderes, Adnan (1967). Menderes Diyorki (Istanbul, Demokrasi Yayinlari).

Mernissi, Fatima (1991). The Veil and the Male Elite (Reading, Massachusetts, Addison-Wesley Publishing Company).

Mills, C. Wright (1959). Sociological Imagination (London, Oxford University Press).

Milward, S. Alan (1984). The Reconstruction of Western Europe, 1945-51 (Berkeley, University of California Press).

Misiroglu, Kadir (1992). Kurtulus Savasinda Sarikli Mucahidler (Istanbul, Sebil Yayinlari).

Moaddel, Mansoor (2001). 'Conditions for Ideological Production: The Origins of Islamic Modernism in India, Egypt, and Iran', Theory and Society, Vol. 30.

Moghadom, Valentine (1991). 'The Islamist Movements and Women's Responses in the Middle East', Gender and History, Vol. 3.

Moinuddin, Hasan (1987). The Charter of the Islamic Conference and Legal Framework of Economic Cooperation Among Its Members (Oxford, Clarendon Press).

Moore, C. Henry (1990). 'Islamic Banks and Competitive Politics in the Arab World and Turkey', The Middle East Journal, Vol. 44.

Morris, Chris (1999). 'New Firms Tap Hidden Wealth of Pious Turks', Guardian Weekly, 23 May 1999.

Mumcu, Ugur (1994a). Tarikat, Siyaset, Ticaret (Istanbul, Tekin Yayinlari).

---------- (1994b). Rabita (Istanbul, Tekin Yayinlari).

MUSIAD (1996). Basbakan Necmettin Erbakan'in Dogu Asya Gezisi ve MUSIAD'in Bosna-Hersek Gezisi Raporu (Istanbul, MUSIAD)

Narayan, Uma (1997). Dislocating Cultures: Identities, Traditions, and Third World Feminism (New York, Routledge).

Nasr, S.V. Reza (1993). 'Islamic Opposition to the Islamic State', International Journal of Middle East Studies, Vol. 25.

National Productivity Center (1973). Kucuk ve Orta Sanayi Tesebbuslerinin Gelistirilmesi Semineri (Ankara, National Productivity Center Publication, No. 120).

Navaro-Yashin, Yael (2002). 'The Market for Identities: Secularism, Islamism, Commodities', in Deniz Kandiyoti and Ayse Saktanber (eds), Fragments of Culture: The Everyday of Modern Turkey (London and New York, I.B. Tauris).

Norton, J. (1992). 'The Soviet Union and Cyprus', in N. Salem (ed.), Cyprus, A Regional Conflict and Its Resolution (New York, St. Martin's Press).

OECD (1983). Turkey: Country Report (Washington, OECD).

---------- (1982). Turkey, Organization for Economic Co-operation and Development Surveys (Paris, OECD).

Okcun, Gunduz (1971). 1920-1930 Yillari Arasinda Kurulan Turk Anonim Sirketlerinde Yabanci Sermaye (Ankara, Ankara Universitesi Siyasal Bilgiler Fakultesi Yayinlari).

---------- (1968). Turkiye Iktisat Kongresi, 1923-Izmir (Ankara, Ankara Universitesi Siyasal Bilgiler Fakultesi Yayinlari).

Okyar, Osman (1976). 'Turkish Industrialization Strategies, the Plan Model, and the EEC', in Osman Okyar and Okan H. Aktan (eds), Economic Relations between Turkey and the EEC (Ankara, Hacettepe University Press).

---------- (1962). Public International Development Financing in Turkey (New York, Columbia University Press).

Oncu, Ayse (1980). 'Chambers of Industry in Turkey: An Inquiry into State-Industry Relations as a Distributive Domain', in Ergun Ozbudun and Ahmet Ulusan (eds), The Political Economy of Income Distribution in Turkey (New York, Holmes and Meier).

Oncu, Ayse and Deniz Gokce (1991). 'Macro-Politics of De-Regulation and Micro-Politics of Banks', in Metin Heper (ed.), Strong State and Economic Interest Groups (Berlin and New York, Walter de Gruyter).

Ongun, M. Tuba (2002). 'Turkiye'de Cari Aciklar ve Ekonomik Krizler', in Omer F. Colak (ed.), Kriz ve IMF Politikalari (Istanbul, Alkim).

Onis, Ziya (1997). 'The Political Economy of Islamic Resurgence in Turkey: The Rise of the Welfare Party in Perspective', Third World Quarterly, Vol. 18, No. 4.

---------- (1991). 'Political Economy of Turkey in the 1980s: Anatomy of Unorthodox Liberalism', in Metin Heper (ed.), Strong State and Economic Interest Groups: The Post-1980 Turkish Experience (Berlin and New York, Walter de Gruyter).

Orhon, Oktay (1989). 'Turkish Contracting Services Abroad', in Erol Manisali (ed.), Turkey's Place in the Middle East (Istanbul, Middle East Business and Banking Publications).

Ostergaard-Nielsen, Eva (2003). Transnational Politics: Turks and Kurds in Germany (London and New York, Routledge).

Ozcan, Azmi (1997). Pan-Islamism: Indian Muslims, the Ottomans, and Britain (1877-1924) (Leiden, New York, and Cologne, Brill).

Ozdalga, Elisabeth (1999). 'Entrepreneurs with a Mission: Turkish Islamists Building Schools Along the Silk Road' (Unpublished Paper Delivered at the Annual Conference of the North American Middle East Studies Association, Washington, D.C., 19-22 November 1999).

Ozdalga, Elisabeth and Sune Persson (eds) (1997). Civil Society, Democracy, and the Muslim World (Surrey, Curzon Press Ltd.).

Ozel, Ismet (1992/1976). Uc Mesele: Teknik, Medeniyet, ve Yabancilasma (Istanbul, Cidam Yayinlari).

Ozgur, O. (1976). Sanayilesme ve Turkiye (Istanbul, Gercek Yayinevi).

Ozyegin, Gul (2001). Untidy Gender: Domestic Service in Turkey (Philadelphia, Temple University Press).

Paine, S. (1974). Exporting Workers: The Turkish Case (London, University of Cambridge, Department of Applied Economics, Occasional Papers 41).

Palmer, Alan (1992). The Decline and Fall of the Ottoman Empire (London, John Murray).

Pamuk, Sevket (1988). 'War, State Economic Policies, and Resistance by Agricultural Producers in Turkey, 1939-1945', New Perspectives on Turkey, Vol. 2, No. 1.

---------- (1987). 'Commodity Production for World Markets and Relations of Production in Ottoman Agriculture, 1840-1913', in Huri Islamoglu-Inan (ed.), The Ottoman Empire and the World Economy (Cambridge, Cambridge University Press).

Panitch, Leo and Sam Gindin (2003). 'American Imperialism and EuroCapitalism: The Making of Neoliberal Globalization', Studies in Political Economy, Vol. 71/72.

Payaslioglu, Arif (1961). Turkiye'de Ozel Sanayi Alanindaki Mutesebbisler ve Tesebbusler (Ankara, Ankara University Press).

Peker, Receb (1984). Inkilap Dersleri (Istanbul, Iletisim Yayinlari).

Petran, T. (1978). Syria: A Modern History (London, Ernest Benn Limited).

Pigg, L. Stacy (1992). 'Inventing Social Categories Through Place: Social Representations and Development in Nepal', Comparative Study of Society and History, Vol. 34.

Piscatori, James (1986). Islam in a World of Nation-States (Cambridge, Cambridge University Press).

Polanyi, Karl (1944). The Great Transformation (Boston, Beacon Press).

Prakash, Gyan (ed.) (1995). After Colonialism: Imperial Histories and Postcolonial Displacements (Princeton, Princeton University Press).

Quataert, Donald (2000). The Ottoman Empire, 1700-1922 (Cambridge, Cambridge University Press).

Rahnema, Ali (1994). 'Ali Shariati: Teacher, Preacher, Rebel', in Ali Rahnema (ed.), Pioneers of Islamic Revival (London and New Jersey, Zed Books).

Rashid, Ahmed (2000). Taliban: Militant Islam, Oil, and Fundamentalism in Central Asia (New Haven, Yale University Press).

Reed, A. Howard (1954). 'Revival of Islam in Secular Turkey', The Middle East Journal, Vol. 3.

Rist, Gilbert (1997). The History of Development (London, Zed Books).

Ritzer, George (2000). The McDonaldization of Society (Thousand Oaks, Pine Forge Press).

Robins, Philip (1991). Turkey and the Middle East (London, Pinter Publishers).

Robinson, D. Robinson (1971). 'Mosque and School in Turkey', The Muslim World, Vol. LXI, No. 4.

Ro'i, Yaacov (1984). 'The Impact of the Islamic Fundamentalist Revival of the Late 1970s on the Soviet View of Islam', in Yaacov Ro'i (ed.), The USSR and the Muslim World: Issues in Domestic and Foreign Policy (London, George Allen & Unwin).

Rozaliyev, Y.N. (1978). Turkiye'de Kapitalizmin Gelisme Ozellikleri, 1923-1960 (Ankara, Onur Yayinlari).

Rubinstein, Z. Alvin (1982). Soviet Policy toward Turkey, Iran, and Afghanistan (New York, Praeger).

---------- (1979). 'The Soviet Union and the Eastern Mediterranean: 1968-1978', Orbis, Summer.

Sachs, Wolfgang (ed.) (1992). The Development Dictionary (London, Zed Books).

Sahiner, N. (1988). Bilinmeyen Taraflariyla Bediuzzaman Said Nursi (Istanbul, Yeni Asya).

Said, Edward (1995). 'East Isn't East: The Impending End of the Age of Orientalism', Times Literary Supplement, 3 February 1995.

---------- (1993). Culture and Imperialism (New York, Alfred A. Knopf).

Said Nursi (1990a). 'Hutbe-i Samiye', in Ictimai Receteler, Vol. 2 (Istanbul, Tenvir Nesriyat).

---------- (1990b). 'Zeylinin Zeyli', in Ictimai Receteler, Vol. 2 (Istanbul, Tenvir Nesriyat).

---------- (1990c). 'Kurtler ve Islamiyet', in Ictimai Receteler, Vol. 2 (Istanbul, Tenvir Nesriyat).

---------- (1939). Hubbab (Ankara, Ali Sukru Matbaasi).

---------- (n.d.). '"Nationalism in the View of Islam"- The Third Subject of the Twenty-Sixth Letter', in Risalat-Un-Nur Collection (Istanbul, Tenvir Nesriyat).

Sakallioglu, U. Cizre (1991). 'Labour: The Battered Community', in Metin Heper (ed.), Strong State and Economic Interest Groups: The Post-1980 Turkish Experience (Berlin and New York, Walter de Gruyter).

Saktanber, Ayse (2002). Living Islam: Women, Religion, and the Politicization of Culture in Turkey (London and New York, I.B. Tauris).

Sanayi Odasi Bulteni. 15 April 1956.

Sander, Oral (1979). Turk-Amerikan Iliskileri, 1947-1964 (Ankara, Ankara Universitesi Yayinlari).

Saribay, A. Yasar (1985). Turkiye'de Modernlesme, Din, ve Parti Politikasi: MSP Ornek Olayi (Istanbul, Alan Yayincilik).

Sassen, Saskia (1996). Losing Control? (New York, Columbia University Press).

Schimmel, Annemarie (1975). Mystical Dimensions of Islam (Chapel Hill, University of North Carolina Press).

Selekler, H. (1945). Ciftciyi Topraklandirma Kanunu Uzerine Aciklamalar (Istanbul).

Senses, Fikret (1990) 'An Assessment of the Pattern of Turkish Manufactured Export Growth in the 1980s and Its Prospects', in Tosun Aricanli and Dani Rodrik (eds), The Political Economy of Turkey: Debt, Adjustment, and Sustainability (London, Macmillan).

Serin, Necdet (1963). Turkiye'nin Sanayilesmesi (Ankara, Ankara Universitesi Yayinlari).

Seton-Watson, Hugh (1977). Nations and States: An Enquiry into the Origins of Nations and the Politics of Nationalism (Boulder, Westview Press).

Sevilgen, M. Gulen (1980). MSP.'de Dort Yil, 1973-1977 (Ankara, Yuksel Matbaasi).

Shanin, Teodor (1997). 'The Idea of Progress', in Majid Rahnema and Victoria Bawtree (eds), The Post Development Reader (London, Dhaka, Halifax, and Cape Town, Zed Books, University Press Ltd., Fernwood Publishing, and David Smith).

Shepard, E. William (1987). 'Islam and Ideology: Towards a Typology', International Journal of Middle East Studies, Vol. 19.

Singer, Amy (2002). Constructing Ottoman Beneficence: An Imperial Soup Kitchen in Jerusalem (Albany, State University of New York Press).

Singer, Morris (1977). The Economic Advance of Turkey, 1938-1960 (Ankara, Turkish Economic Society Publications).

Smith, J.E. (1963). The Defense of Berlin (Baltimore, The Johns Hopkins University Press).

Sodaro, J. Michael (1990). Moscow, Germany, and the West from Khrushchev to Gorbachev (Ithaca, Cornell University Press).

Somel, A. Selcuk (2001). The Modernization of Public Education in the Ottoman Empire, 1839-1908: Islamization, Autocracy, and Discipline (Leiden, Boston, and Cologne, Brill).

Soysal, Yasemin (1997). 'Changing Parameters of Citizenship and Claims-Making: Organized Islam in European Public Spheres', Theory and Society, Vol. 26.

State Institute of Statistics. Statistical Yearbooks of Turkey (Ankara, Office of the Prime Minister).

State Planning Organization (1996). A Comparison of 1994 Temporary Results of National Income (Ankara, Office of the Prime Minister).

---------- (1985). Fifth Five Year Plan (1985-1989) (Ankara, Office of the Prime Minister).

---------- (1983). Milli Kultur: Ozel Ihtisas Komisyonu Raporu (Ankara, Office of the Prime Minister).

---------- (1977). Annual Program for 1977 (Ankara, Office of the Prime Minister).

Szyliowicz, J.S. (1991). Politics, Technology, and Development: Decision Making in the Turkish Iron and Steel Industry (London, Macmillan).

Tanju, S. (1978). Tepedeki Dort Adam (Istanbul).

Tarhanli, B. Istar (1993). Musluman Toplum, 'Laik' Devlet (Istanbul, AFA Yayinlari).

Tekeli, Ilhan (1977). Kirda ve Kentte Donusum Sureci (Ankara, Mimarlar Odasi Yayinlari, No. 18).

Tekeli, Ilhan and Selim Ilkin (1981). Para ve Kredi Sisteminin Olusumunda Bir Asama: T.C. Merkez Bankasi (Ankara, Middle East Technical University Press).

---------- (1977). 1929 Dunya Buhraninda Turkiye'nin Iktisadi Politika Arayislari (Ankara, Middle East Technical University Press).

Tekeli, Ilhan and G. Mentes. (1978). 'Turkiye'de Holdinglesme', Toplum ve Bilim, Winter.

Tezel, Yahya (1982). Cumhuriyet Doneminin Iktisadi Tarihi, 1923-1950 (Ankara, Yurt Yayinlari).

---------- (1977). '1923-1938 Doneminde Turkiye'nin Dis Iktisadi Iliskileri', in Ataturk Doneminin Ekonomik ve Toplumsal Tarihiyle Ilgili Sorunlar Sempozyumu (Istanbul, IITIA).

Thornburg, M.W., G. Spry, and G. Soule (1949). Turkey: An Economic Appraisal (New York, The Twentieth Century Fund).

TIB (1978). 'Kucuk Sanayinin Kredi Sorunu' in Sanayide Kucuk Uretim, Toplumsal ve Mekansal Boyutlar (Ankara, Chamber of Architects Publication).

Tibi, Bissam (1998). The Challenge of Fundamentalism: Political Islam and the New World Disorder (Berkeley, Los Angeles, and London, University of California Press).

Tilly, Charles (1998). Durable Inequality (Berkeley, University of California Press).

---------- (1990). Coercion, Capital, and European States, AD 990-1990 (Cambridge, Basil Blackwell).

TOB (1978). Odemeler Dengesi Sorunlari (Ankara, TOB).

Toprak, Binnaz (1981). Islam and Political Development in Turkey (Leiden, E.J. Brill).

Truman, S. Henri (1955). Years of Decisions: Memoirs Vol.1 (New York, A Signet Book New American Library).

Tunaya, T. Zafer (1962). Islamcilik Cereyani (Istanbul, Baha Matbaasi).

---------- (1952). Turkiye'de Siyasi Partiler, 1859-1962 (Istanbul).

Tuncer, B. (1975). 'External Financing of the Turkish Economy and Its Foreign Policy Implications', in Kemal Karpat (ed.), Turkey's Foreign Policy in Transition, 1950-1974 (Leiden, E.J. Brill).

Turkone, Mumtazer (1991). Siyasi Ideoloji Olarak Islamciligin Dogusu (Istanbul, Iletisim).

TUSIAD (1989). TUSIAD Members' Company Profiles (Istanbul, TUSIAD).

---------- (1982). The Turkish Economy, 1982 (Istanbul, TUSIAD).

---------- (1981). The Turkish Economy, 1981 (Istanbul, TUSIAD).

Ulman, A Haluk and R.H. Dekmejian (1967). 'Changing Patterns in Turkish Foreign Policy, 1959-1967', Orbis, Vol. XI, No. 3.

US Congress (1983). US Interests in the Eastern Mediterranean: Turkey, Greece, and Cyprus. A Report Prepared for the Subcommittee on Europe and the Middle East of the Committee on Foreign Affairs, 98th Congress 1st Session (Washington, US Government Printing Office).

---------- (1981). Congressional-Executive Relations and the Turkish Arms Embargo (Washington, US Government Printing Office).

---------- (1980). Turkey, Greece, and NATO: The Strained Alliance. A Staff Report to the Committee on Foreign Relations, 96th Congress 2nd Session (Washington, US Government Printing Office).

---------- (1979). Congressional Record, House, 21 March 1979.

---------- (1977). Assessing the NATO-Warsaw Pact Military Balance (Washington, US Government Printing Office).

US Department of State (1955). The Conferences at Malta and Yalta, 1945 (Washington, US Government Printing Office).

---------- (1947). The Problem of the Turkish straits (Washington, US Government Printing Office).

US ECA (1949). Turkey, Country Study (Washington, US Economic Cooperation Administration European Recovery Program, US Government Printing Office).

Uyguner (1959). 'Memleketimizde Sanayi ve Kredisi', TIG, 18 December 1959.

Vali, A. Ferenc (1971). Bridge Across the Bosphorus: The Foreign Policy of Turkey (Baltimore, The Johns Hopkins University Press).

van Bruinessen, Martin. (1992a). Kurdistan Uzerine Yazilar (trans. N. Kirac et al) (Istanbul, Iletisim Yayinlari).

---------- (1992b). Agha, Shaikh, and State: The Social and Political Structures of Kurdistan (London and Atlantic Highlands, Zed Books).

van der Pijl, Kees (1989a). 'Restructuring the Atlantic Ruling Class in the 1970s and 1980s', in Stephen Gill (ed.), Atlantic Relations, Beyond the Reagan Era (New York, St. Martin's Press).

---------- (1989b). 'The International Level', in Tom Bottomore and Robert Brym (eds), The Capitalist Class: An International Study (New York, New York University Press).

---------- (1984). The Making of an Atlantic Ruling Class (London, Verso).

Venn, Fiona (1986). Oil Diplomacy in the Twentieth Century (London, Macmillan).

Wallerstein, Immanuel (2000). 'The Agonies of Liberalism: What Hope Progress?', in Immanuel Wallerstein (ed.), The Essential Wallerstein (New York, The New Press).

---------- (1995). After Liberalism (New York, The New Press).

Weber, Max (1971). The Protestant Ethic and the Spirit of Capitalism (London, George Allen & Unwin).

---------- (1947). The Theory of Social and Economic Organization (New York, The Free Press).

White, B. Jenny (2002). Islamist Mobilization in Turkey: A Study in Vernacular Politics (Seattle, University of Washington Press).

Williams, Raymond (1977). Marxism and Literature (Oxford, Oxford University Press).

Wood, Robert (1986). From Marshall Plan to Debt Crisis: Foreign Aid and Development Choices in the World Economy (Berkeley, University of California Press).

World Bank (1987). World Development Report (Washington, The World Bank).

---------- (1984). World Development Report (Washington, The World Bank).

---------- (1982). Turkey: Industrialization and Trade Strategy (Washington, The World Bank).

---------- (1980a). Turkey: Policies and Prospects for Growth (Washington, The World Bank).

---------- (1980b). Turkey: Prospects for Small-Medium Scale Industry Development and Employment Generation, Report No. 2913 (Washington, The World bank).

---------- (1975). Turkey: Prospects and Problems of an Expanding Economy (Washington, The World Bank).

Yalman, Galip (2002). 'The Historical State and Bourgeoisie in Historical Perspective', in Nesecan Balkan and Sungur Savran (ed.), The Politics of Permanent Crisis (New York, Nova Science Publishers).

Yarar, Erol (n.d.). A New Perspective of the World at the Threshold of the 21st Century (Istanbul, MUSIAD).

Yasa, Ibrahim (1966). Ankara'da Gecekondu Aileleri (Ankara, Akin Matbaasi).

Yetkin, Cetin (1983). Turkiye'de Tek Parti Yonetimi (Istanbul, Altin Kitaplar).

Yildiz, H. (1991). Fransiz Belgeleriyle Sevr-Lozan-Musul Ucgeninde Kurdistan (Istanbul, Koral Yayinlari).

Yinanc, M.H. (1969). Milli Tarihimizin Adi (Istanbul, Hareket Yayinlari).

Yucekok, Ahmet (1972). Turkiye'de Dernek Gelisimleri, 1946-1968 (Ankara, Sevinc Matbaasi).

---------- (1971). Turkiye'de Orgutlenmis Dinin Sosyo-Ekonomik Tabani (Ankara, Sevinc Matbaasi).

Zahlan, R.S. (1989). The Making of the Modern Gulf States (London, Unwin & Hyman).

Zeytinoglu, Mumtaz (1981). <u>Ulusal Sanayi</u> (Istanbul, Cagdas Yayinlari).
Zubaida, Sami (1994). 'Human Rights and Cultural Difference: Middle Eastern Perspectives', <u>New Perspectives on Turkey</u>, Vol. 10, Spring.
Zurcher, J. Eric (1993). <u>Turkey: A Modern History</u> (London and New York, I.B. Tauris).

Magazines and newspapers

<u>Cumhuriyet Newspaper</u>
<u>Gunaydin Newspaper</u>
<u>Herald Tribune</u>
<u>Hurriyet Newspaper</u>
<u>Los Angeles Times</u>
<u>Milliyet Newspaper</u>
<u>New York Times</u>
<u>The Economist</u>
<u>Turkish Daily News</u>
<u>Ulus Newspaper</u>, 1945-1966
<u>Vatan Newspaper</u>, 1945-1950
<u>Yon</u>, 1960s

Index

N

O